JOY 365
DEVOTIONAL

Published by LUI Media
P.O. Box 491
Waldorf, Md 20603

ISBN: 978-1-961743-13-7 Hardback
978-1-961743-12-0 Paperback
EPUB: 978-1-961743-11-3
Printed in the United States of America
Edited by Katherine Anderson -Literary World Set in Eb Garamond and Cinzel
Cover Designed by Nadia Monsano

Library of Congress Information available upon request.
Published by LUI Media
P.O. Box 491
Waldorf, Md 20603

Contents

Abdulrazak Abubakar

In the aftermath of a shattered marriage, the echoes of past failures threatened to define my existence, fostering depression and anxiety. However, a transformative journey unfolded, guided by courageous acknowledgment of pain and a commitment to facing the raw truth. The struggle to move on, both external and internal, became a pivotal chapter in my life, leading to a turning point marked by embracing forgiveness for both my ex-partner and me.

Amid the pain, a profound alchemy transpired, turning mistakes into milestones, and propelling me toward personal and emotional growth. Depression and anxiety, intertwined with the trap of past failure, were addressed not just symptomatically but at their root. Professional help, support, and self-care dismantled the walls that held me captive.

As my devotion deepened, my identity emerged, revealing an inner strength and resilience. No longer defined by the failure of my marriage, I embraced purpose, gradually revealed as the shadows of regret lifted. The journey toward healing opened my eyes to new possibilities, transforming me from a prisoner of the past to a pilgrim, walking with intentionality towards a purpose-filled future.

In the tapestry of my days of devotion, redemption unfolded

through the struggle to move on, battles with mental health challenges, and the transformative journey of forgiveness and resilience. This story extends an invitation for others to embark on a similar devotional journey, recognizing that beyond the pain of past failure lies the potential for a breakthrough that can reshape lives. May this devotional serve as a guide, companion, and source of inspiration on the path from brokenness to breakthrough.

<u>Esther Adebayo</u>

Oh, what a wonderful time to be alive and bask in the love the father has bestowed upon us. Contrarily, as seasons would have it, it could also become a time where one tends to feel inadequate and restricted. As a youth, I have found myself in situations where I entertained the notion that "I was unqualified." In Judges 6:12-17, we meet Gideon who, although hiding, was called a "mighty man of [fearless] courage." Gideon furthermore itemized all things that would, in a human sense, disqualify him from being who God has called him to be.

Does this ring a bell? Have you confused WHO God has called you to be, with WHERE you find yourself? Being in the winepress (a place of crushing, stomping, and hiding) as Gideon was, does not mean God sees you as downtrodden, O mighty one! We need to tenaciously learn to accept only the report of the Lord over our lives. This reminds me of a song my parents always played when I was little which goes "whose report would you believe… yes I'll believe the report of the Lord…"

There is a time for everything under the sun, and in some seasons, you might be required to "hide and fortify," however, do not confuse your season in life with your reason for being alive. When you see tasks, relationships, and ministry opportunities that you feel you are UNQUALIFIED for, just remember that God is a master in Qualifying the Unqualified, and He will be with you.

Lakisha Adams

The darkest valleys and shadows of my Breast Cancer Diagnosis took me on another faith testing journey that dimmed the light that shined so brightly in my spirit just the day before. Another battle to fight after overcoming anxiety and self-doubt from traumatic events I experienced only a few short years before. After so many gloomy days, I knew I needed to find the faith, courage, and strength for survival. On the stormiest of all, I found myself alone. The silence was so loud, I could hear my own heartbeat. Questions kept rolling through my mind: Why am I here? How do I overcome this darkness? Why sulk in misery when God has blessed you with this life? My answer…do not allow your faith in God to be broken, and I released bellowing cries until the voice of God said, you are never alone. My heart feverishly poured out prayers of gratefulness, prayers for forgiveness, prayers of affirmation as I already knew that I could do all things through God who strengthens me. The darkness slowly faded, the clouds and rain rolled away and opened my eyes to GOD's LOVE and MERCY. My morning prayers and daily self-affirmations became the foundation for breast cancer survival, shining light on My Journey to Restore my JOY.

My Daily Prayer: Kisha…The righteous cry out and the Lord hears them; he delivers them from their troubles. The Lord is close to the brokenhearted and saves those who are crushed in spirit. Be joyful in hope, patient in affliction, faithful in prayer. The Lord will keep you from all harm, he will watch over your life. The Joy of the LORD is your strength, the trial (suffering) will not last forever. Before long, your generous God has great plans for you.

Evangelist Nicole Adkinson

"Your testimonies are my heritage forever, for they are the joy of my heart." Psalm 119:111 Have you ever felt like you lost your joy? Do you find being with family and friends no longer enjoyable? It's as if the laughter, giggles, and innocence of being happy went silent. You find yourself smiling but with no joy behind that smile. You wonder, where did my joy go? How did it escape me? Why would joy want to leave me? These are emotions and questions I have asked myself for the past 2 years. In a moment's time, my joy lifted. I found myself not happy anymore. I looked and looked, and my joy was nowhere in sight. I pondered. I prayed. I cried.

One winter day, I came across Psalm 119:111 ESV during my devotional time. My eyes lit up, and my soul rejoiced. As I read the scripture, I heard a small whisper, "Here I am, don't you remember? Don't you recall all the times we've laughed, giggled, and shared innocent happiness together? I am here. I never left you. I've been here all along waiting for you. Waiting for you to rejoin me on the path that I have made known to you: the path of life. In my presence, there is fullness of joy. Don't you recall our testimonies? Why are you letting this life get you down?

"Remember it's in my presence and in my testimonies where joy can be sustained. It's where laughter is king, and giggles are made in my presence." As I quietly listened to the Holy Spirit, I began to reemerge. Reflecting on God's goodness and mercy towards me and all the sweet testimonies that sustain me, I reclaimed my joy that winter day.

Dr. Anthea Aikins

"…. Let us go over unto the other side of the lake"
- Luke 8: 22 KJV

Is your current circumstance(storm) shaking your confidence in what God said?

Lesson: Do not be a forgetful hearer of the Word of God! The disciples traveling with Jesus witnessed Him teaching, healing, and raising the dead. Yet, when a storm hit, they feared perishing, even though Jesus was with them! Did they not hear Jesus say, "…let us go to the other side of the lake?" His statement had a clear destination: "The other side."

Did they allow the storm to make them forget Jesus' power? Sometimes, unfamiliar circumstances make us forget God's capabilities and what He's done in the past. We may even feel like God has left us! But know this: such thoughts are not from God. He has promised never to leave or forsake us. God IS with you—YES, HE IS!

Your situation may be unfamiliar to you, but it's not to God. He's not surprised by what you're going through. God can do exactly what He said! What is your "other side?" If He said it, He'll take you there safely. Do NOT be afraid! Do NOT let the enemy steal your joy. God is able! Take your joy back by anchoring your faith in Him and believing ALL His promises concerning you. The joy of the Lord is your strength!

Declaration: *May I NOT be a forgetful hearer of the Word of God in Jesus Name!*

Call to Action: What was the last thing God told you? Write it down & Believe it. What did God say to you about your identity in Christ? Write it down & Believe it!

Israel Akinloye

Though the fig tree may not blossom, nor fruit be on the vines; Though the labor of the olive may fail, And the fields yield no food; Though the flock may be cut off from the fold, And there be no herd in the stalls— Yet I will rejoice in the LORD, I will joy in the God of my salvation. The LORD God is my strength; He will make my feet like deer's feet, And He will make me walk on my high hills. To the Chief Musician. With my stringed instruments.
- Habakkuk 3: 17 - 19

To REJOICE is not a function of circumstances; when things are prospering or unsuccessful, but a sustained knowledge about God who makes all things work for our good. (Rom 8:28)

God works in diverse ways and sometimes, His working process may seem confusing to us. He could choose to withhold blessings, allow difficulties, or cut off things from us, but you can be assured that His words are ever consistent with His doings, even though the ways of His operation may be different.

Knowing that the God of our salvation is here and there for us, and with us, at any phase or season is a major source of strength for our lives.

You may not understand His works at the beginning, and the way He does it may be so strange to you, but His words are the sure Lamp to guide you.

Felicia Alexander-Branch

God will move mountains.

God will move fear.

God will move financial hardship.

But we must lie down and let God do His work.

We must recognize His blessings, as they come in many forms.

Let God do His job, adhere to His signs, and everything will fall into place.

Every day may not be good or bad, but if we let God do His work, all will be well.

Not all things are ours to fight; they belong to God. Lessons come with patience and time.

When we let go and let God, things align with His will. Patience comes through daily practice.

Take time to meditate and rest your mind.

Taking time for self-care aligns the mind, body, and soul.

God has given each of us a purpose, but it takes time and effort to find and fulfill it.

It may not always look easy, but just believe—let go and let God.

When doubt arises, place everything at His feet. Trust that it's no longer in your hands.

Keep life simple, free from worry and second-guessing.

Rev. Dr. Patricia Allen

Today is Joy Day! I pray you will know God's love deep down in your heart, the love that surpasses all understanding (Eph 3:17-19). I was not raised with a lot of affection and words of love, yet the longing deep inside me was to hear the words "I Love You" my entire life. Many people search their entire lives seeking that affirmation and never find it.

I, too, was on that life's journey asking God daily, why was I not enough? When will it be my turn to be loved? Romans 5:18 says, behold, what manner of love God demonstrates towards us, in that while we were yet sinners Christ died for us. Now THAT'S Love! I wanted and needed love, not knowing it was always there for me since the foundation of the world. 1 Corinthians 13:7-8 says, Love bears all things, believes all things, hopes all things, endures all things. LOVE never ends.

I pray that everyone embraces His unconditional love as it flows like a river of joy and life. No one can earn it. This love crosses all barriers of age, race, educational and financial statuses, even religious preferences. Nehemiah 8:10 says, "the joy of the Lord is our strength." God's love language bears fruit throughout eternity. Galatians 5:22-23 says, "But the fruit of the Spirit is love. Against such there is no law." (That means - NO LIMITS.) The measure of love is to love without measure. Let no one take your joy. Please receive this joy in love.

Tangela Allen

In the tapestry of our lives, woven with threads of love and joy, there are moments when our hearts overflow with happiness. We find ourselves immersed in relationships that bring us unparalleled joy, as if our hearts cannot contain the abundance of love we feel. Yet, this blissful tapestry can begin to unravel when mistreatment, disrespect, disloyalty, and heartache creep in. Nothing hurts more deeply than loving someone at a level unmatched, only to feel trapped in a relationship where your love is unreciprocated. In losing ourselves, we discover the painful truth-a lack of self-love.

But during heartbreak, there is hope. Although the journey to reclaim oneself may be intimidating, it is essential. When relationships are good, they are undeniably good, but when they turn sour, the struggle can be overwhelming.

Amidst the pain, consider the joy you once shared with someone who failed to appreciate it. Take that joy and let it resonate within you, making your heart happy. It's a conscious decision to feel all the joy your heart can hold, independent of external circumstances. Reclaiming your joy becomes an act of self-love, a commitment to your own well-being.

Allow this rediscovered joy to fill you to the brim. Only when our heart is overflowing with self-love and joy can you spare and share without fear of losing it again. Reclaiming joy is not only a declaration of independence from the pain of unreciprocated love, but it's also a journey back to the core of who you are.

In the tapestry of life, joy is a resilient thread. It weaves through the fabric of our existence, reminding us that even in the face of heartbreak, we have the power to reclaim our joy, one thread at a time.

Tiffany Alston

Prayer, praise, patience, purpose, and positivity are the keys to Joy when facing challenges and difficult circumstances. Spend moments out of your day to communicate with God because this will bring you joy. Expect miracles to happen in your life, and they will.

I was in my late thirties, married for about thirteen years with three young children. A day before my husband's fortieth birthday we were told that he needed to be on emergency dialysis, or he would not live more than twenty-four hours. He had kidney issues, temporary blindness, and multiple lengthy hospitalizations. This was caused by untreated high blood pressure along with other health factors contributing to kidney failure over the years.

Immediately I begin to pray and build a stronger relationship with God. I had to trust God like never before. While my husband was on dialysis, God used me to author a book called the Journey of Faith. I was able to open and share a multitude of experiences. I began to hear God's voice while maintaining balance and happiness. God gives us the power within ourselves to have inner peace. We must listen to our intuition to perceive and understand the seasons we are in. After my husband had been on dialysis and a kidney transplant list for several years, we finally received the call on Christmas Day for him to have his kidney transplant. Every challenge that you go through in life can help you become a greater version of yourself. Your destiny depends on your faith and trusting God. Speak things into existence.

Thank God for them in advance. Always put God first, love, give generously, forgive quickly, and be kind to others. You will be blessed and experience joy.

Donald C. Alston Jr.

This moment is what we have now. If you are reading this, take a moment and just say thank you God.

Each day I wake up, I tell myself it's a new day for a new story. We, as humans, are highly intelligent beings but all in different areas of life.

Over the years I was told by my physician that I had high blood pressure. My physician would always be on me about taking my medications. At this time, I was not taking it seriously. In 2015 my physician warned me that if I didn't take my medications that it would have a chance of affecting my kidney. I decided to make a change in my eating habits. I started working out & l lost over a hundred pounds within a year span. I was on a roll until my physician said my kidney functions were starting to fail. Within those 3yrs I ended up having kidney failure in 2018 & ended up on emergency dialysis. It was a very dark time for me because I did the best I could to change things around. I ended up being on dialysis for close to 5yrs and during my time going through this, I saw a lot of my family and friends pass away. I see the sadness in everyone, and I see everyone giving up.

I'm here to tell you that through it all, God is the Alpha & Omega. He has the final say. One thing I do Know, if you keep yourself in alignment with God, anything's possible.

Faith of a mustard seed is all it takes. I just received my new kidney on Christmas day of 2022. Never lose hope.

All we have is this moment so embrace it.

Debra Anderson

How can God perform in your life without faith? In the beginning of Exodus, we hear about the oppression of the Israelites by the Egyptians. Like all of us, they had a low point in their story and needed God. God reaches the Israelites through Moses.

He sets them free in such a way that could only be pointed back to God. In this way He establishes himself as above all things seen. As I continued reading, I noticed a pattern that the Israelites constantly fell in.

This pattern started with distrust causing disobedience which resulted in failure to achieve what God had planned for them. How can they really achieve that without closely following the instructions of God?

When asked to battle people greater than they, the Israelites refused, because they were focused on their abilities. What they failed to notice was that their abilities didn't matter. Psalms 5:11 "But let all those rejoice who put their trust in You. Let them ever shout for joy because you defend them."

The part that stuck with me is in the last sentence, "because you defend them." It wasn't on the Israelites to win the battle; they just had to have faith.

Dr. Ivy Anderson

Voila means used to call attention, to express satisfaction or approval, or to suggest an appearance as if by magic! Voila also means "with my thoughts I create my day." Therefore, I call my thoughts to create Joy which is more than a happy feeling. It's an intentional thought to produce a lasting euphoric emotion or peace that comes from the choice to trust that God will fulfill his promises. The promises of God's Word hidden in the heart to mediate on them day and night that the evidence of profiting, progression, and productivity may appear to all. It is the quiet confidence that since God, the creator of the universe be for us who or what can be against us. It is knowing my success or failure begins and ends in what the mind believes is and what the mind believes is possible because all things are possible to him/her that believes and as a man/woman thinks so it will be. When thoughts are formed, next to following are the words of those thoughts so Abracadabra which means as I speak, I create. The Hebrew meaning of Abracadabra is derived from several Hebrew words "ab' (father), 'ben' (son), and "ruach hakodesh" (holy spirit), or from the Aramaic "ayra kadayra", meaning 'it will be created in my words. So, do I create Joy or Sadness, Life or Death, Promotions or Demotions, Marriage or Divorce, Health or Sickness, Poverty or Prosperity? The choice is ours because death and life are in the power of our tongue, so the fruit of our Voila and Abracadabra will be apparent. Let your thoughts create your day because thoughts are things coming from the invisible world to the visible world. Joy is a high vibrational frequency, so develop the magnet of Joyful Thoughts.

Kamisha Anderson

The life of your dreams. You've probably imagined it more times than you can remember. You've probably had everything planned out year by year, detail by detail. You've probably gone as far as to create your vision board, write out words of affirmations, pray for it, attend workshops and seminars for it, work and wrestle for it, gone to colleges, and gotten degrees for it. Then suddenly you realized years have passed. You're no longer a teenager, in your 20's, 30's, 40's, or maybe even 50's. Now discontent sets in. You're sad, disappointed, scared, angry, maybe even jealous, but don't dive too deep into your thoughts and emotions. Your story is still being written. The dreams you dreamed are still alive and they are just as beautiful as the picture you tried to manifest. But today, I want you to stop, relax, and take a deep breath. Yes, that's it. In through your nose, out through your mouth. Feel every breath as you receive it and release it. Do you feel that? That's life. Every breath is life changing and transformative. Now relax in knowing that God makes all things beautiful in its time. The life you imagined is being born of every breath you take, every word you have written and spoken, and every effort taken. Your "life-imagined" has a time to be born, so relax and know that it has already been declared beautiful, but only in its perfect time shall it be fulfilled.

Le'Keshia Atchison

Over a year and half ago, I was thirsty, not for water, but for love. As a 15-year Navy Veteran born in North Carolina to a one parent household where the spirits of rejection, abandonment, narcissistic abuse, and neglect resided with an older sibling was not ideal for love, but for survival. Because of my living situation at the time, I was looking for love in all the wrong places...at the bottom of a pill or alcohol bottle, addiction, within the bisexual and homosexuality communities.

It was not until I met Jesus Christ that I found the love that I was so desperately needing in my life. Accepting Jesus Christ as my Lord and Savior allowed me to experience love from an older sibling (Jesus Christ-Big Brother) which was the way (John 14:6) to receive love from a Father (Abba) that I've never experienced before. This agape...this unconditional love that I thirsted for was filled in me by the Holy Spirit...the Spirit of Truth (John 6:13) and now, my best friend. With receiving and accepting salvation made possible by Jesus Christ, I shall never thirst again! In Jesus Name! Amen! Love may not be what you are thirsty for...it's healing in your body or a breakthrough in your finances. It may be that you thirst for deliverance from demonic covenants made knowingly or unknowingly. It may be generational curses from your bloodline from 18 generations back that you are now becoming aware of. Whatever it may be that you are thirsty for, I promise that you will not find it anywhere else other than in believing in the Blood of Jesus Christ.

Kimberly Babers

"Peace I leave with you, my peace, I give unto you: not as the world giveth, give I unto you. Let not your heart be troubled, neither let it be afraid." (John 14:27 KJV)

This joy that I have, the world did not give it to me, and the world cannot take it away.

There is a distinction between joy and happiness. Happiness is based on conditions.

Joy is an inner flow of peace, tranquility and oneness with God which never changes.

Joy flows like an inward fountain pouring out peace, strength, perseverance, love, hope, forgiveness within the depths of the heart, mind, and soul.

This is what joy is to me. The adversities, challenges, and circumstances that occur and have occurred in my life, often allow me to remember the joyous moments in my life instead of focusing on the pain or past hurts. The joyous times also help me to know, I am an overcomer and no matter what life throws at me. I have joy and the Peace of God, despite the adversity and challenges that I have faced.

I would never have known the true meaning of having joy and peace in my life without the struggles. The hope and reassurance that God has my back, and my life is in His hands brings me much joy.

What a wonderful feeling to know that God is in control. Thank You Lord for your peace and joy that surrounds my life. This is my Joy 365: Having peace every day of the year.

<u>Njabulo Banda</u>

Devotional: To many young black women, the angel (or genie or fairy God mother if you will) has appeared and declared us might women of valor!! Yet the shame, self-doubt and sometimes lack of awareness of who we are is often already entrenched so deeply that we often look behind us to check who is being referred to. Our family backgrounds, the way we look, the color of skin, parts of our body we don't like and the negative words from family and the unapproving looks from community members have gotten to us so much that it takes time for us to realize that we are who we are looking up to, who we are looking for. See when society verbalizes disgust or disapproval towards us, that is, envy, amazement, awe, and utter curiosity of the absolute wonder in front of them. We do things that others want to do but are too scared to attempt, work towards or wait on. Oh, mighty woman of valor, yes, beauty, wisdom and strength live in us. They are entrenched, embedded, God given and naturally in us. So, can we please own our education, experience, masculinity, femininity, emotions, the crazy, grace and absolute vulnerability? Leave the friends who constantly remind us what we looked like when they first met us, spiritual leaders who tell us that being outspoken and feisty are sins against God's plan for women. The lioness in us simply refuses defeat and continues to roar. She roars throughout excellence, our academic performance, our magnificent work ethic, our hard work, perseverance, and ability to go beyond the call of duty. She roars and says, I am here, and I am a mighty woman of valor.

Tanisha Bankston

I want others to know that no matter what you go through in life there is hope, and you can rise above the pain. You are created in the uniqueness of our Father "the creator."
2 Timothy 1:7.

"For God gave us a spirit not of fear but of power, love, and self-control." We must not just say this but live by this. For Faith is moving Forward and Fear is to keep you stuck! Choose to Walk by Faith and cast down Fear. The enemy is a deceiver.

Be not ignorant to his devices but rather Faithful to God's word. Allow the angels to speak to you and for you in order to bloom and blossom.

Juanita Banks-Whittington

Consider it pure joy, my brothers, and sisters, whenever you face trials of many kinds because you know that the testing of your faith produces perseverance. Let perseverance finish its work so that you may be mature and complete, not lacking anything. James 1:2-4 NIV Who am I? The granddaughter of a grandmother who only wanted to break generational curses. Who am I? The daughter of a mother plagued by substance addiction and mental illness.

Who am I? The daughter of a father who was never present.

Who am I? The mother of a daughter who is innocent and looking up to me as a role model.

As humans, we're susceptible to the preconceptions of others, and those life experiences mold you into who you are. Entering the world while in an already broken home has affected me in many ways that were out of my control. I remember always searching for the love of my father and wishing my mother was around more. What I can say is that I was able to foresee the life I did not want for myself through the love of my grandmother and other family members.

The stigma of mental illness and generational curses plague many families, but what matters is the determination to rewrite your story. Experiences growing up are what motivated me to pursue a better understanding of a healthy foundation of wellness. Being open to listening and having difficult conversations is what influences resiliency and breaks generational curses. Remember, although stigmas and traumatic experiences are hard to break, your past will never define who you really are. Through understanding, setting boundaries, and self-awareness, the sky's the limit.

Bartee

When I was young, I never thought about not waking up the next morning. I never took the time to see the changing of the seasons when the leaves turned colors, but I do remember the snow.

On April Fool's Day, 1972, I was very thankful for the blessings God had bestowed upon me and the realization of "Don't Be Stupid – Keep Running." Common sense prevailed that day, but I was at the end of the road.

August 11, 1975, was an incredibly good day and year for me. Thirty-eight months from the ten-to-twenty-five-year sentence had passed, and I was being released on probation.

My time spent inside was used wisely. My goal was to receive a Stationary Engineer License, yet I received a High-Pressure Boiler Operator License. Oh, What a Joy!

When the cell block doors opened, the first thing I yelled was "All Hands-on Deck!" (I had seen that in a movie when someone in authority comes aboard a ship).

I was LEAVING the ship, also known as 3 Northwest Cellblock at Mansfield Reformatory, located in Ohio.

Now, I lay myself down to sleep and pray to the Lord, my soul to keep. Joy comes to those who have struggled to be free; those who have "Gotten Over the Hump," those who have gotten on their knees to pray and chose to get back up with a smile on their face, knowing that to God Be the Glory!

Dr. Angela Basden-Williams

Let your moderation be known unto all men. The Lord is at hand. Be careful for nothing; but in everything by prayer and supplication with thanksgiving let your requests be made known unto God. Philippians 4:5-6, KJV

A good testimony can change our lives. Jesus was the master storyteller. To admit that your life was challenging is not a good feeling to express to others. As I can remember, a family member came into my room and stole my mortgage, daycare, and grocery money. I was devastated, scared, and didn't know what to do. I had children to feed, which was my main concern at the time. I called and asked my birth father for help, but he told me no to avoid asking his mean-spirited wife who didn't care for us or family members. His words made me numb and sick to my core. All I knew to do next was to scream loudly and cry out to God for help. I started praying and talking to God telling Him my needs and a calming spirit comforted me. Psalms 121:1-2, KJV. "I will lift mine eyes to the hills, from whence cometh my help. My help comes from the Lord who made heaven and earth." Afterwards, I called and asked a good friend to lend me three hundred dollars, and thank God she said yes! I gave a date to repay. During this process on the same day, I heard a knock on the front door. I opened the door and saw a car driving down the street. What I noticed on the porch were three brown bags of groceries. It had food that I told God was needed. I jumped for joy and felt restored. God is Awesome and Amazing! I honestly believe God sent an Angel when He heard my cry for help. I thought the car looked familiar and asked someone was it them, but they never confirmed. Pray for favor, financial blessings, and God's protection over your life. Amen.

Aharon J. Beavers

AJ here, and I want to take a moment to talk to you about something important.

Life can be challenging; sometimes, it may feel like everything is working against us. But I'm here to remind you that you are stronger than you think, and you have what it takes to overcome any obstacle that comes your way.

It's okay to feel overwhelmed and hopeless at times.

We all have those moments. But it's important to remember that these moments define us. These are the moments that test our character and our resilience.

So don't give up. Instead, keep pushing forward, one step at a time. Also, take care of yourself along the way. Self-care is essential, and it's okay to prioritize your well-being.

Surround yourself with people who support you and lift you up. Reach out to friends, family, or a professional if you need someone to talk to. You don't have to go through tough times alone.

Remember that you are never alone and have a source of strength and hope greater than anything in this world.

So, my takeaway for you is this: Life can be tricky, but we are stronger than we think. We have the power within us to overcome any obstacle that comes our way.

Cultivate gratitude. Even during difficult circumstances, there are always things for which we can be thankful.

Please take a few moments each day to reflect on the good things in your life, and express gratitude for them.

Gil Beavers

I want to share some encouragement with you on joy after grief from a man's perspective and from someone who has endured tough times and faced the pain of loss.

I want to remind you that hope, and healing are available to us all.

During our heartache, it can be difficult to see a way forward. But I want to assure you that joy can still reach our hearts. It may take time, and there may be challenges along the way, but with patience and persistence, we can overcome our grief and find a renewed sense of purpose and joy in life.

The Bible offers us many words of wisdom and encouragement in times of grief, and I am reminded of *Proverbs 3:5-6* which says, *"Trust in the Lord with all your heart and lean not on your own understanding; in all your ways submit to him, and he will make your paths straight."* These words remind us that we are not alone in our struggles and that we can find the strength and courage we need to move forward with faith and trust in God.

So let us continue to press on, Rich Bro, the journey may be challenging at times, but with a heart full of joy and gratitude, we can overcome any obstacle that comes our way.

Let's choose to find the beauty in each day and cherish every moment we have with the people we love.

Renée M. Beavers

Rich Sis, today I want to talk about a topic close to my heart: joy after grief. As women, we experience so much in life - both the highs and the lows. We love fiercely and deeply, and losing someone we love can feel like our world has shattered into a million pieces.

But let me tell you something; there is hope. Even amid the most profound grief, joy can still find a way to shine through. I know this from personal experience. I have faced loss and heartache in my own life, but I have also learned that our strength and resilience as women can help us rise above the pain and find a way to embrace joy once again.

The Bible offers us guidance and hope in times of grief. For example, in *Psalm 34:18*, we are reminded that *"The Lord is close to the brokenhearted and saves those who are crushed in spirit."* This verse tells us that we are not alone in our pain and that God is always with us, offering comfort and healing in our time of need.

As women, we have the power to support and uplift each other through challenging times. We can offer a listening ear, a shoulder to cry on, and a reminder that joy can still be found during grief. And when we emerge from the darkness of grief, we can embrace the beauty and wonder of life once again with a newfound appreciation for the blessings that surround us.

So, my Rich Sisters, I urge you to hold on to hope and never lose sight of the light that shines within you. Even after the deepest grief, joy can still find a way into your heart.

Remember that you are loved and that you are never alone. And YOU ARE MORE THAN ENOUGH.

Evangelist Angie BEE

In everything give thanks: for this is the will of God in Christ Jesus concerning you. - 1 Thessalonians 5:18 KJV

Ingredients:

- 1 cup of pain in your body.
- ½ cup of emotional trauma.
- ¾ cup of devastation, divorce, or death of a loved one.
- 2 tablespoons of bad credit, lay-offs, underpayment or an empty bank account.
- A dash of faith.

Instructions

Mix all ingredients into a bowl and add the prayers of the righteous. Stir in your grandmother's advice and the instructions from your physician. Slowly pour in a scripture, read it, and pray to understand and apply it. Set the bowl aside for one hour in meditation. Take a bath, listen to music, dance, or enjoy a good cry. Add daily, weekly, and yearly goals. Ask the Lord that His will be done in your life and stir vigorously. Preheat your healing oven! Set a timer and fold in praise and forgiveness. Pour into a mustard seed-based container and spend time with loved ones—call, mail a letter, or use video chat. When the timer goes off, give praise to God and acknowledge your progress. Realize that the pain and mental anguish have fallen away as your new creation cools. Before slicing, cover with 1 Thessalonians 5:18. Allow this word to set into your spirit and reapply daily. Slice and serve. Proclaim, "Therefore, if anyone is in Christ, the new creation has come: The old has gone, the new is here!" 2 Corinthians 5:17 – NIV

Karla Beedles

Each day, we have the power to rewrite our narratives, redefine success, and live a life that is intentional, purposeful, and uniquely our own. Today, we celebrate and affirm the beauty, resilience, and strength within us as we embrace A Lifestyle Reimagined. Living your life intentionally requires self-awareness, the courage to challenge societal norms, and a deep connection with your dreams and desires. Acknowledge who you are, unapologetically, and let go of any limitations imposed by others. You have the power to carve your own path, embracing authenticity, using it as a source of strength, inspiration, and pride. Embrace the power of your voice, as your words can shape minds, galvanize movements, and bridge cultures. Speak up for what you believe in, amplifying unheard voices and championing change for a better tomorrow. Know that your opinions and ideas are invaluable and worthy of being heard. Remember, A Lifestyle Reimagined comes to fruition through setting clear intentions and committed action. Identify your goals and aspirations each day, and then take deliberate steps towards them, no matter how small. Every action you take, every decision you make, can bring you closer to the life you envision. Be patient and gentle with yourself along the way, celebrating each milestone and learning from every setback.

Nurture your mind, body, and soul, for your well-being is the foundation upon which a fulfilling life is built. Prioritize self-care, practice mindfulness, and surround yourself with a supportive community that uplifts and empowers you. Your journey is unique, and it should be nourished with self-love, self-acceptance, and unyielding belief in your own worthiness.

Join me and hundreds of other women intentionally living A Lifestyle Reimagined www.facebook.com/groups/richgirlshq.

Khadisha Benjamin

"Dear God, what am I here for? What is my purpose?" Those are the words I found myself crying out, on numerous occasions, as a child and even more as an adult. My childhood trauma derived from involuntarily being used as a target for the arrows of deep-rooted pain, conflictions, and insecurities of others. Because of that, I developed a false perception of who I am based on what people said and did to me.

One day, at a breaking point, there was an awakening, something that energetically said, "Enough is enough." That is when the most important question I could ask myself developed into the foundation of my healing. "Who am I?" Because of my traumatic childhood I was psychologically stripped of my identity. But "Who am I?" gracefully made itself present and all the answers I needed seemed to already hold a space within me.

Well, of course, all the answers are within. Is that not where God dwells? I was looking for peace, love, and healing through unhealthy, worldly things when all I needed was to look deeper, to search for the God within me. I had been wandering around in the dark for so long looking for the light, unaware that I Am the Light. God is love, therefore "I Am." Coming to that realization gave me strength that I'd never felt. Now, I confidently find joy in embracing my truth and standing in my purpose to help others find their light.

Acknowledge yourself from a higher perspective, face your past and actively heal your broken inner child in order to unblock the many obstacles that are holding you back from allowing God to speak through you.

Dr. Jo Anna Bella Bennerson

Look how far you've come. You took that special "time for you" to accomplish your goals, to seek out your dreams!

Look how far you've come. Whether you were supported or even if everyone turned away, you were sure to carry on and required yourself to dig deeper anyway.

Look how far you've come. To "market you go…reap what you sow!" You did that while helping others and without letting your energy slip low.

Look how far you've come. Creating needed energy without running anyone else's race. Instead, you used resilience and hardworking efforts to create this new space.

Look how far you've come. Turn around and look over your shoulder. Wow, so many steps were taken and you even crushed some boulders!

Look how far you've come. Say it loud . . .to yourself, not just a whisper, "I'm so proud of you!" Say it louder, in the mind and in the mirror.

"I'm so proud of you, too! "Look how far you've come! Take breaks. Rest when you're tired but keep striking!

Keep going! This is your journey! Keep Hiking!

Now look back, look around and see how far you've come! Look ahead and "Forward March!" because you are not done. Look around. Testify today to how far you have come!

Do it! Look around. See how far you have come!

Look how far you have come!

How far you have come!

Keri Bentsen

"I'm free," was my first thought when my divorce became final. And then, blank. I didn't know who I was. I felt lost. After my kids had grown and left home, it was time for me to leave, as well. I was in a narcissistic relationship for 3 decades and I previously thought there was no way out. I went to therapy and finally felt validated for what I was feeling. I've learned to accept that I am enough.

I had long played the role of a people-pleaser, dedicating my existence to the happiness of others, yet clueless about the path to my own joy. I felt like a failure. I retreated within and journaled my deepest thoughts and feelings. This was a journey of unraveling years of manipulation and false beliefs that had diminished my self-esteem.

Thankfully, I was blessed with a supportive and caring family, who uplifted me and encouraged me to live my dreams. They listened to me cry, held space for me, and cheered me on. They believed in me when I doubted myself.

My relentless faith in God has helped me through the toughest moments in my marriage and again in recreating my new life. I listened to affirmations, Christian songs, and prayed…a lot. I vowed to never ignore my intuition ever again and to set healthy boundaries. I decided to "Let Go and Let God." I practiced self-compassion, and self-care. I learned to love myself just as I am. I made a promise to live life for me and find joy in life's simple pleasures and to empower other women to do the same. Now, if you'll excuse me, there's a flower nearby calling me. I must go over and smell it.

Rhonda Berryhill-Castaneda

What does intentionally joyful living mean? How do we live our lives with the intention of being joyful?

Life is full of challenges, heartaches, betrayals, and loss. There are times when we feel like giving up and believe we will never experience healing. What is the answer? The answer is to live life with the intention of being joyful each day. How do we do this? The answer will be different for each one of us, but it is up to everyone to determine what helps.

There are many diverse types of things that can make your heart feel joyful. The first is to focus on your blessings. This will include prayer, meditation, and gratitude. If we wake up with a grateful heart and simply feel happy to live to see another day, that's a great start! We can add a morning prayer and choose what we are truly thankful for each morning. As you are thinking of what you are grateful for, you will automatically smile and feel love.

Another tool I use is to play cheerful, uplifting songs while I get ready each morning. Happy music immediately improves attitude! In addition to my morning routine, I add affirmations. The affirmations change each day according to what is going on in my life. Do I need strength, or clarity? Do I need peace, tolerance and understanding? Or do I need to find forgiveness in my heart? I personalize my affirmations each day.

Affirmations are said as though they have happened and are real. Thank the universe for unknown blessings already on their way!!!

Denise Bethea

For you are fearfully and wonderfully made. Psalm 139:14

Do you realize when God created you, He broke the mold? There is absolutely no one else on this earth that He created like you.

There is not another person that has your DNA. God created you so intricately together that He has the number of each strand of hair upon your head. You are His divine creation that He loves most.

You are beautiful to God. Never feel less than the beautiful creation He has made. This alone should give you all the assurance in the world. He has made you in His image and in His likeness.

How wonderful it is to know that God loves us so much He gave us His DNA, and it is marvelous in His sight. Whenever you're feeling low, just remember the Creator of Heaven and Earth thinks the most of you.

You are amazing and the more you recognize that, the more wonderful, caring, compassionate, powerful, beautiful, brilliant, resilient, attractive, wise, giving, genuine, loving, strong, creative, inspiring, you become.

You are beautiful inside and out. Don't you forget it. God Says So! You are what He says you are because He knows you and you are Beautiful.

Dr. Vernessa Blackwell

Right at this moment, you may be feeling as though you are unable to meet your needs; however, have you considered that there may be someone you could offer a little help, and it would mean the world to them? It could be through gifts or a form of service. The joy that fills their heart as you give so selflessly will put a smile on your face and keep you joyous. Research has shown that lending someone a hand can improve your mood and self-esteem, make you happy and decrease your stress level. Have you lost joy? Look around you; you'll find less privileged people, and you can find organizations that organize outreach for those who desperately need help. Can you volunteer?

With those helping hands of yours, you could restore joy to those you serve. This, in turn, will restore your joy. You may be wondering why helping another gives you that level of satisfaction. It is because we are all God's children, and we belong in one family. We are all created in the image of God, and we are connected and woven together. Each of us is a piece of God's beautiful big picture. As such, it would feel like what you do to someone else you do for yourself. It is little wonder then that Jesus would say,

"do unto others whatever you would like them to do to you…"

(Matthew 7:12 NLT).

If you can, you may invest your time in service to the community in which you live. You may also offer a hand at church to make church programs run smoothly or make an event work better. You will find such fulfillment and joy especially if you know you're appreciated. I find joy in writing and helping others publish their books.

Artiana Bols

In the hustle of daily life, as a wife and mother, it's easy to find joy slipping away amid the demands and responsibilities. Yet, joy is not lost but waiting to be rediscovered. In the quiet moments, God invites you to restore joy. Pause and breathe. Inhale the grace that surrounds you, and exhale the burdens you carry. The journey to joy restoration begins with acknowledging the weariness and surrendering it to God. Remember, His love is steadfast, His mercies are new every morning. Reflect on the beauty of your role as a wife and mother. Each hug, each meal prepared, each bedtime story shared is an offering of love. God sees your sacrifices, and in them, He is weaving a tapestry of joy. Find joy in the small victories, celebrate the love that permeates your home, and embrace the imperfections that make it uniquely yours. Turn to Scripture for strength and guidance. Psalm 30:5 reminds us that "weeping may stay for the night, but rejoicing comes in the morning." Your current challenges are temporary; joy is on the horizon. Trust in God's timing and lean on His promises.

In prayer, pour out your heart. God is not only a listener but a healer. Share your burdens, dreams, and hopes with Him. Let His presence fill your spirit with a renewed sense of purpose and joy. Lastly, cultivate gratitude. In the chaos of life, count your blessings. Gratitude has the power to shift your focus from what's lacking to what's abundant. Keep a joyful journal, noting the moments that bring a smile to your face. As you embark on this journey of joy restoration, know that you are not alone. God walks beside you, ready to lift your burdens and fill your heart with a joy that surpasses all understanding. Embrace each day with a spirit of gratitude and watch as joy is beautifully restored in your life.

Elder Jean Bonds

Is this possible, you may ask? Yes, you can have joy every day. Joy defined by Webster's Dictionary states: immense pleasure or happiness (delight). When I wake-up in the morning, the first thing I do is say "Good Morning Lord." Having joy every day is not based on what's happening around you or even your emotions. Having joy is a mental decision every day when you wake up. You must be intentional!

Command and declare your day. Speak to your day, even if you feel tired, sick, depressed, or unworthy. I ask the Lord for strength and the Holy Spirit to guide me every day. I am thankful for trivial things and that is what brings me joy.

Being joyful every day doesn't mean you don't have any life issues. While we are on this journey, how are we choosing to live it? Are we going to murmur and complain or have joy during our journey? I had to find scriptures to help me understand how to have joy during my sorrows and pain. Some scriptures I use are: (NIV-Life Application Study Bible)

1. Romans 15:13

2. Psalm 30:5

3. Nehemiah 8:10

4. 2 John 1:12

Dr. Shirley Boykins Bryant

During life's journey, we all encounter challenges and setbacks that test our resolve and strength. While it is easy to succumb to despair and defeat, the true mark of a courageous soul lies in our ability to exhibit resilience. Resilience is the steadfast attitude that enables us to bounce back from adversity and find renewed hope and strength. As we embrace the spirit of resilience, we discover that it is not merely a trait but the transformative power of GOD that empowers us to endure and thrive.

Resilience does not deny the existence of challenges; instead, it acknowledges the presence and impact of challenges on our daily lives. By acknowledging the reality of challenges, we free ourselves from the illusion that we will live without difficulties. Adversity is an inevitable part of the human experience, but our response to it is what sets us apart.

Embracing resilience means accepting that storms will come, but we have the power through GOD to rise above them. A resilient heart is one that nurtures a positive mindset, even amidst chaos. It is easy to dwell on negative thoughts and become trapped in a cycle of despair. However, by focusing on the possibilities, lessons, and hidden blessings, we develop an optimistic outlook and attitude of resilience. Life is ever-changing, and resilience involves being adaptable to these shifts. Just as a tree bends in the wind but does not break, so, too, we must learn to adapt while remaining true to our core. Embracing the unknown with courage allows us to discover new opportunities for growth and progress.

TRUE RESILIENCE!

Phyllis Brewer

"Weeping may endure for a night, but joy cometh in the morning."
(Psalms 30:5)

The joy of the Lord is my strength, and it resonates deep down within my heart and soul. This joy that I have did not come overnight. I spent many years caregiving for both of my parents as their health declined. I often lost my joy at the thought of becoming an orphan. It wasn't until God reminded me that He is the joy and strength of my life that I felt like going on and completing my assignment.

It was the word of God that restored my joy and fervent prayer. I understood that one day both of my parents would go back to our Heavenly Father. When I accepted this outcome, I began to face the reality of life which allowed me to continue pressing forward.

I learned through this process the importance of self-care so that I would not lose myself. On those lonely days, I found myself doing things that brought me joy. Going to the nail salon to get manicures and pedicures and taking a ride on my bike around the lake always put a smile on my face which restored joy. It was in those moments of self-care and learning who I am all over again that gave me unspeakable joy that God restored.

Now that my joy has been restored, I'm able to smile on the inside as it radiates on the outside. God has given me renewed hope, peace of mind, and a brand-new smile.

Now that I have been restored, I am able to pour into the lives of others. I'm blessed to share this unspeakable joy.

Antionette Broadnax

"Why am I so sad? Why am I so troubled? I will put my hope in God, and once again I will praise him, my savior, and my God."
(GOODNEWS) *Psalm 42:11*

Take a pause and ask yourself what the cause of your sorrow and sadness is. When you do, you must decide deep within yourself that you will no longer give them the chance to consume you. You must make up your mind that you will not let the situation you are facing rule over you. You have got to take the reins of your life in your own hands because God has already given you power over your life (Luke 10:19). With that power, He has instructed you to resist the devil and he will flee (James 4:7). So long as you are submitting to the authority of God, nothing can take your joy if you don't let it.

The decision that you choose to learn from these experiences no matter how painful they may be, must come from you. You must decide that you will perceive the lessons and not let the pressure put you under. When this becomes your new disposition, you will find joy gradually replacing sorrow and bitterness. Although this may not be instant, with consistency and determination, and with faith in your heart in God's word, joy will soon become your reality.

When the pain grabs you tight in the throat and you are feeling like giving up and giving in, consistently remind yourself that joy comes in the morning. And morning is extremely near. Declaring God's word over your heart also makes the journey worth persisting. God is right there with you no matter what (Isaiah 43:2). Find joy in this!

Allensia Brown

Lasting joy is found in God's goodness, providing us strength during times of weakness and sorrow.

True joy starts from within and overflows as God's love fills us with hope and happiness (*Psalm 30:5*). Focusing on the positive aspects of life and sharing hope and peace with others helps us remember the love and sacrifice of Jesus Christ, who cares for and loves us unconditionally.

In response, we should emulate God's love, loving others unconditionally and without judgment. This practice leads to lasting joy, strengthens our relationships, and creates a world filled with compassion, understanding, and joy. Scripture guides us in deepening our understanding of these values, allowing for spiritual growth and a closer relationship with God.

Compassion is vital, and *Colossians 3:12* encourages us to display it in our daily interactions. To grow spiritually, we should seek God's wisdom and understanding rather than relying solely on our own (*Proverbs 3:5-6*).

The essence of joy is rooted in our relationship with God, and the joy He provides gives us strength in challenging times (*Nehemiah 8:10*).

Galatians 5:22-23 highlights the significance of joy, describing it as a fruit of the Spirit. Cultivating these qualities allows us to experience and share joy with others.

In summary, by seeking God's guidance and embodying compassion, understanding, and joy, we deepen our faith, creating a world filled with love, empathy, and happiness.

Scripture is a valuable resource for spiritual growth, enabling us to become more like Jesus and share His love with others.

<u>Che Brown</u>

The coronavirus pandemic disrupted our lives in unimaginable ways, forcing us to adapt and reconfigure our plans. Yet, amidst the chaos, my son Che Jr. and my wonderful daughter-in-law, Brittanee, managed to create the perfect wedding day almost three years ago. When Che Jr. got engaged a year prior, I was overjoyed as a father. I eagerly anticipated gaining a daughter-in-law and admired the beautiful bond they shared. The infectious happiness they brought to each other's lives was undeniable.

The pandemic, however, threw a wrench into our meticulously crafted wedding plans. Venues closed; social gatherings were limited to 50 people in Maryland. Our wedding dreams were reshaped countless times. Brittanee's mother came to the rescue, creating personalized wedding masks with guests' names, ensuring everyone's safety. With less than 45 days to go, we switched to a new venue, adjusted the plans, and rescheduled the wedding. Despite the obstacles, our pandemic wedding was perfect. Tears of joy flowed as Che and Brittanee exchanged vows, surrounded by loved ones, both physically and virtually. Their unwavering gaze, heartfelt promises, and intimate connection made it a day to remember. From this extraordinary experience, I drew invaluable lessons that resonate not only in personal life but also in the world of influence and business. Everyone Plays a Crucial Role: The pandemic taught us that we are all interconnected and deeply affected by global events. Every individual, in his or her own way, contributes to the bigger picture. Compassion and Patience Are Essential: Navigating through challenging times demanded a shift in communication and resourcefulness. It underscored the importance of empathy and resilience in connecting with our community.

Nui Brown

Have I not commanded you? Be strong and courageous. Do not be frightened, and do not be dismayed, for the LORD your God is with you wherever you go." Joshua 1:9

When I was a small child before I even tried anything sometimes, I used to say the words," I can't." I noticed that I used these two powerful words whenever I tried something before the task was even completed. And instead of looking at whatever I was doing as a challenge, and sticking it out, I immediately threw up my hands in desperation and said I could not do it with whines, sobs, and cries.

My mother in all her wisdom sweetly, but very calmly, said, "I don't know why you keep saying, "I can't" when no one has ever told you that." I was incredibly quiet at that moment as we looked at one another. Her words reverberated all around me and through me. That one moment changed me. I realized that somewhere I picked up two words, not knowing their full impact. If I totally internalized them, I would live in a constant state of disbelief about myself and my abilities for the rest of my life.

I learned that I needed to dig for courage. Circumstances or situations would not diminish my spirit. I had to fight to the end. I needed courage to exercise my faith, even if it were as small as a grain of a mustard seed. I needed to conquer my fears and become the loving, strong, vibrant, resilient, and beautiful person God had created me to be. Stay encouraged and always be courageous. *Knowing this: that the trying of your faith worketh patience. But let patience have her perfect work, that ye may be perfect and entire, lacking nothing. James 1:3-4*

Bray Bryant

Psalm 91:1 (NIV): "Whoever dwells in the shelter of the Highest will rest in the shadow of the Almighty."

Life as a teenager can be exciting, but it can also be filled with challenges and uncertainties. As we navigate through difficulties, it's essential to find a place of refuge and rest. Psalm 91:1 paints a beautiful picture of where that place can be found. To dwell in God's shelter means to make Him your home, your safe place. It means inviting Him into every aspect of your life. When you encounter challenges, fears, or uncertainties, you can turn to God for refuge. Just as you go home after a long day to relax and find comfort in your parents, you can go to God in prayer and seek His guidance, strength, and peace.

Imagine the shadow of a mighty tree as a symbol of God's presence. His shadow is not just any shade; it's a place of ultimate protection. It's where you find safety from the trials of life, just as you find relief from the blazing sun in the shadow of a tree. When you rest in God's shadow, you can trust that He will shield you from harm, comfort you in times of trouble, and provide a place of calm during life's storms.

So, as a teen, remember that you don't have to face life's challenges alone. You have a refuge and a fortress in the Lord. When you dwell in His presence and rest in His shadow, you'll find the strength, peace, and protection you need. Make it a habit to turn to God in prayer, trust in His guidance, and let His love and presence be your constant source of comfort on your journey.

Sherline Burnett

Some things are worth fighting for!

We are at WAR! The Body of Christ is in a spiritual battle and the devil will stop at nothing until he robs us of every gift that God has promised. He tries to bombard our thoughts with oppression, depression, sadness, failure, defeat, etc., so we will abdicate our position in Christ. JOY is a Gift of the Spirit, and we must guard it, and every God-given gift our Heavenly Father has promised us.

The only way that the enemy can steal our joy is if we allow him to. Again, this is a spiritual battle, and we must fight according to the rules of engagement. You wouldn't bring a toothpick to an alligator fight, would you? Therefore, bring the only thing that the enemy must obey, and that is the Word of God! The Apostle Paul declares in 2 Corinthians 10: 4-5, "for the weapons of our warfare are not carnal, but mighty through God to the pulling down of strong holds; casting down imaginations, and every high thing that exalted itself against the knowledge of God,"2 Corinthians 10:4-6 KJV. Believe it, or not, every thought is not your own.

The enemy tries to plant thoughts in our mind that question the validity of God's promises for us. We can have joy even in our greatest challenges. Jesus is our example. He focused on "the joy that was set before Him…" as he endured the cross for us. What looked like tragedy was really Triumph! Never forget, you have victory in Jesus Christ. Read God's Word out loud, sing songs of praise and celebration. Declare His promises against every thought and feeling that is contrary to what the Bible says. Fight the good fight of faith and GO GET YOUR JOY!

Dr. Lori Butler

"To everything there is a season, a time for every purpose under heaven." -Ecclesiastes 3:1 (NKJV)

Oppositions and trials will come to each one of us at some point in our lives.

We will face illness or have a family member affected by an illness. Financial worries also intrude in many lives causing anxiety and worry. People have mental health issues and depression from trauma or an extenuating life event. Others are simply lonely and tired of living life alone.

Whatever the individual case might be, there is always a reason, a season, and a time for all things according to the word of God. What we must remember is to lean solely on God in all circumstances during this journey called life.

Pain does not always have to result in discord. Once we sit in our pain, it teaches us lessons which we can use to find our purpose.

Purpose brings us peace and ultimate satisfaction in our lives. Although the world is constantly changing, and we are living in critical times in the world. The good news is God's word is never void and always dependable.

Experiences may not all be pleasant, but they make us stronger once we conquer each obstacle. All experiences are meaningful and add context to our life.

Further, we are resilient and wonderfully made. If life experiences are not pleasant, bringing us down in the moment, remember consistent positive thoughts and prayer always leads to joy in our daily journey. God is always right on time in every season of our life.

Darlene Caffey

The story of David and Goliath is a familiar passage.

The events leading to the main events of this story affords us the opportunity to reminisce on the many miracles God has performed right before our very eyes.

Once we begin to remember how God made a way for us in the past, the true believer fights his battles with confidence, recognizing that the battle does not belong to him or her, but to the Lord.

On this day, David was given specific instructions by his father, Jesse, to deliver goods to his brothers who were fighting with Israel against the Philistines for the Arc of the Covenant.

On his way to his destination, David heard a conversation between the armies of the Philistines concerning this champion and the Philistine of Gath called Goliath. Goliath was a modern-day bully whom many feared, but David had firsthand knowledge of how God was a master in defeating enemies.

Therefore, David begged Saul to give him the opportunity to defeat Goliath. He kept on begging and pleading until Saul finally gave in saying, "Go, and may the Lord be with you." I don't know who your giant is today, but I am urging you to "go, and may the Lord be with you." Go, until your enemies become your footstool! Go until the Lord shows up and shows out in your life! Go, until your children come back home saved, sanctified, and filled with the Holy Ghost! Go, until you get back what the devil stole! Go, until no weapon formed against you prospers. Go until others see your good works and give God the glory! Go, and may the Lord be with you!

Brianna Calhoun

My upbringing would bring tears to your eyes. I endured many trials with a strict mother, a blunt father, and an over-attentive stepfather. My Godmother, Lillie, was my family's saving grace. She has cared for me since I was 4 weeks old and raised me half of my life while my parents worked. Instead of spending my earlier years in daycare, like most children, she made sure I was academically prepared for kindergarten in the comfort of her own home.

My parents instilled in me the value of loving The Lord at an early age. I never left the house without my mother praying over and with me. Sunday School was a place of solace; grade school, on the other hand, was problematic. I was bullied regularly because of my weight, and I directed my rage toward those who did me wrong. Mentorship, for me, began in the 7th grade. My former grammar teacher, Ms. Odom, took me under her wing and became my school mom. After my first suspension, she introduced me to beauty pageants. I was introduced to life outside of "the desire to fit in." High School came with a whole new set of challenges.

I attended a white high school. I had 6 inspirational educators, Dr. Cox, Ms. McDonald, Ms. Hall, Ms. Hill, Coach McKibben, and Coach West, who dedicated their time to teaching me personal accountability. My adoptive aunt, Christy, joined the administration of my alma mater. She mentored me into womanhood. She taught me how to act like a lady, think like a boss, and demand respect. She's why I joined our sorority's debutant in High School and the sorority in 2018. Her mentorship led to several scholarships that instilled self-security and broke me out of my shell. My story is still being written.

Dr. Shela M. Cameron

On the journey of Joy 365 becoming a motherless daughter is a hard pill to swallow. By no means is coping with the loss of your mother an easy task. Please know that there is no wrong or right way or amount of time to grieve the passing of your mother. Losing your mother at any age can be a traumatic experience. Also, no matter what kind of relationship you had, losing your mother can still feel overwhelming. The initial grief can be severe, followed by moments of sorrow, stress, depression, binge drinking, crying spells, mental breakdown, anger, and mood swings. These effects affect your life daily, weekly, monthly, and probably years to come. It is a statistical fact that women have more intense grief responses and more difficulty adjusting physically and psychologically to the loss of their mother.

The loss can cause a variety of physical effects from high blood pressure, cardiac issues, immune disorders to the psychological effects of regret, emptiness, anxiety, and sadness, all of which are linked to a compromised sense of self. Oftentimes you feel empty from the loss of family traditions and cultural knowledge as well as feeling a loss of an important part of your support system. I know, I did because my mother was my ROCK and provided UNCONDITIONAL love. I knew without any doubt, she would do anything for me.

My Joy 365 journey is the daily memories of the loving and caring Mother-Daughter relationship we had. Although you will miss your mother very much, I smile, knowing she is and was always proud of me as most mothers are. Her words of encouragement will always be near and dear to my heart and forever ring out in my ears as I continue my annual Joy 365 journey.

Robert Campbell

For me, this verse tells of the power and importance of the written, spoken or read Word and how using it can bring us joy or pain. It's about communication, something a lot of us, even me, take for granted. Read *ST John: 1:1* That's why ST John list this first as a means of pointing out its significance.

Whether it's the Word of God or man, how we interpret it makes all the difference in the world. There are two forms of joy and pain, one is physical and the other inflicted by words. For most of us we do our best to avoid physical pain, but pain delivered by word(s) we seem to use as a tool to harm others, either intentional or unintentional and the joy delivered by a word(s) has the opposite effect but can be intentional or unintentional as well.

The unintentional harm due to a word can never be truly directed at one person since people tend to talk to others about things that give them joy or pain and each person receives and processes information differently. Something constructed to harm one can potentially harm others, although they may not be in the direct line of fire. The same goes for joy and this drives the importance and power of words that we choose to use. I've found using words that produce joy are far more rewarding than those used to invoke pain. My words of choice to communicate my thoughts and feelings are guided by my faith in God and the matters of my heart that express the joy I feel about being given the opportunity to show my humanity. So, before you speak to a person, especially one that has experienced a setback or needs a kind word or two to get them through the day, choose your words wisely and let your words come through your faith in God knowing the Word is with God and is God.

LaRae Cantley

We've been made new,

Now,

What do we do about it?

We're living proof of how the truth will bring a change within us. Rearrange our thinking when love starts to sync in and

Take away the heartache and the pain. Now, let's get deeper. Replace it with forgiveness.

Man, I hope we get this.

Realign the purpose, see a whole new vision.

When we rearranged our thinking and love starts to sink in

We put away the heartache and the pain.

Now- let's get deeper!!!

Placing the responsibility in our collective hold

We told one another how important it is.

WE Are

Take on the cloak of relational care.

Share stories that inspire. Encourage and Uplift

Let's give one another restorative hope.

Hold to the highest thought of our fellow creations and treat them as such.

Touch the hem of the garments to grasp a hold the love that surpasses understanding.

Let's step into our favor as we walk into our season.

Keep believing.

Keep seeing.

May we be enough to hold each other up.Hand in hand and with joy in our hearts

It is ours

We create.

We attain.

We sustain the joy of justice.

That is ours!

RaKail Carter

As kings and queens, we sometimes trouble ourselves by allowing our minds to be open to the opinions of naysayers. We know exactly who we are, but sometimes question our abilities. Often, we try to live up to the next persons' expectations while stampeding over our own.

Many may speak about your aspirations and success trying to make it out to what THEY think it should be. You may hear, "Do it this way instead of that way. That's not what's best for you. Take this road and not that one. Listen to me and not them. That's not good enough." Never allow the fear of others not wanting to see you succeed overshadow your faith.

Know who you are. Know what you want. Know what you desire. While you are preparing for success, LET THEM talk. LET THEM try to figure out a way to stop you, but LET GOD take full control and follow his lead. As you are letting them, God himself is prepping you.

Dr. Melodie T. Carr

Have you lost your job? Do you want your joy back? God's sweet, beautiful, soul-saying joy? That deep down unspeakable joy? Well, did you pray for it?! Go ahead, ask for it; pray for it.

Restore my joy, Oh God, in the Holy Name of Jesus, Amen! God takes brokenness, puts it back together again, and makes it better than it previously was. As God promised to us, there is a better way, a better life, and a better future. To renew your spiritual joy is to submit, surrender, and recommitment to God. "Create in me a clean heart, O God; and renew a right spirit within me!" The same applies to restoring the Joy of God's salvation. Simply ask God for it. Pray for it.

"Jesus Christ, my redeemer and healer, come into my heart, Oh Lord, become my Savior, Oh Lord! God, the beginning and the end, the alpha and omega and the most powerful God in heaven, on earth and under the sea, Oh God, I humbly come to you in prayer for the restoration of the joy of your salvation, Oh God, I come in prayer for all your heavenly and spiritual fruits of goodness and blessings, Oh God. Lastly, Oh God, I'm praying for you to restore all your gifts of joy, Oh God, way deep down in my soul, in the holy name, blood and spirit of Jesus Christ, Amen! Amen! Amen!

Restoration Is Always in Abundance

Biblically, restoration is always in abundance. When something is restored, it is always better than it was at its beginning. God not only restores you, but He also restores you abundantly. Always Remember, all that you must do is ask God in prayer through the name of Jesus Christ

Darlene Caviness

"...For the joy of the Lord is your strength. Nehemiah 8:10

There are times in our lives when the cares of life can become so overwhelming that it may cause us to feel weak, especially after losing a loved one, a job, a friendship, your home, or divorce and much more. These life-changing events in our lives can bring about great sadness and we may feel too weak to go on. At times it becomes difficult to see ourselves having life and having it more abundantly after these great losses. We seem to have lost our strength to push beyond what we are currently going through.

However, the word of the Lord reminds us that the joy of the Lord is our strength. He has given us the joy that the world didn't give, and the world cannot take away from us.

This joy gives us the strength to trust and believe in the God of our salvation. He will strengthen us for the journey that lies ahead of us.

This joy gives us the strength to get up and start over again; it strengthens us to love again and to have joy knowing that the Lord is with us no matter what life throws at us.

Father in heaven,

I thank you for giving us your joy that strengthens us to stand on Your word when we are weak.

Thank you for giving us the strength to trust You no matter what comes to distract us or prevent us from seeing that we are strong in You. In Jesus' name, Amen

Dawn Charleston-Green

Have you ever experienced waking up and before you could even begin your day you were already drained just thinking about it? After which, you couldn't rest. You were up, tossing and turning, thinking about the job, the husband, the children, the project, ministry responsibilities, school what you're cooking for dinner, tomorrow's to-do list. It doesn't take long to become consumed with the affairs of life. But no matter what task or circumstance lies ahead, God promises you STRENGTH. You just must acknowledge you need it. As Christians, some of us have a natural proclivity to DO TOO MUCH. We're wired that way for the most part. Did you ever consider that w*e don't have to try to be what God has promised to be for us?* Nehemiah 8:10 (KJV) says, "*...for the joy of the Lord is your strength.* "What?!

You thought you automatically had joy because you were saved and believed in God? Understand, salvation is a remarkable thing for us every day. If we take a deeper look at the scripture, it says, the joy OF THE LORD is our strength. Meaning, it's the Lord's joy in the first place. He has JOY because He IS joy, and He gives it to us. That's good news because it would be naturally impossible to fulfill and sustain your own joy. Life takes too many unexpected turns. His Joy covers and strengthens us, just because we're in His presence. Psalms 16:11 (KJV) says, *"Thou wilt show me the path of life: in thy presence is fullness of joy; at thy right hand there are pleasures for evermore.* "So, there it is. It's not just knowing God that brings us joy. It's being in a relationship that brings us into His presence. Now, who wouldn't want to be around a friend who offered those types of benefits? Today do not try to go it alone Remember to focus on being in God's Presence and believing the promises He offers.

Khalil Chase

Waking up every morning and being able to see the sun rise and feel the warmth of its sunshine against my skin . . . hearing the phone ring and seeing that it's a call from my overbearing mother . . . starting my day realizing that I would get to spend my college years in Fort Lauderdale Florida. . . hearing my older cousins and younger siblings tell me how proud they are of me and my actions . . . .Everyday being able to wake up and chase my dreams, and the few examples above help to specify what brings me joy. You see joy is an interesting topic when broken down; the word itself means a feeling of immense pleasure and happiness, yet a few simple sentences can take all this away.

Sentences that often repeat what some would say are too much in my head. Sentences such as "I'm disappointed in you" or "You'll never be great enough to succeed" are what tears away at my joy like an old scab. The feeling of never being good enough picks and picks away at my joy.

So, what joy is there you might ask. Joy is the feeling that rises in your stomach when you're congratulated on completing a task. Joy is the sun beaming on your skin after a long day of deflating in your room. Don't let people tell you what joy is because it can be whatever you want it to be, Joy is what makes you happy and smile. Find joy within yourself.

I find Joy in my daily walk. life in college is stressful yet Joyful. I am learning and meeting friends from all walks of life. I pledged in a Fraternity, yes, I am a Nuke aka Kappa Alpha Psi that brings me Joy as well.

Takia Chase-Smith

When I think of Joy the first thing that comes to mind is my family: my husband, my three amazing children, my fabulous mom, my hilarious father, my four sisters, one brother and my bonus children (nieces and nephews)! Family has always been important to me. As a little girl I can recall my dreams about my family when I became grown. I can remember my cousins and me playing house with our doll babies and raising our children together. Those were some of the best times then! But now to have these Blessings from Jehovah in its purest form is much better! My bundle of Joy came in there! Two boys and a Queen (Literally). The people they have become and are becoming are truly amazing. My daughter is a mess. She is feisty, fierce, and wise. Hard to believe she is so much like me when I was younger. I sometimes just sit and look at her and say wow it seems like déjà vu. She is an entrepreneur and already about her coins. Her passion is providing for the less fortunate. Next, there is my middle son. My comedian, and bodyguard. He swears he is my dad and likes to be in charge. His personality will make you love him at first encounter. Finally, there's my first born! He is my brainiac… my calming in the storm. He enjoys reading as a hobby! He is striving to be a Real Estate Agent. We grew up together! The Joy that I get from just hugging these three and my bedtime kisses are so worth it. As parents, our babies don't come with a set of instructions. You do what you think is best. You try to guide them based on your experiences. KEEP BEING THAT BEACON OF LIGHT!

Jen Chávez Perdomo

"Do not judge me by my success, judge me by how many times I fell down and got back up again."
Nelson Mandela

How many times have we been judged by how good we are in any area of our lives? Nobody sees all the pain we had to get there; it is easier to judge. Life comes with a lot of tests and sometimes we feel we won't be able to pass them, but the truth is that humans are very resilient and strong, and it is in those moments when we see we have so much light inside of our souls to get through anything.

Heartbroken, death, sadness, loneliness appears without noticing and the body stops to feel all the intensity on them. I know, I've been there, but it was at that exact moment when I understood that my life needed something to live for.

I did it, and I found joy. I found how pain can bring the opportunity to reinvent myself and honor every person that supports me in any crazy dream. Embrace your strength. It is right there inside you. It is the light you have that no one can turn off, and your success is the result of every fight you face.

I have lost so much . . . so many people in my life, but I still want to live. I had to face death to understand I wanted to live so badly to honor my ancestors and to prove to myself that my dreams, my lists of projects are worth fighting for.

Grab the pain, and ask God how strong you have to be to win the fight, and then fight as hard as you can!

Eunise Chery, CCLC

This life we live is full of choices.

When we make a choice to do one thing, we are inevitably choosing not to do something else. Just like life is full of choices, life can be full of difficulties. Amid the changes in life, we make a choice as to how we will respond. These difficulties in life are what cause us to be happy or unhappy. The world places so much emphasis on people to be happy but happiness is fickle and dependent on the circumstances you face from day to day. It is an emotion that is unstable and forever longing to be pursued.

Joy, on the other hand, is not an emotion but a continual state of being. This pursuit of happiness alone leaves a person missing out on the eternal aspect of joy. The Bible tells us that God is our source of joy, and it is something He promises to give us when we are connected to Him. Joy comes from an eternal source and therefore is eternal in nature. Joy will endure any challenge or hardship you may be facing in your life.

As a believer, the key to experiencing His joy is deciding. When we choose joy, we are responding to God's goodness in our lives no matter the circumstances. This choice will ensure that joy is present in every situation. Ask yourself this question, "Do I choose to respond in sadness, hope or despair when the circumstances of my life don't look the way I want them to?" If you do, decide now to choose joy over the pursuit of happiness and empty emotions. Delight exists in knowing that no matter what goes on in our lives, joy can always be present!

Tisha Chin

JOY can be found in Jesus Christ and not in our circumstances. To me JOY can be taken in many contexts. I found JOY when I found Jesus Christ. It was a JOY I had never felt before. It was refreshing having Him in my life, a new beginning for the old me. I have cried tears of JOY, watching my children maturing and taking their respective places in society.

Living to see that my grandchildren and family are still with me is the settled assurance that God is in control. My JOY is a gift from God for me to celebrate and share with others.

Amid JOY there can be tragic circumstances, brokenness, and a loss of one's direction. Before I was baptized on November 20,2022. I went through disrespect, stress, and bitterness, but God placed good Samaritans in my life to uplift me.

I vividly remember when my dad died in September 1983; I cried for a long time. I referred to him as my 'funny man' and I had great conversations with my dad. Whenever he was going to punish my brother Patrick and I, we would get a sheet and roll it up and he would be beating the sheet instead of us. That was hilarious! The passing of my nephew, Zekie, took a toll on me because I was one of his caregivers. I was devastated, but God gave me HIS JOY. My children, church family and Pastor also helped me to restore JOY after all the tragedies.

For those of you reading my devotional in JOY 365 Read Psalm 30:5. I am wishing for you in this season of your life, PEACE, LOVE, JOY, and HAPPINESS.

Dr. Michele D. Clark LMSW

How can the storms of life lead us to the crown of life?
Blessed is the one who perseveres under trial because, having stood the test, that person will receive the crown of life that the Lord has promised to those who love him - James 1:12 (NIV)

In life, we will encounter trials that test our faith. During these times, we may wonder why we experience life's pitfalls or endure its hardships. It's in these moments that we must cling to the promise the Lord has made to those who love Him. When I was diagnosed with Breast Cancer, I struggled with understanding the tribulations of my journey. But embracing God's promise and seeking His strength empowered me to persevere. When was there a time in your life when you experienced strife? Possibly, it was health issues, temptations, toxic relationships, or professional demands. Without challenges, how many would consistently reach out for God's unchanging hand?

It's easy to trust in the Lord when times are good. Praising Him during life's downturns is what brings the Lord's blessing. Just as an athlete pushes through exhaustion and wins the race and is crowned for his or her accomplishments, we also receive a crown for persevering with faith: the crown of life, a symbol of endurance, faith, and unwavering commitment. Facing trials while trusting in God's love and purpose leads us towards that crown of life. As we go about our day, let's be reminded that our trials are not in vain. They are opportunities for growth, faith, and endurance. So, embrace God's promise. The transformative power of facing life's trials and tribulations brings us closer to the crown of life - a promise the Lord has made to those who love Him!

Elle Clarke

It's true that life can be hectic and overwhelming, especially for those of us with many responsibilities like being a mother and a wife. However, it's important to take a step back and appreciate the little moments of happiness that we experience throughout our daily lives. These moments are what I like to call "pockets of joy." Pockets of joy are those small moments of pure happiness that we experience throughout our day. They can be as simple as enjoying a cup of coffee in the morning, watching a beautiful sunset, or laughing with a friend. These moments may seem insignificant, but they can have a profound impact on our overall well-being.

As we go through our busy lives, it's easy to overlook these pockets of joy. We get caught up in our daily routines, to-do lists, and worries. We forget to pause and appreciate the little things that make life worth living.

As a mother and a wife, finding time for myself can be a challenge. But I've learned that taking a few minutes to reflect on my day and appreciate the pockets of joy I experienced can make a big difference.

If you're having trouble recognizing the pockets of joy in your life, try keeping a journal. Write down one thing each day that made you happy or smile.

It's important to take the time to appreciate the pockets of joy in our lives. These small moments of happiness can help us stay positive, motivated, and grateful, even in the face of adversity. So, the next time you're feeling stressed or overwhelmed, take a deep breath and look for the pockets of joy that are waiting for you.

Jasmine Christina Clarke

Proverbs 3:5-6 (NIV)
"Trust in the LORD with all your heart and learn not on your own understanding; in all your ways submit to him, and he will make your paths straight."

Now let's break it down, *"Trust in the LORD with all your heart,"* Trust in God, believe in God, be faithful to God with all your heart.

"And lean not in your own understanding, Don't lean on your knowledge and not what you think is right for you nor what other people think is right for you, only what the Lord thinks is right for you.

"In all your ways submit to him, and he will make your path straight,"

If you do what the Lord tells you to do and follow what the Lord has put on your heart then the way you're living on this earth will be how the Lord wants you to live and know that when you die you're going to go up to heaven proud that you knew you lived for this moment. That's what the verses *Proverbs 3:5-6* mean to me. The scripture could really touch everybody's heart to change if people really understood it. I hope this mini lesson touched everybody's heart as much as it touched me.

God loves you and have a blessed day.

Antron Cobb

John 3:16 For God so loved the world that he gave his begotten son, that whosoever believe in him shall not perish but have everlasting life.

God loves us so much that he sent His Son, Jesus to be born and die on this earth. He gave us His only Son that everyone who believes in Him will not perish but have everlasting life. We, as children of God, should have faith, believe that Christ died for us, and ask Him to forgive us for our sins. We are loved by God and can be forgiven.

Carolyn Coleman

Your quest for Joy must start with you. How good does it feel to soak in the bathtub, each muscle relaxing, cleansing your mind from the stressors of the day; the scent of lavender permeates the air. That is Joy. Yes, we can strive for daily joy, on days you are hurting, you must speak healing and comfort into you. Joy is a sense of being well with yourself. Your joy must begin with you. Set boundaries on how you will allow people to treat you and or what they feel they can say to you. Remember to filter your ears. Being positive and having a good sense of humor can bring you Joy. There are times when you need to omit the daily news or Debby Downer for a day or two to decrease the negativity they can bring.

Joy encompasses how you think, feel, and move. It is not just the smile. It is the essence of why you smile. Was it a random thought, a lovely memory, a recent accomplishment? An accomplishment does not always have to be about you.

You can receive your joy from another person. Yes, joy can be contagious. My niece accomplished a long-awaited goal, when she completed her goal. I praised God for her for it was an answered prayer. It made my heart smile, which brought me joy.

Get those endorphins going. Why? Because releasing them makes you feel better. How do you get your endorphins going? Simply by exercising. No, you do not have to walk or run a 5K, Just walking a few minutes a day, 30 minutes a day, is an effective way to start. It will benefit your body and mind.

So, if your Joy is diminished, get it back. You have the power to do it.

Chanelle Coleman

I'm a best-selling author, playwright, speaker, visionary, CEO, and the creative powerhouse of CeCi's Ink. I created and developed a platform that affirms, supports, and promotes disenfranchised authors. I've fostered a movement that not only motivates and inspires but pours passionately and purposefully into women.

A few years back, I experienced one successive crisis after another. My disease began to rapidly progress. My bubbly, energetic ten-year-old daughter, Taniyah, suffered two anoxic brain injuries that turned her into a multi-complex healthcare kiddo overnight. While doctors urged me to remove her off life support, I chose to hold onto my God and my faith instead. I spoke life while everything around me screamed death. I managed a state that I call happy hurt as I silently grieved all the missed milestones believing they were deferred but not denied. Without warning, my mother died and my second marriage deteriorated. When I thought things couldn't get any worse Taniyah died unexpectedly. Immediately, I started checking out of life and began willing myself to die. But the grace of God covered me! I'm alive today walking in my purpose because of two gifts: my surviving children and intercessory prayer.

We've all suffered losses. Life has the tendency of dealing cards that leave our world in pieces.

How many of you have been there before? Life has knocked you down, and you felt like giving up, but despite every obstacle you've faced, you're still standing.

It's not by chance. It's divine design. God always reveals and ignite our purpose in this life.

Whitney Coleman LICSW, LCSW-C

Joy is a simple, three-letter word that holds heavy weight in our lives. We often get lost in the activities of daily life and we forget joy is not just a fleeting moment; it's a state of being we can actively cultivate. So, how can we bring more joy into our lives? You can start by counting your blessings. It sounds cliché but there's a reason that phrase is used time and again. When you pause and take stock of what you have instead of focusing on what's missing, your perspective shifts. You start to acknowledge the abundance around you, and that brings joy!

You'll find joy in places you never thought to look. The way the sunlight filters through the leaves during a walk, or the way people congregate together. These little moments add up. While we're talking about moments, let's talk about being present. Do you ever find yourself so wrapped up in what's next that you forget about the here and now? This happens to the best of us. Actual joy comes from being fully engaged in what you are doing, whether that's working or even mopping the floor. There's a certain satisfaction, a sense of joy, which comes from giving your all to the present moment.

What is the takeaway? Joy does *not* just come knocking on your door; you've got to invite it in. It's about being proactive and creating an environment where joy can blossom and thrive. This could be as simple as indulging in things that make you happy, spending time with people who uplift you, or setting boundaries to protect your peace. Cultivating joy is an active process; it's a journey filled with discoveries about yourself and the world around you. Are you ready to make joy a priority?

Dawn V. Collins

There's no denying the unquestionable joy of the genesis of our relationship with our Lord Jesus Christ; it's the moment we experience the fullness of joy. We then journey with Him, transforming little by little, day by day, desire by desire, experience after experience, choice after choice, faith to faith. Then suddenly, it happens! You notice you're a bit more loving, and a little less quarrelsome. You intentionally consider others and start feeling lighter because you've emptied yourself of self and feasted on love received from Abba during your personal time together.

As you think on whatever things are true, honest, just, pure, lovely, of good report, have virtue, and are praiseworthy, you serve all. Could that be joy? Yes...Yes! And just like that you've become a container of Joy by living from a heart of humility. Seeing or hearing the word humility can bring thoughts or feelings of melancholy, weakness, and shame...any and everything contrary to joy. The truth is strength is revealed in humility. Jesus is our greatest example of a life lived in humility. It was humility that equipped Him to live both as Son of Man and Son of God; it was with humility He became a servant to creation and lived a sinless life on earth. Humility nailed Him to the cross, our sins killed Him, but it was the Joy set before Him that enabled Him to endure it all!

So, from today on, when we read, hear, think, or choose humility, let's change the collective story we tell ourselves, our children and each other! Let Humility evoke JOY, for Joy IS OUR PORTION!

Sadie Collins

There have been multiple times in my life that I have been faced with challenges that I didn't know which way to turn and was ashamed to ask anyone for assistance.

It was during these times that I found myself relying on my childhood upbringing cliché of "God will not put more on you than you can bare" and as an adult I've learned that this translated into Faith.

We just need a little bit of Faith to hold onto. *Matthew 17:20 (*King James Version*) reads And Jesus said unto them, Because of your unbelief: for verily I say unto you, If ye have faith as a grain of mustard seed, ye shall say unto this mountain, Remove hence to yonder place; and it shall remove; and nothing shall be impossible unto you.*

Learning to stay focused on Christ amid all fleshly viewed impossible things, we learn that through Christ ALL things are possible.

The word "impossible" itself tells you, I'm possible; therefore, it is how you focus your thoughts and attention along with your abilities to succeed that helps you learn to lean on Christ even more with each new endeavor of your life.

I am God's child who has His favor. Will you walk with me and increase your faith?

Heavenly Father, I come to You right now and ask that You open Your loving arms and embrace those that are humbly coming to You with a renewed mind, spirit, and newfound FAITH in You.

In Your darling Son's Name, we pray…. AMEN.

Sheila Conley - Patterson

Who is the GREATEST among you? We understand that everyone wants to be great. But how? You must discover your gift along with your royal gift. Yes, you can have more than one gift. You must become a servant to find your gift. Then you must deploy yourself to the WORLD, only if you want to be GREAT. Deploy, in this context means to come into a position ready for use. You must want to uncover your gift to serve the WORLD with positive energy. Uncovering your gift is to share, listen, motive, train, teach, watch, and learn at every turn or moment in your journey. You must use these five tools:

KNEEOLOGY- Taught me to pray without seeing.

PRAYER- Taught me to seek the Kingdom of GOD.

FASTING- Taught me to make healthy eating choices for my body.

BEING STILL Taught me that NOTHING can happen without GOD's permission.

GRATEFUL-Taught me that the ATTITUDE of GOD's goodness and his mercy shall follow me ALL the days of my life.

LISTENING- Taught me that he/she has an ear to listen to the Spirit of GOD.

We are the treasures that carry the gifts of GOD. Discover and uncover your gift for your children's, children's, children for generations to come.

Dr. James JC Cooley

In life we will experience many disappointments, trials, and tribulations because we lack understanding for what God's purpose is for us. Each one of us has our own unique purpose identified by our Lord and Savior. However, we must be able to stay on course and focus because there will be many destinations that each of us will experience.

Life is hard and will knock us down many times. God's blessing comes from good and bad. We must be able to accept it all regardless of the circumstances.

We must RISE UP and count it all JOY even when we lack understanding of the path that we are on. Destination and destiny, this is the path that God placed on each one of us to discover our purpose that He planned for us. Sometimes in life when we take this path, we lack understanding and want to commit to failure because we do not see a way to achieve our goals. God's plan for us is to be able to accept His blessings regardless of whether we see them as good or bad. We must count His blessings as Joyful. We must stay on a path that helps us understand His purpose for us and our purpose for others, even if the light is not always shining on us.

There will be days when we may feel like the Lord is not protecting us, but life is a path that we must stay focused on. Life is a series of destinations where we must complete each assignment that God places on our hearts leading to our goal in attaining and completing each destination that leads to our destiny.

Count It All Joy. Obtain God's key for us and wisdom.

Dr. Michelle Cooley

Our lives can be so busy that sometimes we find ourselves in such a rush to get everything done, and we don't take time to pause, listen and embrace those moments when the Lord is speaking to us.

The Lord could be showing us something either through another person, a situation or circumstance, but we allow the distractions in life to take away our focus on hearing and receiving His Word..

Distractions are used by the enemy to keep you from the purpose God has for your life. JUST like Martha, we may allow the urgency of the temporary things in life to distract us from receiving the blessing of God's Word which will provide enlightenment and guide us to the purpose for our lives.

The enemy tries to distract us from our identity by using the things of the world to keep your focus off God's Word. However, when we remember that the things on earth are only temporal and our focus should be on the eternal, we will take the time to be quiet, still, and listen to what truly matters.

My point is when we listen and pay attention to God's voice, this prepares us to prioritize our focus on the things that truly matter.

Therefore, make the best use of your time. Do not be distracted by the temporary cares of this world and use every opportunity to pause and listen when the Lord speaks to you.

Teresa M. Cooper

Hello, my friend: If you've been acquainted with any faith community, especially one with roots in Pentecostal/charismatic traditions you've heard the song lyrics, *" Fill my cup, Lord, I lift it up, Lord. Come and quench this thirst of my soul."*

Whether we've known it or not we've all at one time or another found ourselves depleted, running on empty. In a blink we become complacent with the necessary care of our own life. Soul care is something that happens when we're conscious of our emptiness.

Joy is a spiritual and divine attribute deposited by our creator, and I would dare say it's not a part of our natural senses to maintain. When Joy is withering, the soul knows the only remedy is the source of that Joy. Empty cups are needing only what the giver of Joy can supply. The journey of life carries many lessons, experiences and heartbreaks that erode the faith, hope and optimism we have toward our unique life experience.

Our critical eye, greed, selfishness, pride, and expectations chisel away at our Joy, and we find ourselves in need of restorative deposits. I believe our daily position should be one of empty cups lifted daily to our Heavenly Father for a never-ending filling. My friend, that posture facilitates spiritual encounters that expand beyond what is temporal for the eternal. The joy of the Lord is our strength, and He teaches us Joy that produces fulfillment. The next time you have an empty cup, lift it up knowing He takes delight in filling you up!

Lakisha Copeland

The most imperative things when it comes to self-love to me are self-worth, self-esteem, self-awareness, and self-care. Take a few moments to think about the most important things that come to your mind when it comes to self-love. What are some those things? Sometimes it can take a little longer to fully love yourself; however, this is something that comes along with growth.

Loving yourself also can consist of having a clear understanding of your strengths and your weaknesses. When it comes to some of my weaknesses, I would try to find a way to turn that weakness into a strength, to be able to maneuver throughout life.

We must continue to remind ourselves every day that we are unstoppable when we genuinely love ourselves from the inside out, nothing or no one can get in our way. The overall goal is to love the natural you. Think about it like this: for example, we all love to take selfies, and some of us like to add a filter onto the picture once captured in order to alter it in some way.

The beauty of self-love would be to love yourself before adding any filters onto your life. Although times can get a little rocky at some point, we must continuously get up every day and look in the mirror and say to yourself I GOT THIS. We determine our own happiness and must keep in mind that everything starts with loving YOU from the inside out.

Dr. Nina R. Copeland

Many are the afflictions of the righteous, but the LORD delivers him out of them all. - Psalms 34:19

Have you ever been in a desolate, barren, or suffering place in your life? It can be a painful place.

We sometimes question God, "Why am I here, and why is this happening to me?"

Going through the valley is the shortest distance to where God wants to take you. During this time, it is important to understand that God has a way of preparing His people for victory.

In the valley, you can identify who you are in Christ.

We must sit, pause, reflect, meditate, and sharpen our skills in the valley; but most importantly, we must first lean on God. Why in the valley? Because God has a gift for you in the valley. He wants you! Your attention! He is waiting for you to surrender fully. The valley experience helps you find the greatness inside of you. So, there is also joy in the valley! It comes from knowing that God is always with you to protect and guide you in all things.

Embrace your "low place" and ask God for navigational instructions in the valley. Endure the process and accept the circumstances. God has instructions for you to retrieve your gift. Your purpose! A renewed mindset! God wants to transform you in the valley.

Are you ready to change for God? If so, don't miss your gift in the valley, which will elevate you to new dimensions.

Encourage yourself today! Decree and declare, "I am a WINNER! I have already WON!"

Sharon Coulberson

Due to overwhelming feelings of grief, subconsciously we sometimes block memories of loved ones who have transitioned from this life. Being emotionally submerged can sometimes negatively take precedence over our lives. Grief can have us in a world-wind of emotions and even keep us mentally stagnate. The relationship between grief and joy are interconnected. Joy really does come in the morning. The same memories that once had us in a defective choke hold of sorrow can be the same memories that have our faces and stomachs hurting, while crouched in a fetal position, from laughter and joy as happy tears are rolling down our faces. Actively remembering our loved ones will keep them very much alive. It is ok to allow the memories to flood our thoughts. It is ok to cry on holidays when their presence is mostly missed. We should openly allow ourselves to feel every intense emotion that comes to mind. Until we can see them again, we must understand that creating a safe space to share in the joy of their memories and the time we had with them are most important. Joy 365 is a dedication to my family and friends who have lost someone significant to them. In Loving Memory: Mona Ann Coulberson, Claudia Marie Collins, Ella Bell White, Gregory Coleman, Malik James Sheets, Darrell Coulberson, Denise Jackson, Donterrius "Jade" Potter, Andrew and Geneva Burns, Elizabeth Johnson, Dr. Princess Jackson, David "Fat Dude" Jackson, Melvin Dewayne Jackson, Donnell Ray Bennett, Vince Pardue, Brandon "Boogie" Montrell, Flora Mae Jones, Gwendolyn Gale Jackson, Geraldine Jones, Theresa Mae Hensley, Zola Mae Christopher, Glenn Kline, Wesley "Uncle Big Boy" Johnson, Kaden Storm Brown, Kaneshia Logan, Vince Pardue, Kimbra Richard, Donald Ray Louis and Willie Hines

Psalm 30:5 KJV

Jennifer Covello

Did you know that God has authored a book about you?

It's a heavenly bestseller! Every page is filled with His plans for your life. Long before the universe was created, God had you in mind. He knits you in your mother's womb and knows everything about you. He sent His Son Jesus and ordered your steps so that you would have a life filled with peace, hope, and purpose. God has also given you specific gifts and talents so that you can be all He designed you to be.

"Each one should use whatever gift he has received to serve others, faithfully administering God's grace in its various forms." (NKJV)

The Bible says that you are to use your gifts to serve others and to give glory to God. These gifts are not to be left dormant or downplayed. God made you to be uniquely you! You are His masterpiece. However, we live in a broken world and walking out God's plan is not always easy. We get caught up in the busyness of life and put other people, places, and things ahead of Him. When we do this, we can miss or delay His plan for us.

Yet God loves us so much that He will get us back on track. He will help us with the bumps in the road and the storms that come along. Our part is to diligently seek Him every day, listen for His guidance, and walk in obedience.

God has a great plan for you – one filled with hope and a great future.

Detra Cowan-White

Why should I continue when it seems so little is gained. Why should I continue when lately through all my efforts, all I feel is pain. Why should I continue when I can't see the light. Why should I continue in this nasty everlasting fight.

Why should I continue when my heart's broken. I feel like a used unwanted token. Why should I continue if I'm already alone in a house with no resemblance to a home. Why should I continue when I lost it all. It feels like I am continuously spiraling down this awful fall. Why should I continue when I love and give my all but can't seem to get anything back from any of you?

Why should I continue after all of the mistakes. I never seem to ever get a break. Why should I continue when it appears all is lost. My failures and attempts have led to a horrible cost. Why should I continue when my mind is unclear. I don't know what to do because, God, I can't hear, see, or feel you.

Why should I continue if I have no hope or motivation to live or grow. I feel like a closed up, closed off room with no windows or doors. Just a pit full of sadness covered in sores.

I continue because I am prepared and equipped. These are only temporary feelings and not who I am. The one and only God who created me says who I am. I was created on purpose, with a life purpose. *Ephesians 2:10*; *Romans 8:16-17 I know that my God will deliver me, and He will deliver you as well. Hold on as better days are coming, Keep praying your joy will be restored.*

Deborah Crowley

I am a beacon of radiant joy, embracing my roles as a loving mother, grandmother, and entrepreneur with unwavering faith. Each day, I am filled with the divine presence, radiating joy, and spreading love to those around me with unwavering faith. With a heartfelt reminder of the joy that fills my life during my busy schedule and various roles, it's important to pause, reflect, and nurture your spirit. It is important to embrace gratitude and take a moment to reflect on the blessings in your life. I give thanks for the joyous moments, the loving relationships, and the opportunities that have come my way. Personally, I am culticating an attitude of gratitude and letting it fill my heart with joy. My strength and challenges sometimes appear in a moment of dismay. As an entrepreneur, I face challenges and obstacles along my journey. I must remember that my strength comes from the Lord. I find comfort in knowing that I am not alone, and God equips me with everything I need to overcome any adversity. As a loving mother and grandmother, my relationship was a source of great unforeseen joy being a child of the unknown. Now I take time to nurture these bonds, expressing love, kindness, and respect. My joy for family relationships reminds me of the depth of God's love for me. I spend my quiet time Resting and Renewing my goals for my future endeavors, as well as gaining insight on how to move forward to leave a legacy for my grandchildren. I demonstrate strength and endurance in the face of inner hurt and pains from my past life. To all the mothers, grandmothers, and entrepreneurs, your impact on society is immeasurable. May you continue to inspire, uplift, and provide joy along the way. Dedication to: Terrell Wallace, Devon Wallace, Braylen Wallace, Wes Wallace

AJ Cuggy

"Truly, truly, I say to you, that you will weep and lament, but the world will rejoice; you will grieve, but your grief will be turned into joy."
John 16:20 (NASBA95)

When I think of Joy, two loves come to mind - my pets and grandchildren. What a source of happiness they are. This would be tested when suddenly one of our beloved dogs came to the end of her life.

Juliette, a gorgeous harlequin miniature dachshund was sick for 7 months with autoimmune anemia. We were counting the precious days. The many transfusions sustained her during this time. That fateful morning all was well. Suddenly she could barely walk. My vet had predicted that soon enough the transfusions would no longer work. Two and half weeks later, post transfusion, her fate arrived. Grief stricken! How could we babysit my two youngest grandchildren today? Compassionate Vets were contacted, and home euthanasia was arranged. Meantime, Juliette just lay there. With tears and a cracking voice, I asked my daughter to still bring the children over and their presence would allow us to get through the sad event and restore our smiles. My oldest grandson and his dad agreed to come over to help bury our sweet girl.

God answered my prayers not in totality but in part. The miracle of a recovery was denied, but He heard my request for summer enjoyment and her 13th birthday celebration. She passed away three days after this milestone, surrounded by love in the arms of her daddy. Love and kindness changed the tears of sorrow to tears of joy. God had not forsaken us. He gave us not only the life and love of Juliette but our beautiful grandchildren too. Our hearts and love are restored in her memory.

Siobhan Cunningham

Listen to your Heavenly Father when you don't know what steps to take is the ultimate act of faith. As an independent and stubborn woman, my intuition flawlessly moved me in the right direction throughout life. However, my love life decisions often made me feel less than empty. I finally listened to the voice that told me, "He's not for you." I took a leap of faith to undo our holy union. My decision was one of my strengths, to put myself first. To be the woman my daughters, my dear, sweet babies, deserve, a mother who is confident enough to be herself. Trying times continue. Faith is the key to joy. Appreciate the precious moments of love and kindness that God gifts us. When intolerance creeps into your heart, consider this prayer:

Dear God,

I ask for Your guidance and wisdom as we navigate this new phase in our lives and strive to co-parent in a way that honors You and puts our children's well-being first.

I pray that You help us let go of the negative emotions or attachments that hurt our ability to work together effectively. And we ask that you heal any wounds that have caused our separation, and help us forgive each other and ourselves. As Your child, I pray that You give me the strength and patience to communicate respectfully and constructively, grant us grace as we make joint decisions that reflect our children's best interests, and support each other as co-parents. I ask that You bless our children with Your love and protection and help us raise them in a healthy, nurturing, and stable environment.

I commit to Your care and guidance and trust Your plan for our family. In Jesus' name, I pray. Amen.

Remember, you are His child. Therefore, you are enough.

TaiSheena Cunningham

"I can do all things through Christ which strengtheneth me." - Philippians 4:13

Moving seven times (two different countries and three different states) over the course of two years is HARD. Completing twenty-six rounds of chemotherapy in eighteen months is hard. Having seven surgeries in the span of 2 years is HARD.

These are all things that I thought would break me, but through God I have learned I can do the hard things. When I heard the words "Yes, you have cancer" I felt as though the wind was knocked out of me. Those words rang in my head repeatedly. For a month I felt like I walked around in a fog. What does this mean for me? What does this mean for my family? Will I see my grandchildren grow up?

So many questions went through my head. The answer to it all was, YES, you will get through this. Your story is not done. You still must secure your legacy. Each day of this tumultuous battle I woke up and showed gratitude for the little things in life. Some days, it was hard to find something to be grateful for, but on those days, it was the breath that I was still able to have fill my lungs.

When I speak about finding joy it does not mean that I'm always happy. It means that I understand what it's like to be down, and I'm thankful and joyful to still be here. I changed my mind set to be able to understand that my joy comes from what has been put into ME. It's not the circumstances in which I find myself or the feelings I have. It's the peace of knowing I will make it through.

Pastor Michelle Curtis

This is the day the Lord has made; it is our choice to rejoice and be glad in it! There is no denying that we live in a world that calls good evil and evil good. We live in a sin sick secular society that is bankrupt in morality. It will get worse before it gets better but not for the believing Believer! We may live in a bankrupt society surrounded by corruption, but our God has deposited His joy on the inside of us. The Father's checks don't bounce yet the onus is on us to make consistent deposits until the joy overflows and completes the checks and balances. It's an inside job! The world seeks out happiness that is predicated on happenstance, the situations and circumstances surrounding them. The believing Believer finds strength and solace in the Joy of the Lord. Joy is synonymous with Chara. According to the Strong's Concordance, "Chara means joy, calm delight, or inner gladness." INNER GLADNESS! It's an inside job! Chara is related to Chairo meaning to rejoice and Charis, which means grace. In other words, Chara means to rejoice because of grace. It's an inside job! We can rejoice because we know that God has given us the grace to still have joy repeatedly despite the situation or circumstance. The enemy is a thief who sometimes uses sorrow and grief to steal our joy and peace; remember that weeping may endure for a night, but joy comes in the morning and sometimes through our mourning. Jesus is the Balm of Gilead; the only One Who can soothe our souls. We must guard our hearts for out of them flow the issues of life; joy is an issue. The devil is a robber who only comes for what he deems valuable. The thief comes to steal, kill, and to destroy but Jesus came that we might have life, life more abundantly. In the Lord's presence there is the fullness of joy; praise Him; commune with Him and yield to the Holy Spirit's guidance in the bearing of great fruit. Joy! It's an inside job!

Sheila Curtis

As a teenager, my first boyfriend/girlfriend relationship was not ideal. My first job didn't offer me an ideal exit. My first trip out of the state, as an adult, was not an ideal trip. My first child was not born under ideal circumstances. My first marriage was not ideal. Within those seasons of what wasn't ideal, I was heartbroken, bruised, and damaged adding to the familiarities of insecurity and rejection.

As I reflect on the very worst moments in those experiences, I can remember struggling to make the best of it to get through it. And I did with the help of the Lord. I vowed not to be found in certain circumstances again. My innate ability to Trust God helped me rebuild my faith through His promises. It fueled my tenacity to persevere no matter the situation because I could do nothing without faith in God. I realized my most joyful times were and are directly connected to my faith and inner peace to live and be better. It's more than trusting God in situations; it's becoming a living testimony of a changed lifestyle throughout life's situations.

Trust in the Lord with all your heart and Lean Not on Your Own understanding; in all your ways, acknowledge Him, and He will direct your path (Proverbs 3:5–6). With that, I reconnected my natural life to my spiritual life; not just in "church but also and especially outside of "church". Now, I am fully persuaded that my faith and joy are directly connected to God's peace, which surpasses all my understanding and will guard my heart and mind through Christ Jesus (Philippians 4:7).

Dr. Doris H. Dancy

Sometimes God presents us with challenges that require great faith… a belief in Him more than anything else. In the story of Esther when she is asked to go to see the King to save her people, she reminds Mordecai that the king has not requested her presence for over thirty days. Visiting without permission means death. However, because Haman is planning to kill all Jews, Mordecai tells her she must go. There's no escape for her just because she lives in the Palace. She is in a battle, and in the battle, God demonstrates His glory and His power. It is in the battle that God plucks Hagar from the wilderness, takes Joseph from the pit to a family reunion, finds David in a shepherd's field and places him on a throne.

Repeatedly, God teaches it's in the battle where blessings materialize, and where His vision is actualized. If we cast the battle away, we lose the blessing. Here, God reveals His master plan. Will Esther trust God and go forth into the battle or will she refuse and protect herself? Her first response is self-serving. Her concern is with maintaining her position and not with fulfilling a purpose for God. She must decide if her relationship with God will take priority over her comfort. She's faced with one of life's most difficult tests, and she must make an important decision. In our lives we, too, are faced with the same kinds of tests. There are times when Christ requires us to trust Him. NEVER give up the opportunity to fight in the battle because it's in the battle that we are blessed. God's DIVINE PURPOSE calls for us to yield to things that seem impossible.

Biodun Dapherede

It was the great winter of 2010...

It was tame on the East Coast, but I didn't feel that way then. I had just moved to the US, and the weather threw me for a loop. It had a horrific effect on my mental health, resulted in aggressive skin reactions, and upset my regular cycle. And that was how it began, a secret tug of war with the weather that had me cramming dreams into 3-4 summer months and barely functioning in the remaining months of the year.

I've learned that expecting happiness in every season will lead to frustration, but the secret to wholeness is cultivating Joy. We rarely see these words together - Cultivate and Joy. Cultivating is developing something through its growth stages and cultivating relationships that keep us grounded—cultivating a posture of patience and empathy.

We experience a life of vulnerability, even though it was never modeled in your family or circle. When we let our feelings crowd everything else out, we risk losing our way and missing the winning seasons. Don't get me wrong, I'm still a summer girl at heart, but I have learned to cultivate joy even in the winter months. There'll always be seasons of uncertainty and fear but remember that just like the winter and the summer, they don't last forever.

Joy is exactly what the Lord prescribes.

"Therefore, the redeemed of the LORD shall return, and come with singing unto Zion, and everlasting joy shall be upon their head: they shall obtain gladness and joy, and sorrow and mourning shall flee away." Isaiah 51:11

Cynthia Davis

Depression once pressed me down, paralyzed, and kept me from moving forward in God's plan and purpose for my life. In despair, thoughts of suicide plagued me nightly as I suffered in silence. Overwhelmed and mentally tormented, sleep would flee from me, and I was almost ready to give up, so I had to expose what I was experiencing because I was sinking to my lowest point and could no longer handle this alone. After revealing what I was experiencing, a few great women of God stood with me in prayer through this mentally agonizing battle. They did not abandon me and are still instrumental in my life today.

They imparted strength to help me lift myself out of this low state of despair and sadness. Hope returned and canceled out the thoughts that played over and over in my head and not only am I living again, but I am also functioning as an instrument for God's use. Love and care stepped in and gave me the boost I needed to begin to live on purpose as life's pressures are given to God. Loneliness and isolation meant to cause mental desolation, are no longer my companions because God surrounded me with the right laborers on my journey of hopelessness. Crying out to God while in mental anguish was primarily my acknowledging that I needed help and that I could not handle this prison of internal pain to my own potential self-destruction. God showed His love for me through His people as they supported me in my time of need during this dark season. My life and mental state were altered and under fire, but God's love marched in and helped me walk out of this trial of sorrow so that I could experience the *Joy of Arising from the Ashes.*

Danita Davis

In the ebb and flow of life, we encounter moments of both difficulties. It's during the downward spirals that we often retreat into solitude, seeking solutions in isolation. Yet, it is precisely in these moments that staying connected becomes paramount—mentally, emotionally, and spiritually.

It is through our connections that we find our Power Source. This connection can provide you with the surge that you need to overcome the challenge. When you relate to people, they may be able to present you with ideas and or solutions that you have not considered while in your alone state. Remember, 'iron sharpens iron,' and diamonds emerge more brilliant from the crucible of adversity.

It's important that we think of thoughts as seeds for emotions, which then shape our feelings. Navigating this emotional journey is where connections come in. Sharing our thoughts and feelings with trusted individuals provides support, clarity, and a fresh perspective. It's like having a secret weapon for understanding and managing our inner world, lightening the emotional load and making the journey more bearable.

Now comes the faith connector. It is when we are connected to our power source that we gain our strength. It is where we are reminded that we CAN DO ALL THINGS! Being confident and knowing that greater is (He) that is within us than he who is (alone) in the world. Because it is through our source to Him that we move and have our being. So let this be a reminder to stay connected to your energy source, while you are in the valley, so that you can have the strength you need to get to the mountain top!

Susan Deal

Many know the story of the resilient tree, firmly planted, seeking the life-giving water (Psalms 1:3). Just as the tree flourishes and stands strong, our well-being thrives when we nourish ourselves with self-love and care. Embody the wisdom of a tree planted by the water by embracing the power of positive values and exploring a path of growth and authentic living. Begin with the art of growing.

Grow: Cultivate Personal Development - In your soul's garden, plant seeds of personal growth. Commit to continuous learning, self-discovery, and embrace challenges that foster evolution. Explore the rich soil of your potential to discover the resilience needed to overcome burnout to blossom into your truest form. *Live: Nurture the Essence of Self-Care and Self-Love*

Living radiantly is tending to your garden of well-being by recognizing and offering your body and mind profound self-love. Find time and space for healing, restoration, and daily self-care, whether prayer, meditation, a nature walk, or doing something you enjoy. Prioritize moments that rejuvenate your body and mind to spark the joy of radiant living.

Radiate: Experience Joy, Peace, and Beauty- Radiance is more than reflections of moments of joy and peace; it's a powerful projection originating from within. Like the sun casting its glow, you can illuminate beauty within and around you. When you immerse yourself in joy, your soul radiates a luminosity that transcends the physical. Here's a challenge: Sow positivity by sharing a compliment or performing an act of kindness each day. In doing so, you vibrate higher, radiate energy inside, and inspire hope that lights the path for you and others. As you cultivate a life filled with joy, radiance, and beauty, take a moment today to embrace the brilliance within.

Carla Ginebra De Garcia

"And I John saw the holy city, new Jerusalem, coming down from God out of heaven, prepared as a bride adorned for her husband (Revelation 21:2)."

There are 4 actionverbs introduced in the above verse which are *saw, coming, prepared, and adorned.* Do you think that it is referring to a joyful wedding ceremony that pointing us towards a Great Feast? Well, the answer is Yes! The Feast of Tabernacles/Sukkot comes 4 days after Yom Kippur Feast, and it is a celebration! The sukkah is a temporary structure that symbolizes the booths the Israelites lived in while wandering through the desert (Leviticus 23:42-44). Has a life situation invited you to wander in the desert? In Israel, during the days leading up to this feast, you will find people building sukkahs outside their homes, in their courtyards, and on their balconies. During the holiday families will eat in their sukkahs and some will even sleep there. In the Jewish rabbinic tradition, it is customary to host seven "tzadikim" This custom in Aramaic is called Upsizing, meaning "guests." <u>Reflection:</u> Have you welcomed the greatest joy, Yeshua, in your life? As we are here on earth in transition, let us seek to abundantly give hospitality to others through Yeshua, the GREAT I AM. Enlarge your territory, by embracing His consecrated pure joy that only comes from the chambers of His throne to His Bride. Are you ready? Miracles happen when you are adorned with joy! Heaven is coming to dwell in a new Earth Prepare the Bride in joy, see Your Bridegroom is coming!

Dr. Destiny

If Moses held up his hands, the Israelites were winning, but whenever he lowered his hands, the Amalekites were winning. - Exodus 17:11

The Israelites went to battle with the Amalekites. God instructed us to raise His hands. When His hands were raised the Israelites won, when His hands lowered the Amalekites won. Aaron raised one of Moses' arms and Hur raised the other. They took the initiative and supported Moses until sunset when Joshua won the battle with his sword. What if Aaron and Hur criticized Moses? What if they whispered among the people to build a camp against Moses for their own selfish ambition? Instead, they trusted in God and respected His plans.

Are you Hur and Aaron at this moment? Do you need to develop a supportive mindset? Who are you attached to? Will they support you through tough times? Time is short and tomorrow isn't promised! God requires full surrender. You must seek His face and turn from your wicked ways, and He will forgive sin, and heal you. You are an instrument, conduit, liaison, never lose sight of the fact that you are in a spiritual war. So, do you choose to be an instrument of sin or blessings? You can lead people to darkness or to the light. Jesus and the Holy Ghost defends you and pleads your case in the courts of the spiritual realm. Jesus and Holy Ghost defends us but remember it is based on the character of our heart and evidence. If there is evidence of unrepented sin, you will be guilty as charged. Yet through His grace we can be vulnerable and pray for Godly relationships that guide us through life's storms. God is calling for His children to Get real. Remember, together we win!

Tyrone Dicks

Slowly inhale... Exhale... Relax... Breathe... Focus...

I have struggled, sweated, bled, cried, and loved. My motivation has been ripped apart, although I still press forward from the shards.

I would do it all over again just to see the blessings that I'm about to receive. Everything I go through is meant for me by "*my design.*" As my Ancestor's, my Orisha's, my God, my Allah, my Creator, The Universe will yield my mind's intent through "*free will.* "I'm built for this. The contents of my paradigm will be in motion and will be pushed freely. Every thought processed, every decision made, every action rendered, I care*fully* analyzed before carrying it out. So, if anything goes wrong, I can only blame myself.

No worries... No Pressure... Because I'm built for this. I will not put any more on myself than I can handle. I create my path inspired by my dreams and ambition. As my Ancestor's, my Orisha's, my God, my Allah, my Creator and The Universe will yield my mind's intent. *"We set the tone for our livelihood and how other's approach, communicate, associate, or disengage with us.* "So, stay in-tune with yourself and your core beliefs that move your soul. Let no-one or nothing stop you from attaining your goals. Anything you set forth in your mind to do is already blueprinted and accomplished. All you must do is carry your *will* out. And your support system will promote it *freely*. Do not let the bumps in the road detour or discourage you. It's building your character and chiseling your attributes for success. Do not fold or conform. It's only one of you.

Be yourself. You got this... You're built for it

Tiphanie Thee Doll

I know, I know, so often we hear the phrase "Trust the Process" a phrase that is easier said than done and let's face it, with so much going on how can we really "Trust the Process". Trusting the process is like having that thing called FAITH, knowing that God is going to show up on time every time. Often when trouble arises, or things are not happening according to our plan we go into panic mode. Honestly going into panic mode is a natural human reaction, and let me tell you, if you don't go into panic mode, I'm looking at you sideways, lol. But when trusting the process comes into play, you go into panic mode, you don't stay there, you have what we call a "woosah" moment because you know everything is going to be alright. As a mother I have had to train myself to have a million "woosah" moments because let's be real, becoming a mother changes you. It changes the physical you, the mental you, the emotional you, and the spiritual you, and if you are not equipped or prepared it will send you in a whirlwind. From Day 1 my motherhood reality is nothing like I envisioned. Eventually I found myself asking those questions: Why is my child not talking like everyone else? Why did her father and I do not make it? etc.; I had to realize things have not gone according to my plan before so what makes this any different. We get so caught up in our way not working that it deters us from the REAL or believing that God is still in the picture.

Know that your steps have been ordered since you were in the womb. Trust the process: even if it doesn't look clear right now, it won't always look like that.

Eventually the process will be so clear that you'll laugh at everything you went through.

Milicent Driver

At times, life can seem difficult, and joy can seem far away from us. We all face those moments in life that may cause us to question our faith and moments that rob us of our joy. Instead of focusing on the pains that are part of this life, let's take a moment to reflect on what brings us true joy. Let's remember what it really means when we talk about "the joy of the Lord"—it is far greater than any earthly pleasure or satisfaction. It is a rich blessing found when we devote ourselves to God! When we focus on Him, no matter the circumstances in our lives, joy is sure to follow. Let's not forget that Jesus is the source of our greatest joy and the ultimate answer to all of life's struggles. Through Jesus Christ, we CAN find true and lasting joy.

Let us remember that *"the joy of the Lord is our strength" (Nehemiah 8:10)*. In His presence is where our souls will be truly satisfied and it's only through Him that we can experience that *unspeakable* joy. When we come to Him each day with thanksgiving, we may be filled with His peace and joy. As we continually invest our time in prayer and reading God's word, let us remember that our joy will be fully rooted in Him. Let us seek Him first and all other things will be added unto us (Matthew 6:33).

He is the ultimate source of our joy, contentment, and peace. Let us find our greatest joy in Jesus and share it with others around us. Together, let's celebrate the Joy of the Lord! Amen.

Glendora Dvine

Psalm 34:4-5 reminds us that fear cannot coexist with the unwavering belief in God's presence: "I pray to the Lord, and he answered me. He freed me from all my fears. Those who look to him for help will be radiant with joy; no shadow of shame will darken their faces." It is time to make a conscious choice, to shift our mindset from fear to faith. Too often, we vocalize our fears, both the visible and the unseen, even as we profess our love for the Lord. It's time to intentionally choose the Lord's side, breaking the habit of giving voice to our fears. This shift will demand a change in thinking, but it will allow God to work His wonders within us. Embracing faith over fear means granting the Lord full access to our hearts and minds, knowing that His love covers us like no other. To help you break free from the chokehold of fear, consider these three steps:

Give Yourself Grace: Understand that life is meant to have storms; they are part of the journey. Expect them, but also have faith that you will weather them. Have Mercy for Yourself: Recognize that you are divinely created, but you are not meant to be always the smartest in the room. Embrace each moment as an opportunity to learn, grow, and draw closer to the love of the Lord. Activate Thanksgiving: In every situation, good or bad, choose to praise the Lord out loud. Even when fear attempts to grip you, let your praises resound. With faith, take bold steps forward, knowing that you are never alone. In changing your mindset from fear to faith, you empower yourself to change your world. By embracing the love and guidance of the Lord, you can overcome any obstacle that comes your way.

Denise E. Edwards

John 8:36 "whom the son sets free is free indeed."

Growing up I can recall being teased and taunted by everyone I met, including those in my own home. There wasn't a day that went by that I wasn't ridiculed and laughed at. I was called all kinds of degrading names.

You see I was born with a severe form of eczema, a dry, itchy, and irritating skin disorder that would cause breakouts of painful white blisters all over my body. No one wanted to be around me, let alone be my friend so I withdrew, turning to food, drugs, and alcohol as my only means of solace. For years, I suffered in silence with addiction, deep depression, loneliness, sadness, and poor self-esteem. I became a suicidal introvert who wanted nothing more than to escape life and die.

But God…He had a different plan for me.

In May 1992, during a church service, I heard God saying to me, "Denise you are my daughter, I did not make a mistake in creating you; you were created on purpose with purpose". It was then and there that I accepted Jesus as my Lord and Savior; from that day on my life has never been the same. Jesus freed me from the life of torment and addiction. He took the taste of drugs out of my mouth. I went to church that day bound and drug addicted and came home delivered and set free, never to touch drugs again. I no longer listen to or believe the lies of the enemy, nor seek the approval from others, but I live now only to please God.

I walk in that freedom in which Christ has made me free. To God be the glory. I'm free.

Mrs. Benita M. Elcock

Prior to the loss of my mother, I never knew grief.

I felt my heart break and immediately become numb. Grief for me looked strong, disciplined, and focused. Grief had taken away my ability to feel. I would still show up for discipleship training. With this group, God is constantly at my center, and one morning the sun beamed through the window. I can still remember the warmth caressing my face, I basked in it. I was then moved to sit with *Psalm 30:5-6*. I want to encourage you to know that Joy truly indeed comes in the morning. There was a shift; I was feeling again.

Now everything meant something. I cared about everything. There was a feeling of wanting to make it count. This loss triggered me to think about my own mortality. I clung to my children when meeting strangers and the exchange was meaningful. I encouraged others to consciously love. Grief doesn't just subside, it transforms. Grief taught me resilience and appreciation. Through this transformation I found myself healing, and the healing came by way of understanding life's cycle and where I fall in this process.

Life is a journey full of so many experiences that are meant to teach and grow us. We can then use the experience to pave the way. In this understanding I have found peace, and, in my peace, I can see characteristics of my mother in my children and this realization allows me to take comfort in their laughter and know I have not lost.

I want to empower anyone experiencing grief to know this: With time and work, the initial feeling will subside, and with renewed heart and mind, you will be transformed. Just keep God at your center.

Amber Enfinger

Fifteen years! That is how long I was an active addict.

I grew up a preacher's daughter. I knew at an early age who Jesus was. Yet, I allowed myself to become entangled with the yoke of bondage, as Paul warns us against in Galatians.

It started at age 16. I met a boy and went from respectful, humble teenager to runaway teen in a few, short months. I was caught in Houston, TX, 10 hours away from home, and sent to juvie. My Mom came to pick me up. Once home, my parents gave me an ultimatum; marry or part ways. I chose to marry. What seemed like love, quickly became destructive. When that marriage ended, it didn't take me long to find another husband. I was seeking validation in the wrong place. The next few years consisted of a myriad of every kind of drug, as I tried to find solace for my life. I had one child with my first husband, two children by my second.

Eventually I lost custody, became homeless, jobless, clueless and without hope. Now, let me tell you how God changed me. He's my rescue story. He picked me up out of the mess and saved me. My home and vehicle are paid for. I'm a successful business owner. I have full custody of my children. I have peace in my heart, joy in my soul. He turned a nobody like me into somebody.

Jesus is the answer.

Gloria Evans

I didn't understand why people complimented me with the words, "You are so strong." They didn't see the pain and suffering I was experiencing as a single mother of two sons, whom I had at a very young age after marrying and divorcing young too. For me it was like a banner I was given to show I did not need any help. Not only was this not true, but unfortunately there was no real help given.

The expectation was for me to make it on my own, find my way and figure it out. After the trauma of that kind of pain back-to-back, with no relief or help, I found my strength to keep moving from the joy of the Lord, knowing He cares for me.

Through all the tears and sleepless nights, not knowing what to do next, dealing with school issues, absent father, lack of support, there was something on the inside pushing me to keep moving. Even at my lowest and most devastating mistakes, I never felt God turn His back on me. Although this all took a toll on my health, I always found joy in praise and worship because of my attitude toward Him. He is High and Lifted UP! The Almighty King of Kings cares for me! That gave me joy to keep going and strength to endure all that I encountered.

Don't lose your praise, and you won't lose your joy!

Psalms 27:6; And now shall mine head be lifted above mine enemies round about me: therefore, will I offer in his tabernacle sacrifices of joy; I will sing, yea, I will sing praises unto the LORD.

Pastor Kaye Ross Faison

There is a certain level of aspiration that comes forth out of us when we Look Up. A sense of optimism, hope, and expectancy, suddenly seems to become possible when we Look Up. Looking up brings about an assurance of new answers, understanding, and determination. It is like looking into Heaven for the very counsel of God. Such questions can arise like; "What should I do?" "Lord, where are you?" Or we finally reach the mindset which says, "No matter what Lord, I trust you." That alone can bring us to a place called better.

The opposite of Looking Up is down, and it can indicate unhappiness, hopelessness, shame, and defeat. In this regard, there is no joy, hope, or apparent possibilities. It feels like we are stuck, and this is all it will ever be. As we settle, it changes our posture, demeanor, and emotions. We become negative and faithless. Personally, I believe that no matter what comes our way, if we can just get to the place where we lift our heads and look up, things will start to shift. It is conducive to our deliverance and restoration.

No wonder, the bible encourages us to: *"Lift up your heads, O ye gates; and be ye lifted, ye everlasting doors; and the King of Glory shall come in. Who is this King of Glory? The Lord strong and mighty, the Lord mighty in battle. Lift your heads, O ye gates; even lift them up, ye everlasting doors; and the King of Glory shall come in. Who is this King of Glory? The Lord of hosts, he is the King of Glory. Selah." ~Psalm 24:7-10*

Notice, our help is in Looking up and depending on the King of Glory. So, Look Up & Live!

Dr. Blanche Farrish

ll my life God has been faithful. Thank you, Holy Spirit, that dwells inside of me, motivating and encouraging me through prayer to speak directly to God, our Lord and Savior.

Make a joyful noise unto the Lord, all ye lands! Serve the Lord with gladness; Come before His presence with singing. (PSALM 100 NKJV)

I shout Hallelujah! God is our King, King of Kings, and Lord of Lords. I shout Hallelujah! God loves me; the joy of the Lord is my strength.

I shout Hallelujah! God made me in His image. I am beautiful, brave, and bold.

I shout Hallelujah! God has forgiven me; I am at peace (Jehovah Shalom, the God of Peace).

I shout Hallelujah! God will never leave or forsake me because He is omnipotent and omnipresent.

I shout Hallelujah! God has healed me. I am no longer bound but free, Jehovah Rapha (God the Healer).

Shout Hallelujah! No weapons formed against me will prosper. I was not given the spirit of fear.

Shout Hallelujah! Light over darkness; Jesus is the light of the world.

Shout Hallelujah! Love over hate. Fight the Good Fight of Faith.

Shout Hallelujah! I am rich, not poor; God will supply all my needs.

Shout Hallelujah! Grace always wins. Encourage yourself; you are a winner. Win! Win! Win!

"Encourage yourself in the Lord and let your light shine so that others may see."

Artisa Felder

Because of HIS love for you, you are never alone. During your darkest days if you look back you will notice that it was God that carried you through. It is easy for us to allow everything that is going wrong to consume us to a point that we overlook the things that are going right, the things that are falling in place. God never said that the weapons wouldn't form, and the storms would not come. He simply said that they would not prosper.

Consider this:

Storms come through to clear a path. Once the path is clear we can now see that there is something good in every storm. Once you come out on the other side, not only will you see the rainbow, but you will be stronger, more confident, and ready to conquer the next storm in your life because you will know that God will be there with you. Finding joy in situations allows you to learn the lesson in every test that comes your way.

Prayer:

Father, I thank you for not allowing me to face the troubles of my life alone. Your word stands firm in truth, and you said that you would never leave me nor forsake me. Not my will, but let your will be done, Lord. I am trusting you to lead me on this journey. Restore my faith, my joy and forgive me if I have ever allowed my storm to doubt your power.

In Jesus' name, Amen.

Author L. Fitz

"The Lord is close to the brokenhearted and saves those who are crushed in spirit." Psalm 34:18

During heartbreaking times, we tend to get angry with God and abandon His word due to our pain and broken hearts. We feel like we cannot get through, but we can always depend on Him. God will use our pain to show others His power. It's never about us but always about Him getting the glory. The trials we go through prepare us for the greater that is within us.

Today is our last day claiming broken heartedness and crushed spirits! He placed purpose in our hearts! We must minister to others and demonstrate what the real Power of God really does when we lean and depend on Him through our storms!

Growing up a daddy-less daughter cut me to the core. It's one of the most heartbreaking things that I've experienced in life. It hurts. At one point, I felt like I would never find healing. BUT GOD! I made it through the storm through praise. I still fight the pain daily, but God gives me strength to continue the fight. Whatever caused your broken heartedness and crushed spirit, I'm calling all broken hearts to tell you to cry out to God and thank Him for choosing you! He only gives His battles to His strongest warriors! Stand strong and look the enemy in the face, and keep praising, praying, pressing, and striving to do the work to heal! Our crushed spirits are temporary zones of brokenness that God will help us get through. He is the only constant and permanent thing in our lives. Share the good truth about His love with others and let's always remember to thank Him in the mist of our storms.

Kemonte Fleet

In life, there are moments when threads of joy unravel, leaving behind a sense of emptiness and weariness. As a 25-year-old, navigating the complexities of adulthood, you may find yourself entangled in the challenges of the journey. Yet, within the chaos, there exists a divine invitation to embark on a transformative quest — a journey towards joy restoration. Life has its way of dimming the vibrant hues of joy, whether through setbacks, disappointments, or the weight of responsibilities. In these moments, it's easy to lose sight of the joy that once animated your spirit. But take heart, for joy restoration is not only possible but also a sacred calling. Just as dawn follows the darkest hour of the night, your journey toward joy begins with the acknowledgment of your own narrative. Embrace the authenticity of your experiences, both triumphs, and trials, for they are the raw materials of growth. Reflect on the sources of your joy, those moments that once made your heart dance, and dare to reclaim them. Renewal requires a deliberate choice to cultivate gratitude, even during adversity. Seek out the small, insignificant moments that sparkle with joy, and let them weave a new tapestry of hope in your life. In the company of supportive relationships and a resilient spirit, you will discover that joy is not just a fleeting emotion but a resilient force that can be rekindled. As you embark on this journey of joy restoration, remember that it is okay to seek guidance, to ask for help, and to lean on faith. The very essence of your being is intertwined with the potential for joy, waiting to be reignited. May this devotional serve as a compass, guiding you towards the rediscovery of joy, a journey that leads not only to personal fulfillment but also to a deeper connection with the divine rhythm of life.

Khyeema Fleet

***"Restore to me the joy of your salvation and uphold me with a willing spirit."* Psalm 51:12 (ESV)**

Sometimes, life's challenges, trials and confusions can overshadow the inherent joy within us. They may even lead us to forget or ignore. Yet, rediscovering joy is not a destination but a continuous, transformative experience, and path.

This joy is a fundamental aspect of your being, not external, and can never be lost even though it may be temporarily obscured or overshadowed. Also, the acknowledgment of the words of Jesus in John 16:33 (NIV) *"I have told you these things, so that in me you may have peace. In this world, you will have trouble. But take heart! I have overcome the world."* helps you understand that it's normal to go through phases where joy feels distant.

This knowledge builds strength in you to journey into rediscovery. How? By peeling away the layers of negative emotions, stress, and worries that have accumulated over time. You'll discover that these layers may have been responsible for concealing that innate joy. As such, praying *"Create in me a clean heart, O God, and renew a right spirit within me."* - Psalm 51:10 (ESV) as you engage in self-exploration and self-awareness, will remove these barriers or layers. Soon, you will begin to experience the restoration of joy from your inside out. You will see how it has always been rightfully yours as your inherent birthright and not something to be earned or achieved.

Minister Karen Foote

    Life is full of challenges, suffering, pain, and disappointments. Our souls can become wounded and crushed by them all. Jesus, Himself, said we would have them (see John 16:33). There is healing in the Word of God. I've created an acronym from the word **A.B.I.D.E.** to make this strategy easy and memorable: The "**A**" stands for ***acquire*** an ***applicable*** scripture. Find scriptures that relate to your problem or issue. For example: for financial problems you can select Philippians 4:19. Write the scriptures down. The **B** stands for ***believe***. First, we must believe God is able. Second, we must believe that the Bible is, in fact, the Word of God and that it is true. The **I** stands for ***internalize.*** The root word here is internal. We must get the word, the truth, inside of us like a lie detector in our spirits. We do that by ***memorizing*** and ***meditating*** on it. Learn the scripture by heart. Biblical meditation is to focus one's thoughts: to ponder, to think on or muse on the Word of God. The **D** stands for ***declare***. Declare means to proclaim to speak out. "Thou shalt also decree a thing, and it shall be established unto thee: and the light shall shine upon thy ways (Job 22:28). The **E** stands for ***expect***. Face every day with the expectation that it could be the day of your breakthrough or healing. Expect it in faith.

    Pray and **A.B.I.D.E.** That is your solution to all of life's issues.

Myairah Fongsue

JOY means something different to everyone. There are so many ways and instances where Joy can be experienced. Accomplishing something, a significant moment, even the simplest things of life can cause joy.

To me JOY means the pure bliss of another form of happiness, completing a daunting task, having fun, meeting a famous person, visiting a beautiful place, a pleasant memory and having time away, such as a vacation. Being Joyful makes me feel free and hopeful. I hope to be joyful and find more of what makes me happy throughout the course of my life.

I remember losing my JOY because I failed at Physical Education but found comfort in knowing I had received 'As' in all my other subjects. When my cats passed away, I lost my JOY but was comforted by the fact that I had my Yorkie, named Julie who is energetic and very playful. Julie filled that void of not having my cats.

When I wake up to a new day and is given the privilege to see another beautiful sunrise, I get immense JOY. I find JOY in being with my mom and doing a variety of activities. I feel so JOYFUL knowing that I am a part of this phenomenal group of Co-authors in 'JOY 365' I am so grateful for this awesome and superb opportunity granted to me by Dr. Vernessa Blackwell, our Visionaire.

For the persons reading my chapter who may be feeling a bit overwhelmed, unhappy, and alone, I leave with you this comforting Bible verse. Psalm 126 :5 NIV.

(Those who sow in Tears will reap with songs of JOY).

Darkema Freeman

"⁵ Don't worry about anything; instead, pray about everything. Tell God what you need and thank him for all he has done. **4: 6 (NLT)**

There's a scripture for every situation or storm of life you may be going through. Pick the scripture that speaks to you concerning the storm you are in and present it to God. This is like speaking God's word back to Him. Put aside the worries just as our scripture of the day says. Rather, table every single concern before God. Why? This is because one biblical principle says God *"...magnifies Your word above all His name"* (Psalm 138:2 NKJV). Therefore, consciously call God's attention to your situation. Insert your request between your thanksgiving. This is because your thanksgiving keeps you joyous even though you are telling God your problems. I know you may be feeling so mad and overwhelmed. But understand that God loves you and cares about you and is willing and *"able to do exceedingly abundantly above all you could ever ask or think..."* (Ephesians 3:20 NKJV).

Another principle is as seen in Genesis 8:22 (NKJV); *"While the earth remains, seedtime and harvest, cold and heat, winter and summer, and day and night shall not cease."* Dearest, no matter what you're passing through, it's only for a season. This too shall pass. So long as seasons come and go, you'll come forth victorious. As you read these words, allow them to sink into your heart. You'll find that joy simmers in your heart and gives you strength while you wait.

Sakinah Nacole Freeman

This is the day the Lord has made. We will rejoice and be glad in it"
(Psalm 118:24, NLT)

Life is a joyful journey filled with profound happiness, experiences, and challenges. From the moment we take our first breath, we embark on a unique voyage filled with twists and turns, shaping the narrative of our existence. The journey of life is characterized by growth and self-discovery.

Challenges become our steppingstones, propelling us forward on this exhilarating expedition. Each obstacle is an opportunity to learn, to adapt and to find resilience within us.

One of life's greatest joys lies in the relationship with our Lord and Savior Jesus Christ. Through faith and a personal relationship with Jesus, will transcend to the changes in one's life.

Jesus brings joy through the profound aspects of salvation, purpose, peace, hope and unconditional love. The assurance that Jesus is with you during times of uncertainty, and that you can find strength and comfort in HIM brings forth a sense of joy and tranquility. The scripture says, "Always be full of joy in the Lord, I say it again – rejoice! (Philippians 4:4, NLT).

Tyquan Freeman

"⁵ Trust in the LORD with all your heart. Never rely on what you think
you know."
Proverbs 3:5-6 (GOODNEWS)

Surrendering seems easier said than done. Most times we profess with our mouths that we have surrendered. We even believe it so much at the time we confess it but the next moment when the situation comes knocking, we begin trying to figure it out. And when we fail, we sink into anger and confusion. If we then take a pause, we realize that what we have done did not indicate surrender in the slightest bit. Surrendering requires that you TRUST God in ALL things no matter how uncomfortable you may feel. It requires that you find a sense of purpose in the will and way of God even if you don't understand. What surrendering means is giving up your desires, plans, and weaknesses to Him because He works in us to shape the image of Christ in us. What you get in exchange for surrendering totally is a relief from the burden that being in control exerts on you. Also, it'll be easier to embrace God's unconditional love, His provision, and the kind of peace that comes from Him alone. Furthermore, you'll find that you begin to work/walk in alignment with His will. To cap it all, you'll find that you'll be spiritually growing and making progress on that journey irrespective of all the hurdles on your way. When you sit back to recount these, real joy that all your planning and calculations could not have afforded you, will be yours consistently. Choose to surrender today, and alway

Rosalie Funderburk

I searched and searched, but never found a name.

as sweet as the name of Jesus.

I did all I could, and through it all, it was Jesus.

I knew beyond a doubt, He was the one I could count on

He was my only way out.

But, no, instead of Him, I did it my own way

I laughed and I cried, every day.

I had my share of loss: to think I'd win the toss.

I was sadly mistaken; I was surely not the boss.

Yes, there were times I thought I knew.

I thought I had all the answers.

But what is to be gained from this ole' world?

But to protect my soul a priceless pearl

The choices we make stick with us like glue.

We make decisions, change our minds.

And wonder what to do We like playing cops and robbers.

It's just a silly game.

The moment we step out of line, Life becomes insane.

We ponder and ponder about life's situations.

We've come a long way - blessed indeed.

But here we go again hitting that same brick wall.

Yearning to be freed before we fall.

But wait, we rise above our circumstances.

It says so in God's word.

We walk by faith, and not by sight.

It's not something we just heard.

We continue to live day to day, still having choices to make.

My records show that Christ took the blows.

He did it God's way. Regrets, I would never know.

For His saving grace sustained me

As He wrapped His loving arms around me

May I say in a wonderful way "I AM FREE"

Tarshia Galloway

The Messiah, Lion of Judah, Redeemer, and Deliverer Deliver us from ourselves, pain, hurt, destruction and most of all our strongholds That is why we rejoice! Our father turns our sorrows into gladness. That's why we rejoice! What a life changer He is. That's why We rejoice!

Oh God Thank You for chasing and never giving up on us.

That's why we rejoice when scared, lonely, talked about, judged, and persecuted. Lord it was You who was there pulling us through.

That's why we rejoice! There were so many trials that have come. But your still small voice spoke words that sustained us. That's why we rejoice! Many times, the words would project out. But you said why not you. That's why we rejoice! The humiliation built us as a strong tower searching for no more validation. That's why we rejoice! During our time of reflection, we think of how you knew what was best when we could not see your plan. Oh, Savior

Thank you for your unfailing love, grace, and mercies. That's why we rejoice! When we think of your goodness That's why we rejoice!

You healed the affected areas in our lives and set us free.

That's why we rejoice! Father, your evidence is all around us.

That's why we rejoice!! It was you who chose us and set us apart. And for that we rejoice! Psalm 151.......

Catrina Garcia

2 Samuel 6:12-15 After a recent volleyball game, a sense of defeat and disappointment was over me, rooting from my performance on the court. The weight of my mistakes during the game had overshadowed my knowledge of technique, causing frustrating disconnection between what I knew and my execution during the match. However, God was teaching me a valuable lesson. During the ride home the song *"Dance Like David* '' by Joshua Aaron started playing. When I began to sing and dance, I felt the weight and heaviness lift off me, and I experienced true joy from the Lord. I had been allowing defeat to overshadow the opportunity God gave me for joy and celebration in His presence. In the testimony of David, God points out the importance of a steadfast pursuit to praise Him in any moment, with the movement of your body and the sound of your voice; no matter what your circumstances are, who's watching you, or your past.

Release your inhibitions, take a posture of praise. Go under His yoke, dwell in His presence, that's the ultimate source of joy. It would take eternity to praise Him in the manner He deserves, however, why not start praising Him today? We are appointed ambassadors of the Kingdom, we have the undeserved privilege to praise Him, because we are restored through the Blood of Yahweh! *Lord, thank You for this day, for allowing us to use our mouth to shout Your glory, arms to lift in praise, and knees to bow to You in surrender. Forgive us for the times we doubted the power of the sound. Thank you for our bodies as your temple which you made us fearfully and wonderfully created to dwell with You. Help us to recognize every opportunity to praise You, because it is in the praise that we experience Your Presence, the source of our joy. In Jesus' name, Amen.*

Toni Garnett

"These hard times are small potatoes compared to the coming good times; the lavish celebration prepared for us"
2 Corinthians 4:17 (MSG)

Things are usually never as bad as they seem. We know this just by looking back over our lives at what we thought would surely devour us… yet we're still here. During those challenging times, we get so busy seeing the negative of the situation, that we forget to seek God. We tend to try to fix things ourselves, instead of holding on to God's unchanging hands. Doubt and fear creep in and the feeling of defeat begins to surround us. Recognize this is where the devil wants you.

But God! This verse reminds us that these tough times are nothing but "small potatoes"! In other words, the hurt, the pain, the uncomfortable feelings that we experience during challenging times are insignificant compared to the good times to come. These are the times when we must lean not into our own understanding of what we see, but rather know that we serve a God that will go before us . . .a God that will never leave us, even in the toughest situations.

In challenging times, keep praying and never give up no matter how bad it seems. God promised us that things we see now are here today, gone tomorrow. But things we can't see now will last forever (2 Corinthians 4:18, MSG). These are the times to stand strong in God's word because on the other side of the pain, the hurt, and the disappointment is assuredly a lavish celebration prepared for us!

Abidemi Gboluwaga

JOY is one of the most beautiful feelings in this world. I receive JOY when I am being kind to someone. The JOY spills over from me to them. The JOY of the Lord is truly my strength. We do not have to be rich to be happy and to have JOY. Our JOY is innate; we have it to share with everyone on our life's journey. Listening to my favorite song, watching a good movie, preparing, and decorating for a party or cooking a delicious meal for my family give me immense JOY. To me JOY also means peace and tranquility. JOY is happiness to me as it dwells within me, and because of this, I find JOY in every situation I encounter daily.

My chosen vocation is Nursing. Initially, it was a big challenge for me, but now I am finding so much JOY in pursuance of becoming one of the best nurses on this planet earth. I am an overcomer. I feel JOYOUS whenever I look back and see how far I have progressed in pursuance of my dream, to the place I am now. God indeed is a good God. I could not have done this without Him.

I encourage everyone reading my chapter in 'JOY 365' to keep moving forward with their goals and aspirations. The beginning of most projects seems daunting at times, but do not fear, step out in faith, and keep telling yourself that not only can it be done, but it will be done. I am also wishing JOY to those who are currently sad, feeling helpless and hopeless. In the Bible it is written:

"A JOYFUL heart is good medicine, but a broken Spirit dries up the Bones." Proverbs 17:22

Tekhari Ghee

In second grade, a brain tumor unpredictably disrupted my academic journey, leading to three years filled with four surgeries and challenges to my physical and emotional well-being. Facing the reality that certain activities I once enjoyed were no longer possible, I developed a fervent desire to find alternative pursuits aligned with my interests and passions. Unexpectedly, I discovered robotics and S.T.E.M. programs, which not only captivated me but propelled me to excel, providing a glimpse into a boundless future career.

This transformative experience compelled me to explore uncharted territories, reshaping my perspective and instilling valuable lessons in resilience and adaptability. Reflecting on my past, I recognize the medical issue as a hidden blessing, as the limitations imposed during my childhood guided me toward a path uniquely suited to my talents and aspirations. While others may perceive my experience as a hindrance, I embrace a different viewpoint. The frame surrounding my journey is a testament to my faith in God, strength, and individuality, allowing me to break free from societal expectations.

Life's detours redirect us towards untapped potential and unforeseen adventures. I now understand that alternative paths always exist, leading to our desired destinations. We must remember that obstacles do not define us; instead, they shape us into individuals capable of achieving greatness. As we embrace our distinctive journeys, let us inspire ourselves & others to be extraordinary, paving the way for a future brimming with boundless potential, endless possibilities, and joy.

Patricia T. Gilchrist

James 1:2 KJV
My brethren, count it all joy when ye fall into divers' temptations.
Philippians 4:4 KJV

Rejoice in the Lord always; and again, I say rejoice.

As a young Christian woman going through some fiery trials, when I would pray about them, I kept hearing the same answer…James 1:2 Of course, that was not the answer I wanted, but as I obeyed and practiced this word, instead of lying down and being depressed, I began to praise and rejoice. It was dry at first, but I did it in faith. As a result, I no longer laid down feeling down and depressed. Over the years, it has led to a life of praise and joy. When we count it all joy by praising God in and through different temptations, tests, and trials, it keeps us from becoming depressed, bitter, or saddened.

When you praise God, the joy of the Lord will rise and drive those negative feelings of unhappiness, depression, and bitterness away, or from taking root. Your patience to wait on God becomes easier when you're in an attitude of praise. God tells us to rejoice in the Lord always and again I say rejoice. So, I encourage you by faith to count all joy when you find yourself going through different trials, tests, or temptations. You want to regret practicing what His word says in James 1:2, it will become second nature. With this practice you will see the spirit of joy rising in you more freely and frequently. It will become a lifestyle. Prayer: Father, I pray your grace upon me to count it all joy when I find myself in different temptations, tests, and trials. I pray never to allow them to take my joy. Amen

Dr. Antoria Gillon

Though it was a new day when I opened my eyes, I could still see yesterday as if it were not far away.

The walls still carry the aroma of yesterday's cooking.

I checked the news to see what I missed while asleep.

Today waits for new mysteries to be explored, but before I can do that, I must discover who I am. Who did I wake up to be? What will I serve? And how will they serve me?

I want to be still, yet I can feel the outside world tugging at me.

QUIT! Is how I feel which means I'm at a loss for what to do. I should stop, drop to my knees, and pray: "God grant me the serenity to accept the things I cannot change, the courage to change the things I can, and the wisdom to know the difference."

Breathe! Even if I've stopped moving, my mind is still operating automatically and gradually. Keep in mind that we are still living and that innovative ideas are being activated by our thinking.

Display! yesterday, as there will be plenty of experiences today.

You're capable of this!

Because your strength for today was demonstrated yesterday.

Sarah Gillet-Couto

In John 14:6, it is written: Jesus said to him, "I am the way, the truth, and the life. No one comes to the Father except through Me." In Matthew 7:13-14, we read, "Enter by the narrow gate; for wide is the gate and broad is the way that leads to destruction, and there are many who go in by it. Because narrow is the gate and difficult is the way which leads to life, and there are few who find it."

When we fully surrender to Jesus Christ as our Savior, we understand that following HIM might cost us our family, friendships, or fleshy pleasures. Still, we underestimate the joy HE is for us. Because Jesus died for our sins, we can rejoice in His blessings. The narrow path to eternal life becomes easier because we are not walking alone: "[His] word is a lamp to [our] feet, And a light to [our] path (Psalms 119:105)." Instead of searching for happiness, we must fill our hearts with His joy no matter our circumstances. Jesus is our only path to an incomparable joy that we can only experience when we walk in His steps.

One of the most powerful ways to find joy in the Lord is through prayer and worship. I am joyful because of HIM, rejoicing always, praying without ceasing, and giving thanks in everything, for this is the will of God in Christ Jesus for me (1 Thessalonians 5:16-18).

Make a list of what makes you joyful today and keep it as a reminder of His promises. As you pray, praise, and worship God, thank Him for teaching you how to be joyful.

Sanerica Gipson

"…looking unto Jesus, the author and finisher of our faith, who for the joy that was set before Him endured the cross, despising the shame, and has sat down at the right hand of the throne of God."
Hebrews 12:2 NKJV

It doesn't matter who you are, there are things that must be endured in this life. There will be situations where the benefit, the purpose for, or the joy in the outcome will not always be seen. Joy will be the last thing one would expect to see when dealing with difficulty. However, with God, it's possible, especially when circumstances are viewed from a right perspective. Jesus was able to endure the cross because He beheld the joy that was set before Him. What was the joy? Us! He set His eyes on the eternal ramifications of what He was doing instead of the agony.

He physically felt. He set His eyes on the millions that would come to know the Father through Him instead of the shame He was bearing. He set His eyes on those that would be delivered from the bondage of the enemy. He set His eyes upon doing the will of the Father. He set His eyes on those that the Father gave Him for all eternity. He saw beyond the cross and beheld His Bride. He saw beyond the cross and beheld the promise of His glorification. He sat down at the right hand of the throne of God. As born-again believers, according to Ephesians 2:6, we are seated with Him in heavenly places. We are not physically there, but this is speaking about the authority that we have in Him. When opposition and certain situations come, we must view them from that place. This allows us to have an optimal viewpoint to see the joy that's on the other side, the lessons to be learned, the lives to be reached, and the glory to be revealed.

Laurie Governor-Curtis

God is our refuge and our strength (Psalm 46:1-3)

I finally see her for who she is.

One that has self-doubt and fear like everyone else. However, she sees the bigger picture. . . the one of hope, love, and community. And she works to better herself so that she can create the life she wants by pouring into others . . . Others that are lost and frightened by life's struggles.

My prayer is that she capitalizes on her gift knowing that all she has endured was for a purpose. Not doing so will be a loss not only to herself but to all that encounter her.

The world needs the gift she must give. She must trust the journey knowing she can lean on, trust in, and put her confidence in the Lord. She doesn't have to fear, because she is safe and set apart. God has a plan and a purpose for her life. It is through that plan that many will be blessed.

I am her; she is you!

Sharing your gifts and talents with others can be scary, but know that God is your refuge and your strength. And the good news is that *"His strength is made perfect in your weakness" (2 Corinthians 12:9)*.

You are not in this by yourself. God has a plan for your life. Trust Him and focus on what sharing your gifts and talents will do for those around and in your community.

All that you have endured was for a purpose, and only you can share it!

April Green

The Power of Prayer

And when they had prayed, the place in which they were gathered was shaken, and they were all filled with the Holy Spirit and continued to speak the word of God with boldness.

Acts 4:31

Prayer has the power to change things. Prayer will change your life, prayer will change your circumstances, prayer will change your outlook on hurt and disappointment, prayer will put gladness in your heart, and prayer will provide you with the strength you need when you need it if you call on Him in prayer.

Do not fool yourself into thinking that God does not hear your prayers. He wants you to bring all your burdens, worries and concerns to Him in prayer. Prayer is your opportunity to commune with God, your time to give thanks and praise, your time to ask for forgiveness and repent of your sins, your time to meditate on the goodness of the Lord. Through prayer, strong holds can be broken, hearts can be healed, and your heart's desires can be sought through the Holy Spirit as you strengthen your walk with Christ.

Marilyn Green

Nehemiah 8:10 (KJV) "This is the day which the Lord hath made; we will be rejoice and be glad in it." (Psalm 118:24 KJV) When I think of the word "rejoice," without the formal definition of the word, I think of having joy over and over repeatedly.

It is a consistent pattern of finding beauty out of ashes, the balm of Gilead and a place of comfort for each of us. It is only in knowing that the God we serve is pleased with us when we are in a state of rejoicing. The Bible says to, "Rejoice in the Lord always: and again, I say, Rejoice" – (Philippians 4:4 KJV). Knowing that bringing joy to the Lord is our strength makes it a strategically intentional goal every day. Setting your morning and evening in a pattern of joy is the requirement to always have the strength of the Lord by faith and with His grace.

Being joyful is the starting point of God pouring more of the blessings that you have been praying for into your life and your loved ones. Having an attitude of thankfulness begins with a joyful heart. You cannot get around working to be joyful in your spirit because that joyfulness will then be seen on the outside by others. Your bubbly, radiating spirit, will give you the opportunity to share the love of our God to someone who does not know Him and/or to someone who needs an encouraging word.

Tiffany Green

Embracing Joy in Everyday Life

As we journey through life's ups and downs, it's easy to get caught up in the hustle and bustle, losing sight of the joy that surrounds us. In those moments, we may feel disconnected from our inner peace and purpose. Pause, take a deep breath, and let us embark on a journey of joy. It starts with acknowledging that joy is not an elusive destination, but a divine gift bestowed upon us. Each day, we can find joy in the simplest of things—the warmth of the morning sun, the laughter of loved ones, or the embrace of a friend. Incorporating a daily practice of gratitude helps us shift our focus from what's lacking to the abundance around us. Gratitude enables us to see the blessings that may have otherwise gone unnoticed, infusing our hearts with profound joy. Taking moments of stillness and self-reflection allows us to tap into the wellspring of joy within. Whether through meditation, prayer, or journaling, these practices nourish our souls.

Ultimately, joy is a state of being—an inner radiance that illuminates our lives and touches the lives of others. As we infuse our daily interactions with kindness, gratitude, and purpose, we become ambassadors of joy, inspiring a ripple effect of positivity and transformation. So, let us journey together, savoring each day with hearts brimming with joy. In our collective devotionals, we offer words of inspiration and prayers to ignite the spark of joy in every reader. May this anthology, "Joy 365 Devotional," serve as a reminder that joy is not a fleeting emotion but a powerful force residing within us, waiting to be embraced and shared with the world.

Nicole Gribstad

"And my God will meet all your needs according to the riches of his glory in Christ Jesus."

- **Philippians 4:19 (NIV)** Oftentimes I have waited patiently and even impatiently for the Lord's providence. Waiting for the Lord to meet my needs and worrying wondering if the Lord will come through for me when I need Him most. As I finally hit my breaking point multiple times, when I had almost given up on Him, He lovingly whispers to me that He will be the glue that holds me together. He also appeals to me to double-check my needs, only to realize that mine didn't always match the ones He dreams of for me. We tend to want God to approve of our desires and dreams instead of seeking and living out His perfect desires and plans for us. When you can trade in your dreams for God's, you will feel more complete and more blessed and content.

When your needs match His, you will experience continual "heaven on earth" bliss! If when you don't feel that your needs are being met, it is because what you are desiring, hoping, and dreaming perhaps, does not match God 's dreams! By talking to God, reading His word, meditating on it daily, listening to what the Holy Spirit is whispering to you with the biblical insights that only He can give, over time you can transform your dreams, your emotions, thoughts, and desires to His. When you transform your mind to that of Christ, you will experience your needs met in Abba Father. This is when joy, promises, and contentment are truly experienced. No matter the circumstances, you will be able to be worshipful, grateful, and be able to live the Christian attitude of gratitude lifestyle, meeting all your needs!

Deborah A. Griffiths

Shake yourself from the dust, rise, No captive Jerusalem.
Loose yourself from the chains around your neck,
O captive daughter of Zion…. Isaiah 52:2 NASB

Several years ago, I confessed to a priest that I struggled with loneliness. My youngest child had left for college, leaving me an empty nester. Eighteen years prior, I left an abusive marriage, where my ex said, "You will never make it, and no one will ever love you." Those words stung. I rebuilt my professional life to provide for my kids and move up the corporate ladder, but those pesky negative thoughts that I was not worthy of being loved stuck in my mind. Finally, the priest indicated I had chains binding me and suggested an annulment. I was already legally divorced, but being Catholic, I had not considered having the marriage annulled.

Completing the annulment paperwork was an arduous task. There was one question that stopped me in my tracks. I recounted an incident where my husband, unbeknownst to me, took my oldest son into the bathroom and began beating him. I was six months pregnant with my third child. When I heard my son screaming, I ran to the bathroom, opened the door, and begged my husband to stop. My son stared at me with a look that asked, "Why did you allow this to happen?" I lived with this guilt for years which became the chains that bound me. I was in a no-win situation and felt I sacrificed my son to protect my unborn child. That night, I broke down with gut-wrenching tears. God had forgiven me. My son had forgiven me, but I learned that night that I needed to forgive myself, and in doing so, I was set free.

Challon Hall

As my girlfriends and I (age 9) were enjoying a sleepover, we somehow started discussing family members being sick, and something came over me before I decided to go to sleep in the wee hours of the morning. I asked God to please release my mother of any pain she was feeling, and to take her to a better place. That morning I received a call to come home as soon as possible. Not thinking anything of it, I ran across the street and to my surprise everyone there was saddened by whatever news was about to be presented to me. "Challon, your mom has passed away." It was October 24,1993 and she was only 34 years young at the time. As we drove to my grandmother's house, I thought to myself, "Did God really answer my prayers this morning?" As the house filled with loved ones, I asked my grandmother could I speak with her for a moment. I expressed to her that I had said a prayer to God about taking Mom to another place. At that moment my little brother (age 5) overheard the conversation and screamed, "You killed Mommy; it was your fault!" That was something that will never be forgotten, but at our age, it was understandable.

I am thankful to my younger brother's father for taking me in as his own even after the death of our mother. I stayed until I became of age. I found out he wasn't my real father after finding my Birth Certificate and our relationship was never the same. Even though my biological father wasn't involved, and several stories were presented to me about him, I never thought to try to find him or reach out to him. One main reason is because, if he wanted to find me, he could have because my name is unique. Another reason is that my mother is not here to defend herself, and I wasn't going to allow anyone to try to say anything to offend her.

My grandmother was my mother from that point on. She held down the WHOLE family, taking in all of us regardless of our ages. As I got older, I felt as though she was being taken advantage of and it was time that WE needed to take care of her. As years went by, I had my first son named Karson (2007), which is so blessed because he was able to see and spend time with her. Throughout the next years, she remained ill with several cancers. Unfortunately, on Black Friday, 11/25/2011 she passed away at 74 years young. This took a toll on me at the age of 27, feeling all alone and my Best Friend now gone forever. At that time, I realized our family wouldn't be the same since she was the one to keep it all together and as time passed, everyone went their own way.

At the age of 33, I had my second son, Ammon II "Deuce" (2018). It became easier to deal with the loss of my mother and grandmother as I began to grow into a woman, have children and a family I could call my own. They are the strength I needed to be the mother I am today. Even though these traumatic life changes happened, and I always wondered "WHY, ME?" I found the good in it all. I have the best two sons; I wouldn't trade them for the world. Their fathers are wonderful, and their side of the family is EVERYTHING I could imagine for my sons, especially since I didn't have it.

I must thank my mother's brother, Uncle Ronald Sr, for stepping in with no expectations and being the father figure I craved for all my life. Also, to Auntie/Bestie/Mom Ericka for always being the mother figure I needed to share the wisdom she had and for taking my son's and me in as her own. (She is also Ammon II "Deuce" god mommy). They are my angels in Human form. THANK YOU ALL! Hopefully, some strength can come from my testimony.

Celine Hamilton

Amid sorrow, in the depths of pain,

It's hard to see the beauty, hard to feel the gain.

But don't give up, dear friend, for hope is on the way,

With every step you take, with every new day.

Remember that joy is not a thing to be found,

But a feeling that can be cultivated, grown, and bound.

It's in the way the sun shines on your face,

In the way the birds sing in the morning grace.

It's in the way your loved ones hold your hand,

In the way a stranger offers a helping hand.

It's in the way the leaves fall from the trees,

In the way the flowers bloom with ease.

It's in the way the stars light up the night,

In the way the moon reflects the sunlight.

It's in the way the waves crash on the shore,

In the way the wind whispers, "there's so much more."
So, take a deep breath and look around,
See the beauty that surrounds.
Find joy in the insignificant things,
And let it fill your heart like a symphony rings.

And when the clouds roll in, and the skies are grey,
Just remember that joy is on its way.
It may be hidden, but it's always there,
Waiting for you to claim it, to let it be repaired.
So don't give up, dear friend, keep on climbing,

For joy is your birthright, it's yours for the finding.
It's a light that will guide you, through the darkest night,
It will restore your hope, it will make everything right.

Megan M. Hamm

In life there are situations, interactions, and/or experiences that have caused us to worry. Worry is that phenomenon that can cause nervousness, can keep us up at night, can alter our health, and can cause us to cry out for help. Worry will take away our joy. We worry about our relationships, our finances, and ourselves. We worry about things that have happened, things that are going on, and things that may never happen.

Worry happens when we do not have a plan, or we feel that our plan is inadequate. It is important for us to remember that we won't be able to control every situation, but we can grow and learn to increase our preparedness for it. Consider a firefighter. They are trained to run into the fire while we run away. The difference is the training and preparedness to deal with it. The fire fighter may not know how the fire started but they are confident of their skills to end the fire. The worries in our life are our personal fires.

Fire fighters learn to fight fires. Believers learn to believe. We learn to believe in the promises that were made to us. Matthew 6:26 says, "Look at the birds of the air: They do not sow or reap or gather into barns— and yet your heavenly Father feeds them. Are you not much more valuable than them?" Our worry decreases as our faith increases. We have faith in God's promises and faith in our willingness to learn and grow from life's experiences.

Today, I want us to consider this, "firefighters run into the building and birds don't worry about food."

How are we increasing our skills & faith today, so that we'll be prepared for the fires of tomorrow?

Christy Harris

The Lord is my strength and my shield; my heart trusted in him, and I am helped: Therefore, my heart rejoiced; and with my song will I praise him. Psalm 28:7

Joy is priceless and cannot be stolen when one understands the value and what it means to be filled with the gift daily. When you choose to embrace the beautiful and unlimited moments that each day blesses us with, it is then you begin to live a life of joy, gratitude, and thankfulness. Joy is a mindset and a daily choice. When gratitude is expressed, our joy is evident in that moment. Be grateful for every experience while staying in a place of peace and joy. Respond with a heart of joy to life experiences and challenges with gratitude. Your test is part of your testimony. Choose joy in all things and watch the giant in you stand tall in every situation.

Lean in and pull from all your sources of joy, connect with the power being released, fill up on what you need at that moment, and release what you can give to others. Make room for more of what brings you joy. Whether it's forming new relationships, sharing love through service, renewing bonds with family, connections remind us of the importance of servanthood and our duty as humans to a world that can be selfish. Be a beacon of light, compassion, and understanding through your joy.

Enjoy the ongoing journey to finding what brings you joy and make it personal to your needs. This journey requires more love, gratitude, thankfulness, and the ability to see joy in simple and beautiful moments. It's choosing to see the possibility in the impossible and strength in times of weakness. Choose joy today!

Joy Harris

JOY means everything to me. It is the foundation of everything positive – compassion, divinity, and empathy, JOY goes beyond borders, and is not barred by gender, language, nationality, or religion.

Who is better at expressing these words than I, Joy? I was given this name by my beloved mom. I wept bitter tears as I migrated from my homeland of Jamaica to search for a better life, and I struggled to find my place in a country that seemed unwelcoming. I felt that I did not belong here in the US.

On February 14, 2016, I started my journey towards emancipation in the first world. I was restricted legally, politically, and socially. My question was. "Will I ever experience JOY?" I met someone during my tumultuous time who offered to assist me to reach the heights I desired to attain. I became pregnant and was given an ultimatum: have an abortion or disconnect from the lifeline that had been offered to me. I chose the latter and thought to myself again, "Will I ever experience JOY?" I was plunged into a dark space of loneliness, regret, shame, and sadness. I felt defeated, but God had a motive for my life. "For I know the plans I have for you saith the Lord, plans to prosper you, to give you hope and a future" (Jeremiah 29:11).

Simple things can give us JOY, like birds chirping in the morning; nature brings us extraordinary JOY. I currently get true JOY from going beyond for others who are in a dark place. I help to restore their joy. Weeping may last for a night, but JOY cometh in the morning. (Psalm 30:5). God restored the JOY of my salvation and upheld me with HIS free spirit.

Marshelle Harris

Paul provides a beautiful and profound description of love's nature and attributes. Love is Patient: patience is a virtue that is in short supply. True love is patient and understanding. Love others with patience, offer grace and space to grow, to make mistakes or fall short. Remember the incredible patience that God has shown you and extend that to others. Love is Kind: Kindness is a powerful expression of love. Love with kindness, compassion, seek to uplift and encourage others. Small acts of kindness can brighten someone's day and demonstrate the love of Christ to a hurting world. Love Does Not Envy or Boast: Love is humble and content. It rejoices in the successes of others. Let's focus on loving others genuinely. Love is Not Easily Angered and Keeps No Record of Wrongs: Love is quick to forgive and slow to anger. It does not hold grudges or keep a tally of past offenses. God's love for you is full of forgiveness, so extend the same forgiveness to those who wrong you. Love Delights in Truth: Genuine love does not compromise the truth but rejoices in it. As followers of Christ, you are called to love others with honesty and integrity, always speaking the truth in love. Love Always Protects, Trusts, Hopes, and Perseveres: Love is not conditional; it is steadfast and unwavering. It protects and cares for others, trusting in God's plan even in uncertain times. Love holds onto hope and perseveres through challenges and hardships, never giving up on what truly matters.

Love Never Fails: Human relationships may falter, and circumstances may change, but God's love remains constant and unfailing. Love others with the love of Christ, which is a love that transcends time and circumstance.

1 Corinthians 13:4-8

Yonder Harrison

As your eyes are shut you can see what you need to see. Stand back. Let them stay shut... now look at what you can accomplish...

Close your eyes and breathe The thoughts . . . the actions . . . your vision is all within reach it's the constant of slowing down and listening to a higher power

You can have more, but that's hard when you already have it all. Days and situations and people make us doubt our own happiness. Some others have passed away, but we have been given favor.

Close your eyes and breathe.

Another night has made its way into the morning, and yes, joy has come to the day.

My happiness is within me, so don't wake me. I have Peace, as my Savior sits talking with me like my daddy does.

Comfort my soul as I thought I needed something or someone else or just not sure

Close your eyes and breathe so you can see.....

Giving you the best of me so you don't fear or desire anything or anyone outside of yourself

I made you like this... it's my testimony for a saved soul. Remember to close your eyes and breathe. then make your next move.

Tiffany Harvey

"When you go through deep waters, I will be with you. When you go through rivers of difficulty, you will not drown. When you walk through the fire of oppression, you will not be burned up; the flames will not consume you."- Isaiah 43:2 (NLT)

Listen, there is going to be a time in your life where a storm is going to reap havoc on you and cause you to question everything around you, even your own life. You're going to try to outrun it, but you can't. You're going to try to hide from it, but you can't. This storm, this one storm you must face head on. As you listen to the winds howling and raging around you, your first thought is I'm not going to survive this, it's too much for me to handle, I can't swim in these deep waters, I'm used to the shallow end, I'm not ready or built for this; however, deep down you are ready, because God prepared you way before this storm came into your life. Don't worry, don't fear because you have the strength of Isaiah running through your veins and the faith of Moses at the center of your heart. Hold on to this as you walk through this storm that's trying to take your life. You tell that storm, no matter how big or small, you tell it "I'm built for this. My Father prepared me for this, and there is no water deep enough I can't make it through because I'm built for this."

You are built and prepared for everything life tries to throw your way. Trust and stand on His word.

Lorinda Hawkins Smith, MBA

***"Weeping may endure for a night, but joy comes in the morning." -
Psalm 30:5b NKJV***

Sometimes it seems easier to just sleep the pain away. If we just close our eyes to grief, somehow it will pass. Maybe if we don't see it to begin with, we can somehow avoid it altogether. But God does not call us to be easier. But instead, to fellowship in His suffering. How much easier would it be to not feel anything? But is that easier? To not feel anything would mean we would be numb. There are some that would give anything to be able to feel their legs. They would sacrifice great pain if it meant they could run.

There are some that would give anything to have been able to love someone and know how it feels to be loved. Even if it means there would come a time that they would have to say goodbye to that love. To experience that pain. I have had the privilege of giving birth twice in my life. The first time, I was numb, having to have a C-section which rendered me numb from the waist down. As a result, I did not feel my son leave my body.

At the second birth, my daughter was delivered in the water. I was fully awake and cognizant. Both times I was able to feel and experience a love I've never known before. When I had to be separated from my children, the pain was immense. I wouldn't trade the experience of knowing that kind of love. We are called to be prisoners of hope. This is only possible with the Hope of Glory who will be there with us through it all . . . even until joy comes in the morning. Because the joy of the Lord is our strength. And the strength of the Lord is my joy.

Teresa Hawley-Howard

The joy of little moments is a treasure that often goes unnoticed in the hustle of our daily lives. These tiny sparks of happiness may seem insignificant individually, but when accumulated, they form the colorful mosaic of our existence. It is in these unassuming instances that life's true magic lies. Imagine the bliss of sipping a warm cup of tea on a rainy afternoon, the aroma wafting through the air, soothing your senses, and bringing comfort to your soul. Or imagine the simple pleasure of witnessing a radiant sunrise, painting the sky with a palette of vibrant colors, filling your heart with wonder and hope for the day ahead. These moments remind us of the beauty that surrounds us daily. The laughter shared with loved ones, the touch of a gentle breeze on your face during an evening stroll, the taste of a perfectly ripe strawberry – all these tiny encounters hold the power to uplift our spirits and make us feel truly alive. Moreover, little moments offer us a chance to practice gratitude. When we take the time to appreciate the small joys, we develop a profound sense of appreciation for life's blessings. This mindset shift brings contentment and perspective, reminding us that happiness isn't always tied to grand events but can be found in the ordinary. The beauty of little moments lies in its accessibility. They don't demand grand gestures or elaborate planning. Instead, they gently invite us to pause, breathe, and soak in the simple pleasures that surround us every day. As we cultivate an awareness of the joy of little moments, we enrich our lives and foster a sense of fulfillment. So, let us cherish these humble treasures and be open to the magic they weave into the tapestry of our lives.

Myrrie Hayes

   Life can be challenging and uncertain, making us tired and losing our happiness. But just like a flickering candle, our spirits can shine brightly again. Deep inside us, there is an important truth: joy is not temporary, but a special gift. It's like a gentle breeze that reminds us of the little things. Sharing laughter can connect us even when we're far apart. And when we face tough times, our strength helps us overcome and find success. In a world that can seem cloudy, we have a choice: let the difficulties take away our light, or

   rise above them and bring hope and restoration. Open your heart to the beauty around you. The colors of nature can make you feel thankful. The sound of rain can bring comfort and refreshment. The warmth of the sun can give you energy and courage. Build meaningful relationships that bring you joy and stability in tough times. Seek comfort from those who understand and support you when you're struggling. It's also important to be a blessing to others. When you live honestly and with kindness, your actions and words can make a positive impact. Help those in need and share your talents to inspire and uplift others. By giving to others, you not only bring them joy but also find fulfillment within yourself. Remember, joy doesn't depend on your circumstances; it comes from within you. Find strength inside to guide you through challenging times. Every day is a chance for new beginnings and discovering what brings you happiness. As you go on this journey, appreciate the good things in life and be grateful for them. Let your inner light shine brightly, spreading joy that cannot be easily explained. In your heart, joy is always present, waiting to be noticed, celebrated, and shared with others. May you be a source of happiness and make a positive difference in the lives of those around you.

Victoria E. Henderson

Nehemiah 8:10 (NIV)
Do not grieve, for the joy of the Lord is your strength.

I must be honest with you - there are days when I am so tired that all I can do is ask God to give me the strength to bear it. Living with chronic pain is no joke. Working full time, being a parent, and doing my side pursuits keeps me busy. But pain doesn't care about any of that. It is my constant companion.

Despite that, I wake up joyful. My mother tells me that she should have named me Joy. She says that as a baby, I woke up smiling and ready to play. That I couldn't keep still and went to anyone.

I still wake up with a song in my heart. I am grateful for another day. I acknowledge that if God gives me breath, there is a purpose for my life. I choose joy.

It is ok to acknowledge that I hurt. But I can't stay there. I must press on and live out my purpose. If you are hurting, depressed, or feel alone, you can't stay there.

Whatever you face tonight, today, whenever you read this – truly give it to Him! Don't give it to Him, then take it back and worry. Trust that He has you! The joy of the Lord is indeed our strength.

Real talk – my body still hurts and, physically, I am still very tired, but my soul rests in Him. I choose to have joy in my heart knowing that God is by my side. He gives me joy for the journey!

I pray you will rest in Him fully! It's joy unspeakable!

Lorieen Henry

"But blessed is the one who trusts in the Lord, whose confidence is in him." Jeremiah 17:7

God has bestowed greatness upon you! Get up and reset! You started off with a great vision and solid plans. For days, weeks, months, or years, you gave your all and experienced some success. You felt accomplished until life hit. BAM! You suddenly see a decline in productivity. Or you derailed because tragedy struck. Stagnation grips you due to life's untimely blows. Now, you feel plunged into a black hole of defeat. Let me remind you to Hope in God! Don't give up on that thing that God gave you to do. For as long as God has given you breath in your body, you can begin again. RESET!

Resetting is not failure so erase that from your mind. Forgive yourself for stopping, slacking or whatever happened. Don't wear guilt and shame as your necklace. Life happened, now reset. God has given you the gift of life. Use it.

Step One: Reset with the word of God! Go back and improve your initial plans. Rework them, but this time hear from God. And plan to reset quarterly ensuring that your aim is fixed on glorifying God. The quarterly reset is to look again ensuring that you are still on track with your God approved vision.

Step Two: Reset by putting in the work. James 2:26 tells us that faith without works is dead. So, stop trying to prove yourself to people. Instead, please God. Review your successes and failures. Study, train and become an expert in your craft. Whatever you do, work heartily for God. Channel the fire and passion that God placed on the inside of you. Put in the work! Reset often!

Patricia A. Henry

Isaiah 61:3

(Noted for your reading)

A few years ago, as I was scrolling through the YouTube site, I came across a video that was titled "Rag Man." The video was short but very inspirational. It incited me to reflect on a moment in scripture in the book of Isaiah, which speaks of a great exchange.

The word "exchange" means the act of giving or taking one thing in return for another. To trade, swap, or switch. The Word of God tells us that we can receive beauty for ashes, the oil of joy for our sorrows, the garment of praise for the spirit of heaviness, so that we might be called the trees of righteousness, the planting of the Lord that He might be glorified.

As in the movie clip, the rag man was doing a great exchange by taking the old rags from those who were hurt or mourned and giving them new ones. In other words, He was restoring them to a place of wholeness. God is a healer and a deliverer, and by our faith we can expect His love to be displayed as He gives us a greater hope, greater strength, and greater peace. God tells us to cast our cares upon Him because He cares for us. God, in His unconditional love, makes a great exchange, and all to His glory!

Reagan Henry

"I can do all things through Christ which strengthens me."
Philippians 4:13 KJV

How many times have you been told to do something and, in the moment, it didn't seem very appealing? How long did you procrastinate? Or did you stop altogether? Hopefully, someone was there to tell you that you can do it. You see, in order to finish a goal, people often have the mindset of 'Is there an end product? What do I get out of this?' At the end of the day, we want some kind of reward or something at the end of the rainbow. That is the main focus! A personal example, in fact, would be me writing this devotional. People, I'm 14 at the time of writing this. Teen years! We're usually texting friends, doing our thing, eating, sleeping, repeating. My mama pipes up one day, 'Hey Rea, you want to be part of Joy 365? Get started writing a devotional!' She's uber-excited, loving the idea of us being side-by-side in the book because of our last names. Some time passes with barely any progress besides a title and a scripture. If you have a military parent, let alone TWO, progress is a must, or face the consequences. 'OK, Rea, have that done by tomorrow, or gimme that phone.' Boom!!! There it was…My end-of-the-rainbow-goal, keeping my phone. God showed it to me, and I hit the ground running. It is worth it! I now have a story to tell and a word to say. So go ahead, lose those ten pounds, use your phone less, write that book, or do whatever you have been putting off. All you need to do is ask God to show you your end results, trust in him, and say *'I Can.'*

Dr. Serelda L. Herbin, MBA, DSL, CDE

There are days I wake up and say, "NOPE. I DO NOT FEEL LIKE IT." There were times in my life when I did not want to push or pray or show up. I knew I did not have an option. I knew my circumstances could not consume me because I was anchored by the most reliable source: God. God continues to push me when I want to quit. He whispers to me when I want to find a way out of my purpose or assignments. I knew at an early age a few things: I was different, I did not fit in, and I loved God's covering. God is the only person that has never done me wrong so my full dependence to live out this life in joy is non-negotiable.

Growing up through the obstacles of a drug-abusive parent, an absent father, a grandmother who was doing the best she could, I knew that God protected me-and my joy- long ago. I knew that life was destined to hand me a life and purpose worth living. I am now a living witness that joy must be planted on the inside of me, and I cannot do that alone. I must do the work. I must make the time. I must show up for me so that the joy of the Lord can do the same. Don't ever stop trying. Don't ever stop believing. Don't ever stop pressing toward your purpose.

Be still and know but be ready and understand that you are NOT your circumstance and despite it all, you can push through it with the joy of the Lord anchoring you.

Judy A. Hewitt

Life, with its ever-changing seasons, can sometimes challenge our faith and steal our joy. But let us be reminded of the timeless wisdom found in Ecclesiastes 3:1 (KJV): "To everything there is a season, and a time to every purpose under heaven." Imagine a lush garden, where a gardener tends to a variety of plants. Spring boasts vibrant blossoms, summer yields abundant fruits, autumn displays a canvas of colors, and winter provides a time of rest and rejuvenation. Each plant has its season, purpose, and unique beauty.

Much like the garden, our lives are filled with seasons. Sometimes, we are basking in the warmth of joy and success, while other times, we endure the cold winds of sorrow and hardship. It is during these shifting seasons that we must remember God's divine plan.

When you are in a season of struggle, remember that God has a purpose for it. Just as winter prepares the ground for spring's new growth, your trials are preparing you for a season of growth and abundance. And in those joyful seasons, remember to share your blessings with others, for Ecclesiastes 3:12 (KJV) reminds us, "I know that there is no good in them, but for a man to rejoice, and to do good in his life."

I invite you to embark on a journey of rediscovering joy in every season of life. Through reflections on Ecclesiastes 3:1, let us learn to trust in God's perfect timing, finding joy in the knowledge that He is the Master Gardener, orchestrating our lives with divine wisdom. Whether in sorrow or in celebration, may we embrace each season with faith, hope, and the promise of eternal joy.

Tekesha Hicks

There are many different storms that we as believers go through. These storms may be in the form of a personal loss of someone or something, legal issues, financial hardship, broken relationships, and/or sickness. When these trials and tribulations come it can cause us to get off course. We wonder, why is this happening to me? Did I do something wrong? These storms can also feel like we are being punished for something we have done or something we were supposed to do that we did not get done. Life's storms can threaten our peace, comfort, and joy and often bring about fear, doubt, and hopelessness. Even though we may not understand at the time why we are going through these tough times, God wants us to remember that He has our backs. We must remember *Isaiah 41:10 "Fear not I am with you; be not dismayed, for I am your God; I will strengthen you, I will help you, I will uphold you with my righteous hand.* This scripture is telling us about how God encourages and reassures us not to be afraid of whatever situation we go through. We must trust that God will give us strength to overcome every obstacle that comes our way. God wants us to trust in Him and take Him at His Word. He is a faithful God, who is ever present in times of need. God did not give us a spirit of fear; He gave us His spirit and a sound mind. God is with us always … He will never leave us.

Yenisen Hidalgo

As a mom of two small kids, I'm always hearing them complain about simple things. For example, today, I asked my kids to walk and look for something. That something was near me, and I told them to forget it. Seconds later, I hear my son saying, "I walked all the way over there for nothing." I explained to him by saying 'that nothing is for nothing.' He needs to find the positive in everything. I replied, "That's not true, you got to exercise!" You can apply this same mentality to everything in life. How many times have you focused on the negative instead of focusing on the positive? How many times have you missed out on thanking God for the blessings because you are too busy complaining about the problems or things of the past?

As children of God, we are mandated to always be joyful, even during the trials. In Ezra 3:10-13, the Levites were praising God because the new foundation of the Lord's house was completed. While they were praising God and being joyful, the older priest, Levites, and family leaders, who had seen the first temple, were weeping loudly when they saw the foundation completed. They were too focused on reminiscing on the past and that the old temple was no longer there. On verse 13, it says that the people were not able to distinguish between the weeping and the joyful shouting. Which team do you want to be in, the weeping team or the joyful team? Both were in the same scenario but had completely different perspectives. If you are feeling defeated, just remember that God is with you. Remember that that feeling of defeat is only temporary and that victory is near. Focus on God's blessings and not the trials at hand. Be joyful!

Andrea L. Hines

God, in his infinite wisdom, places folks in our lives every day. They are our divine appointments and there's something we must do or say.

One day as I was shopping, a young man caught my eye in line. There was something about him that made me ask,

"Could this appointment be mine?"

I tried to engage him in conversation, but he didn't have much to say. Then God whispered, "Tell him I love him."

When I did, he turned away. I don't know what burdens he carried, or what was troubling him so.

I don't know why his demeanor was down, but here is one thing I know – whatever caused his discouragement no longer had to be. I heard the Father whisper, "He just needs to get to know ME! "While we may not have had a discussion, and while no real dialog ensued as I tried my best just to be polite and he tried not to be rude, I know that a seed was planted. I watched as he hurried by. Though he tried to hide, I could see the tear that fell from the corner of his eye. In that split second, he glanced my way with a smile forming on his face.

And I knew right then, God was entering in, and filling an

empty place with His love, with His joy, His peace and His power as divine appointments are meant to do.

Restoration: refreshment of the many blessings that comewhen God is at work through you.

Jescika Holloway

Matthew 17:20 Truly I tell you. If you have faith as small as a mustard seed, you can say to this mountain "move and it will be moved. Nothing will be impossible for you.

I was told many stories about my birthday, born November 1972. I am an identical twin, but Sabella went back to be with the Lord after 3 days of our birth. I weighed 1 lb. and was about 12lbs. 13 ounces (about 384.46 ml) and was an inch longer than a ruler. As I think about my life, and knowing the word, in my mind I feel and believe that my sister Sabella was not ready for this life.

She asked God in the spirit to" let me be a redeemed soul. and bring me back to you. No way am I an expert, but I believe in my mind that is what happened. Why I do not know. I also died, at birth but was given my life back and a second chance to live for Him. After many months in the hospital, I was released and taken home, but still, I was a tiny baby, I could only wear baby doll clothes, and my diapers had to be cut into 4ths. So I believe when a baby dies at birth, God does not throw away those babies.

Sabella went back to heaven and was raised there and taught the ways of the Lord. Shé is a grown woman like me, looks just like me, however my hair is, so is hers. And when I get to heaven, she will be the first person I meet. We will know each other immediately as sisters, she will be waiting upon my return. I have had many questions throughout my life about life. I often used to ask God" Why me God and not Sabella? "I have double God given gifts and Talents to share with the world. I am commissioned to touch lives, make a difference one person at a time. I have a purpose.

Lisa T. Horton

Repentance is a Command not an option.

And Peter said to them, *"Repent and be baptized every one of you in the name of Jesus Christ for the forgiveness of your sins, and you will receive the gift of the Holy Spirit. - Act 2:38*

True repentance isn't just saying you are sorry, but it is actually being sorry in your heart.

True repentance is about changing your mindset and asking for help when needed.

True repentance brings Godly sorrow that will cause us to change our actions and choices.

Repentance is a lifestyle.

Francine Houston

Nehemiah said, "Go and enjoy choice food and sweet drinks, and send some to those who have nothing prepared. This day is holy to our Lord. Do not grieve, for the joy of the Lord is your strength.
- Nehemiah 8:10 New International Version

Joy is not only joy from the Lord but also a fruit of the spirit. When someone is going through mourning or grief, some tend to lean on others when they should lean on God. Leaning on the Lord will give you strength and comfort during your time of bereavement.

How do you find joy during sorrow? By learning to be grateful for every single day you have on the earth. For not taking the little things in life for granted and enjoying each moment of happiness that life can bring you. There is always a silver lining in the midst of a storm.

Grief is something people go through in life. Losing a loved one or something you know can be difficult. Prayer, thanksgiving, and plain gratitude are some ways to cope with grief.

Think of the memories you had with them and fun moments you shared. Mourning should not last too long. Crying is a natural response to grief when losing someone. Listening to music, singing a song, keeping praise on your mouth and heart, can keep you uplifted.

Happiness is based on external circumstances you experience in life. While joy is internal, it helps to be joyful in spite of what is happening in your life. Joy is from having a total surrender to the Lord, and He gives you strength to live a life lead by the Holy Spirit.

Gwendolyn Hubbard-Harrison

Dear fellow traveler on this journey of loss and healing,

In the depths of our grief as widows, we carry the pain of losing our beloved spouses. The ache within us seems insurmountable, yet in our darkest hours, let us dare to embrace a glimmer of hope—a hope that transcends earthly boundaries and leads us to the assurance of eternal love.

Though death has separated us from our husbands, their spirits remain alive, and their legacies live on in our hearts.

Through our role as widows, we navigate the depths of loss, finding meaning in our own existence and witnessing the beauty of God's grace unfolding in our lives. In this journey of healing, we are never alone. The Divine is our constant companion, offering comfort and strength when we are weary. Through the power of prayer, we have a direct line of communication with a loving God who understands our pain. Amidst sorrow, let us cultivate gratitude for the time we shared together. Cherishing memories helps weave joy amidst grief. As each new day dawns, let us live fully, honoring their memory through acts of love, kindness, and service.

Together, as widows, let us hold each other's hands, offer encouragement, and share the lessons we learn. May this book be a testament to the resilient human spirit, the power of love, and unwavering hope that sustains us.

Scripture: "The Lord is close to the brokenhearted and saves those who are crushed in spirit." - Psalm 34:18 (NIV)

May God's comforting presence surround you, guiding you through valleys and leading you to renewed purpose and joy.

<u>Joy Hutchinson</u>

If it was not for the Lord, I would not be here today. He has taken me through many dangers, and He has sustained me through it all. I have had many trials, but God saw me through. The loss of my eldest brother was devastating for me because we were close. He was my confidant and my best friend. Upon hearing of his death, I was unable to sleep, or work, I was so depressed. I felt like I, too, was going to die. I could not console myself and there was no support system in place. I grieved for a long time and the memories of his love towards me as an older brother were always in the forefront of my mind. I was so weak I had to pray and depend on the strength of the Lord to uphold me and to keep me sane. My life in America has been tumultuous, but I always held on to my faith in God. I resumed one of my favorite activities after the loss of my brother, that of sewing. I sewed for my daughter's prom; I was also sewing my son's school uniforms. I was sewing with my hand before I was able to purchase a sewing machine. The most rewarding and happy time of my life is being immersed in the work of God. I sing in the choir, and I am also a part of a singing group called '*THE JOYBELLS.*' At times I volunteer in the Pantry serving the general Public. I was constantly reminded during my sad times that if I stayed in Christ my future was secure.

For those of you reading my story today, meditate on these words and remember that the JOY of the Lord is your strength

They that sow in tears shall reap in JOY. Psalm 126:5

*I MUST MAKE A JOYFUL NOISE UNTO THE LORD.
MY NAME IS JOY!!*

Deborah Ivey

For his anger endures but a moment, in his favor is life weeping may endure for a night, but joy comes in the morning. Psalms 30:5

There was a time in my life where there was a lot of sorrow. My brother passed away. My father passed away, and lastly, my mother passed away. I felt like a parentless child even though I was a grown up. My sister, my younger brother and I were what was left of my immediate family. I had to pick myself up and realize that my family would want me to go on with life. I couldn't dwell on what I lost. God doesn't make mistakes. I had to rest on Psalms 30:5 to get my joy.

Joy is defined as a feeling of great pleasure and happiness. I felt those things in my life. I had so much to feel joy for. I was living, I had life in my body, and I had family. I was working and I was getting food, and I had a roof over my head.

I had to give myself a pep talk. Give your parents and your brother something to be proud of. I went to college, and I retired from the military. I have worked in the Federal Government for over 30 years. I am an author with two of my own books under my belt. I'm always striving every day to be better than I was yesterday. I love being a grandmother to three beautiful girls. These things bring me joy.

Charlotte Izzard

"I can do all things through Christ who strengthens me"
Philippians 4:13

Have you ever just stood at the playground, observing the enchanting motion of the merry-go-round? This timeless piece of equipment has been a mainstay in play areas for years. Kids adore the experience of spinning around and around on a merry-go-round, and it's something most adults can look back fondly on from their childhoods. The innocence of childhood can be reflected upon when looking at such a timeless classic, yet as an adult, you look at the merry-go-round from a completely different perspective of understanding. Why? As we grow older and gain a better understanding of the world, we realize just how dangerous it can be to get stuck in a rut and go in circles with our lives. Fear of the unknown can cause us to become apprehensive about jumping off the merry-go-round when certain situations start to become too precarious. When we were kids, riding on a merry-go-round was indescribable - spinning around with our friends and trusting the ground would be there to support us when we decided to jump off. When you are stuck in an endless loop of the same problems, it can be difficult to break free. However, it is essential to take a step back and get off the endless merry-go-round to gain perspective and make progress. At first, the ground beneath you might feel a bit unsteady, and you may even find yourself feeling uncertain. This is when you must allow Him to be your source of strength to experience life through an entirely new and enlightened perspective.

LaShonda Jack

Joy so sweet, joy so beautiful, joy so peaceful, joy so mindful is such a harmonious sound deep in my soul. To be present is to be aware, to be resilient is to be an inspiration, & to create is to understand there's a choice which lies between provocation and response in this Life.

In the world you have tribulation, trials, distress, and suffering; but be courageous; be confident, be filled with joy. John 16:33 (amp)

Reminiscing on the past 6,106 days of motherhood I brought forth life a second time. At the time of conception or the weeks that followed, I wasn't aware that I was pregnant with twins. In the same breath, devastated to find out that I had Twin-Twin Transfusion Syndrome. A rare abnormality in the blood vessel connection causing blood to flow unevenly between my babies. Immediately, my soul began to cry out, "God where are you?" I never heard of TTTS; the doctors & nurses were trying to figure it out. The survival rate for twins with this condition is 1 out of 2 or in some cases both babes will not survive; however, as I looked around, I saw that I was in good hands, because my babies and I were in His (God's) hands. In that very moment, the joy of the Lord became my strength. How we respond or react to the journey for which we have been called lives deep inside of us all..

Dr. Maisha L. Jack

"Have you ever watched a baby on the verge of walking? This small being who has used crawling as a method to navigate surroundings, now feels a sudden urge to not only stand, but to also take steps. The standing and steps are monumental, for the baby must be able to maintain balance while transitioning from using four limbs to now using only two. It is a scary and challenging task for this baby transitioning to toddler. Balancing, taking steps, being aware of surroundings, and all the while, we adults are cheering and encouraging them to be strong and courageous. When they take one step, we cheer. When they fall, we tell them it is okay and to keep going. Adults transition, as well, for we are babes in Christ who start out crawling and gradually stand up, ready to take steps out into the world. As an entrepreneur, new parent, preacher, coach, whatever it may be, we are initially afraid to take those steps to start walking. Even when we know that our FATHER is there to encourage, support, and catch us if we fall. Whatever you are crawling away from and stepping into at this juncture in your life; "Be strong and courageous. Do not be afraid; do not be discouraged, for the LORD your God will be with you wherever you go." There are arms in front of you to lead you toward your next biggest step and there to catch you if you fall. Like toddlers that keep falling, they get better and stronger with every step to master the art of walking. Whatever you feel is blocking you in your life, the crawling period is over. It is time that you relinquish that baby stage and stand up to walk on the path that God has set before you.

Queen Jackie A.

John 3:16
For God so loved the world, that he gave his only begotten son, that whosoever believeth in him should not perish, but have everlasting life.

In 1988, I found out that I was pregnant. Now, I was told because I was an epileptic that I could not bear children. Imagine my excitement once I was told I was carrying life within me. When I had my first physical, my doctor informed me that due to the medication I was taking, that my child would have a 15% birth defect. It bothered me, and I kept wondering what I could do to prevent this. I could never go more than two days without medication, because I would have a major grand mal seizure. I decided to forego my medicine for the remainder of the pregnancy, which was an additional six months. A decision like this was not easy, however, I stepped out on faith, and I knew that God was going to protect me and my unborn child. Once I went into labor, it was a shock to my system. I began to have multiple seizures during the delivery. The doctors were concerned that my child and I would not survive labor. I had a healthy baby boy, who is now 35 years old. I often refer to my son as my miracle baby.

God sacrificed His Son for our sins, and I was willing to sacrifice my life for my child because God's grace is amazing and imagine if we loved each other as God loved us. I believe in the power of love, and I know that the love we pour into the world will be received tenfold. It starts with us.

Mirta I. Jackson

"For the Spirit God gave us does not make us timid, but gives us power, love, and self-discipline." 2 Timothy 1:7 NIV

How many times have we doubted ourselves? It seems more than we should, so let us change that. God gave us that power to take leaps and see our self-worth. Taking a leap can lead you to feel uncomfortable - scared, worthless, and as if you do not deserve this or that. Please know, it is OKAY to feel this way; you are human. It's important not to let those fears overcome your strength in trying something new. You are worthy of all things; you have that blind faith, so I encourage you to take the risk!

Those that you admire and look up to once took that enlightened chance. Most failed but they continued to move forward. That is when you take another leap of faith and try something else. Even though I have self-doubted my personal life and professional career, I will say that those leaps got me here - A place I dreamed about; however, I doubted my self-worth; I now see myself as an example of those exact words "taking those leaps." It will be scary, but it is worth it! God bless you and know you will get to where you want to be, so take that leap and trust in God.

Prayer - God, you have gotten me this far and I ask that you guide me while I take those leaps. Even if I fail, I will get back up because of my self-discipline. I thank You for allowing me to take those leaps because I have the power to be fearless. In your name I pray, AMEN.

Karen Jackson

Trust in the Lord with all your heart and lean not on your own understanding; in all your ways acknowledge Him and he shall direct your paths. Proverbs 3:5-6

The definition of trust is belief in the reliability, truth, ability, or strength of someone or something.

Examples of trust: We trust that we're going to get a paycheck for fulfilling our job duties. In a marriage or in a relationship, we trust that our partner will remain faithful. We trust elected officials to do what they've promised. We trust our vehicles to run and our GPS to guide us. Let's be honest; some of those things have let us down! What do we do? Where do we turn? Who do we trust? GOD. God wants to be a part of our daily occupation, not just the monumental things, terrifying things, or when we've exhausted all other resources. Therefore, we need to continually seek Him for guidance. Always let God be a part of our decision making, because we can't even trust ourselves to make the right decisions. If God wasn't involved, was it even the right decision? How do we build that trust? We build trust by getting to know God intimately. Start by reading His Word and praying for understanding. Open your heart to Him. Lean on Him; He will not let you fall. Acknowledge that He is the great I AM. God is always in the background working things out for our good. You are loved, you are valuable, you are a jewel. Why? Because God created you and He always gives His best.

So, today, will you choose your own understanding, or will you acknowledge God and ask him to direct your paths? Will you trust Him?

Shawne Jackson

Scripture: Psalm 118:24 (KJV) – "This is the day which the Lord hath made; we will rejoice and be glad in it."

Discovering daily joy may seem daunting in a world fraught with chaos and uncertainty. We are constantly bombarded with news of turmoil and personal challenges that threaten to overshadow life's beauty and blessings. Yet, God's word reminds us that each day is a precious gift, an opportunity to experience His radiant joy. Psalm 118:24 gently but powerfully affirms this truth: *"This is the day which the Lord hath made; we will rejoice and be glad in it."* These words encourage us to shift our focus from life's trials toward the blessings that fill our daily existence.

Radiant joy isn't fleeting; it springs from our relationship with God. The smile graces our faces as we witness a sunrise, the warmth in the company of loved ones, and the peace during moments of reflection. To embrace radiant joy, cultivate gratitude. Each day, pause to recognize the blessings around you—the sun's warmth, children's laughter, a friend's embrace, random acts of kindness. These moments are divine gifts, tokens of God's love.

Share your joy. Acts of kindness, encouragement, and love ripple through communities, spreading joy. Embrace the radiant joy daily, becoming beacons of hope in a world in need. In our collaboration, "Joy 365," we commit to discovering and sharing joy. God's blessings abound regardless of circumstances, and His joy is ever-present. We'll find our lives radiating with His love as we rejoice in each day He's made.

J. Ms. Chardae Jennings

When I was a child, I spoke as a child, I understood as a child, I thought as a child: When I grew up, I threw away all my childish toys.
—- 1 Corinthians 13:11, King James Version 1.

Some of us are walking around in adult bodies but have the same mindset and behaviors of a child. I don't know whether you are in your 20's, 30's, 40's, 50's, etc. Time waits for nobody. It is never too late to change. If you want to change. You can only change yourself. You cannot change anybody or force them to change. When people tell or show you who they really are, believe them the 1st time. ———-Mayo Angelou. People can pretend very well if it is beneficial to them. When the benefits stop, they show you who they truly are. Your life happiness is your choice, your responsibility; it is not your responsibility for anyone else's happiness. So, wipe away those tears, get up, dust yourself off and get back into the game. You have only one life to live. Throw away those old mindsets and practice new ways. People will leave you. If people want to leave you, let them go. They weren't meant to be with you anyway. God will never leave or forsake you. You will meet new people and have opportunities to build healthier relationships if you put in the work. Start with loving yourself; put your needs first before anyone else's, with only the exception of your children. Stop trying to convince, justify, prove your worthiness to people who are already committed to disliking you. Life is too short to waste your time, energy, resources on people who don't appreciate you. Let them stay where they are.

Lakeisha Jennings

In the journey of life, we all encounter moments when joy seems to fade away, leaving us feeling empty and weary. It's not uncommon for a 47-year-old woman to face such challenges. However, the beauty of life lies in our ability to restore joy, to rekindle the light within us. Joy restoration begins with self-compassion. Allow yourself to acknowledge your struggles and imperfections without self-judgment. It's through these challenges that we find the strength to heal and rediscover joy. Take time to nourish your spirit through self-care. Explore activities that bring you happiness and fulfillment, whether it's a long walk-in nature, indulging in your favorite hobby, or spending time with loved ones who lift your spirits.

Gratitude is a powerful tool for restoring joy. Reflect on the blessings in your life, both big and small. A heart filled with gratitude can overcome even the darkest of days. Release the weight of the past. Forgiveness, both for others and for yourself, can be a key to joy restoration. Holding onto grudges or guilt can block the path to happiness. Free yourself from these burdens and allow joy to flow back into your life. Lastly, remember that joy is not a constant state; it ebbs and flows like the tides. Embrace the natural rhythms of life and accept that there will be moments of sorrow. But also know that joy will return, brighter and more beautiful than before.

May your journey toward joy restoration be filled with self-compassion, self-care, gratitude, forgiveness, and an understanding that joy is always within reach. You are strong, resilient, and capable of bringing light and joy back into your life.

Nathan Jennings Jr.

In the rhythm of buzzing clippers and the harmony of scissor snips, I find a sacred space where I, a humble barber, become more than a craftsman. Every day, as I trim away the physical, I also weave conversations that trim the soul.

Amidst the hum of the shop, stories unfold. From laughter-laden tales to the quiet confessions whispered between strands of hair, I become a silent witness to joys and sorrows. In these moments, I've come to understand that my craft extends beyond the shearing of locks—it's about shearing away burdens, restoring joy. The chair becomes a confessional, a sanctuary where burdens are laid bare and where, through the therapeutic rhythm of my work, joy finds its way back. There's an unspoken trust between me and my clients, a bond formed in the sharing of life's intricacies.

Restoring joy is an art as delicate as sculpting the perfect fade. I listen not just to the words spoken but to the emotions echoing within them. With each precise cut, I aim to release the weight carried on weary shoulders, offering a tangible metamorphosis that mirrors the internal renewal. As the day unfolds, I witness transformations beyond the physical. Smiles that were dimmed by life's storms gradually rekindle. Through the gentle strokes of a straight razor or the artful shaping of a beard, I engage in a form of therapy—a joy restoration.

In this humble barbershop, I am not just a keeper of aesthetics but a custodian of stories, a facilitator of renewal. The joy restored in these moments transcends the mirror's reflection; it permeates the soul, leaving a lasting impact beyond the chair. For me, barbering is not just a profession; it's a vocation of joy restoration—one haircut, one conversation at a time.

Tasha Jennings

"²³ "My lips will shout for joy when I sing praise to you—I whom you have delivered."²⁴ "My tongue will tell of your righteous acts all day long…A song writer says, "when I think of the goodness of Jesus and all he has done for me, my very soul shall shout hallelujah, praise God for saving me". Psalm 71:23, 24 (NIV)

Many times, we focus so much on all the negative things we have had to experience. How about you cast your mind back on the good things God did for you even in those troubled days? I tell you, you will pin-point those times when you had it bad, but you were rescued. You will recall those times when you had come to the end of yourself and were about to give up but somehow, salvation came for you. Now, allow your mind to remain on those thoughts. Allow your mind to drink in the feeling of being loved by a big awesome God (Ps. 103:1-5). Then, let the gratitude that wells up in your heart spread. You will find that songs of Praise and worship are forming within you, allowing these to flow out like rivers cascading gently down the hills. Sing those songs of Praise and worship to God. Praise Him with a dance if your feet can take it. Praise Him with sounds and cymbals and other instruments you can lay your hands on (If you know how to play). Praise the Lord! Praise Him the best way you can.

Don't stop! Keep praising! As you go, you'll find unspeakable joy bubbling from the inside out. It is because; *"out of your belly shall flow rivers of living waters"* (John 7:38). Sometimes, this joy may push you to tears. Let it flow.

Heidi Jensen

I don't remember what I was complaining about… our family's 18-month journey in the "valley of the shadow of death?" 9-11 in NYC? A broken heart? My commute or computer issue? The complaint doesn't matter, but I'll never forget my colleague's, *"Have you thanked God for that yet?" What?!!!* Emotionally, I felt like I'd been slapped by this Godly Father, but His words became super-glued to my soul. Thanking God during difficulties is rarely my immediate response, but when I do, I'm reminded that God is with me, and I am not alone; remembering this timeless truth restores my peace and joy. So, how can we thank God *always*? Remember: Jesus, with us in our storms, can calm them with a word (Matthew 8:23-27). Our Heavenly Father loves us and wants to give good gifts to us! (Matthew 7:9-11) By faith, we can overcome our emotions and obey His command in Philippians 4:6, *"Do not be anxious about anything, but in every situation, by prayer and petition, with thanksgiving, present your requests to God.* "Did you see that "in every situation"? That means *ALWAYS!* Facing challenges today, I still may need to process the situation by journaling or talking with a close friend, but thanking God for the trial restores my perspective. When frustrated by things that have gone wrong, I can thank God the situation isn't worse! In grieving a loss, I can thank God for the blessings I had! Whatever the situation, God promised to work *all things* together for good, and *nothing* would be able to separate us from His love (Romans 8:28-39); I can truly thank God for that! *Can you?*

Thank you, Lord, for Your presence, power, love, and grace. Please help me to thank You *always*!

Zontayvia Solomon Jiles

"You are the light of the world. A town built on a hill cannot be hidden. Neither do people light a lamp and put it under a bowl. Instead, they put it on its stand, and it gives light to everyone in the house. In the same way, let your light shine before others, so that they may see your honorable deeds and glorify your Father in heaven."
— Matthew 5:14-16, NIV

For God is the creator of light. Nothing can be hidden as the light will always shine even when we believe that the darkness is upon us. The light within us is to be placed at our forefront and we are to shine it in any space we are in. In doing this we allow others to see the magnificent things that our good deeds present when we abide by our Savior.

Lord God,

I come to you with thanksgiving in my heart and soul. As You are the beginning and the end, the light and creator of all things. For the lights You have given me I will utilize them to lead others in the path to seek their light. Many times, we do not know our route, but in our faith, we move because we know You are in our midst. This is why we say Thank You in advance.

Thank You for the light so that I may bless the people far away and, in my presence, so when they see a glow and shine, they are reminded that it is You, oh God. It is You that gives me the light for all to see. It is You that gives strength when the light is dimming. It is You that allows me to continue to shine during it all.

Thank You for all that is in store.

Amen

Alexandria Evelyn Johnson

"I consider that our present sufferings are not worth comparing with the glory that will be revealed in us." Romans 8:18 NIV

How full is your joy during suffering? Life may not offer us many promises with

absolute certainty. We can be certain that we will experience joy and we will experience suffering. We should not believe that the human experience is merely a symphony of lullabies and laughter or an orchestra of silky-scented rose gardens during springtime. The human experience is an unscripted blend of joy and suffering. Human experience shifts us from laughter at the birth of a baby, at a wedding, or during an achievement to sorrow at the loss of a loved one, friend, relationship, or opportunity.

In times of laughter, it's easy for our joy to be full. It is easy to fill up with worry, fear, jealousy, bitterness, and unforgiveness when we are experiencing suffering. Fill up with joy during suffering. This demonstrates our faith in God. It makes a loud declaration that we believe that God can deliver us from suffering. It reflects that we acknowledge that there is a purpose in our suffering. It demonstrates our ability to be vulnerable with God. These postures allow for God to be glorified. It allows for glory to be revealed in us and through us.

Accept this invitation to fill up with joy during suffering. Joy is our weapon of power to get us through seasons of suffering.

Lakeisha Johnson

For many years I lived in a state of anger and depression due to circumstances and traumatic events that happened in my life. I was molested and raped in my teenage years. I was betrayed, humiliated, and beaten by men that I felt as though I could not live without. I thought I was worthless, nothing and nobody. I no longer wanted to live because at that time, I felt life was terrible and seemed to keep getting worse.

One Sunday morning I decided to go to church. During church service I began to cry, and my tears would not cease. That day I experienced a supernatural event that ignited a fire in my soul. It was at that moment I realized why traumatic events plagued my life. I soon understood it is my testimony that will help others overcome it as well. Traumatic events that happened in my life and how I was able to overcome the obstacles and succeed inspired me to start a nonprofit organization. My purpose is to empower women by providing them with the necessary tools to overcome life's obstacles and continue to succeed.

The days I find to be difficult, I continue to pray, praise, and thank God for the good times and the troubled times in my life. This solidifies my Joy 365. My blessings of overcoming are now having a husband that loves and adores me, five amazing children and two beautiful granddaughters. I also have a book 'I Am an Overcomer' that will be released in 2024! I pray this inspires you and helps you find joy 365 days throughout the year in situations that were meant to break you.

Michelle Johnson

Today's scripture reading comes from Isaiah 61:3, which says, "To appoint unto them that mourn in Zion, to give unto them beauty for ashes, the oil of joy for mourning, the garment of praise for the spirit of heaviness; that they might be called trees of righteousness, the planting of the Lord, that he might be glorified."

This verse is a beautiful reminder of God's ability to turn our sorrows into joy, our mourning into dancing, and our ashes into beauty. It speaks of God's desire to bring healing and restoration to the hurting and brokenhearted.

Looking at my life, I have experienced God's faithfulness in turning my pain into something beautiful. When I have felt overwhelmed by grief, disappointment, or failure, God has always lifted me and brought me out of the darkness. Reflecting on a painful breakup that devastated my life, I prayed to God and sought His comfort. God began to heal my broken heart, restore my joy, and bring new friendships into my life. God opened doors of opportunity and showed me there was still so much beauty amid my pain. God's promise to turn our ashes into beauty is not just a nice sentiment; It's the reality we can experience. God can turn the most broken and hopeless situations around for His glory. God can heal our hearts, restore our joy, and give us a new perspective on life.

Today, I am grateful for the reminder that God is in the business of transforming our ashes into something beautiful. I am encouraged to trust God with my pain and allow God to work in and through me. As I surrender my hurts and disappointments to Him, I know God will bring beauty and joy in ways I cannot imagine.

Norma Johnson

Let the words of my mouth and the meditation of my heart be acceptable in thy sight. O Lord my strength and my redeemer. Psalm 19:14

Our days can be filled with so much happening around us from family to friends, business, leisure and so much more. But it is important to keep God near; He will never lead us wrong. We should never be so busy that we forget that He is the one that sustains us, the air we breathe, the breaths we take as we wake up.

Hence why it is important to watch what we say, and think, as well as what we add to our eyes and our ears daily.

1: I will lift mine eyes unto the hills, from whence cometh my help

2: My help cometh from the Lord, which made heaven and earth: Psalm 121:1&2

Our days tend to get long when we get busy and we can easily forget the one true and living God who gives us all the energy and power we need. If we put in the effort, however, it will be so easy to remember what God does for us.

Let's give reverence to the One making it possible to get the help when we need it. Our Creator is always ready to give us the help we desire.

Dr. Sasha Johnson

When you go through certain things in life, it doesn't seem very easy to find your way back to joy. The truth is life can throw us so many curveballs, and we often do not realize the meaning behind those obstacles and challenges. The truth is God will test us at times, and we must remember that without a test, it is difficult to accomplish the desirable things we want. I often say we must endure tough times and pain to get to space or become the person we want to be. This aligns with how we should be looking at joy. Joy is an indescribable feeling that comes upon our spirit, touches our hearts, and relieves our minds.

Unfortunately, for you to understand your joy, you must also understand your pain, and you're suffering. To reclaim your joy, I would like you to take control of the obstacles that come your way. God wants you to be able to use the power that He has given you to retake battle adversity and use your unmatched strength to reclaim your joy and happiness. Take control of your life in the way that God wants you to.

Stop losing to challenges where you already have the tools necessary to win. Joy means that I understand my pain and struggles, but they do not define me, and my proclaimed wealth is filled with happiness. You deserve joy, so remember that despite how hard it may seem, you have all control with the armor of God supporting you.

Rev. Dr. Patricia Ann Johnson-Dowtin

We see in The Message (MSG) Bible as recorded in the Book of Psalms, Chapter 30:1-5 A Psalm of David. A song at the dedication of the temple. (1)I give you all the credit, GOD—[YOU] got me out of that mess, you didn't let my foes gloat. (2-3) GOD, my [GOD], I yelled for help, and you put me together. GOD, you pulled me out of the grave gave me another chance at life when I was down-and-out.(4-5) All you saints! Sing your hearts out to GOD! Thank [HIM] to [HIS] face! HE gets angry occasionally, but across a lifetime there is only love. The nights of crying your eyes give way to days of laughter. In the King James Version (KJV) of the Bible, Verse 5 teaches us: (5) For [HIS] anger [endures] but a moment; in [HIS] [favor] is life: Weeping may endure for a night, *[but joy cometh in the morning]*.

I have learned there is only one way, only one genuine way *"JOY SHALL COME IN THE MORNING"* - it shall only come in having a relationship with *GOD*! Your relationship shall be with TRIUNE *GODHEAD*. Other names may be the *HOLY TRINITY*, or the *BLESSED TRINITY* yet the name means the *UNION OF THREE PERSONS*, the *FATHER*, the *SON*, and *HOLY SPIRIT* in one *GODHEAD*.

Yes, "a RELATIONSHIP" is:

the way two or more concepts, objects, connect.

the state of being connected by blood or marriage.

an emotional and sexual association between two people. Spending quality time with HIM reading your BIBLE, PRAYING, LISTENING to HIM, and PLEASING HIM is all a part of bonding and having *JOY... MORNING!*

Dr. Celeste Johnson-Matheson

In our lifetime, we will have our share of adversities. Adversity and turbulence are a part of the life cycle. During those times of Trouble, when our circumstances are overpowering, we must trust God, remain calm, and ride out the waves during the storms. The waves represent a metaphor for life's adversities. Waves are generated by friction between the water's surface and the wind. When there is a disturbance, onshore waves will become unstable and get bumpy and choppy, like our life circumstances. Life can get rocky and rough at times.

We can experience a continuous cycle of challenging issues such as personal failures, financial struggles, loss of loved ones, unhealthy relationships, parenting, and health issues. The list goes on and on. Life's adversities can cover us like a tidal wave in a storm with a rippling effect without any end. During the stormy times when life becomes unpredictable, unstable, and choppy like the waves in the ocean, stay focused, adapt, remain resilient, and trust God.

As a child growing up, I always heard the phrase, "Trouble doesn't last always," which is true. Like incoming waves, the water calms when it reaches the shore and ends its journey. Miraculously the wave will disappear, so does our life crisis. God never said our life would be without trials. God did promise to be our refuge in times of trouble and carry us through the storms. Just like the waves in the ocean, rough times will stabilize and end. Stay strong, be bold, maintain a positive mindset, embrace life's trials, and remain calm during life's storms, and you will persevere.

Pastor Janice Stepney-Jones

You will be my people and I will be your God.

God has given us His word for a purpose. It is the daily guide by which we walk and become familiar with His ways. From my experience, I know God is a "I will" God. He speaks clearly to us. He loves us so deeply that He sent his only Son, Jesus so that we could have life more abundantly. God wants to give us a new heart.

Ez 36:29 The message I'll give you a new heart and put a new spirit in you and I will remove the stone heart from your body and replace it with a heart that's God-willed, not self-willed. I'll put my spirit in you and make it possible for you to do what I tell you and live by my commands. He will replace the old heart with an obedient heart,

Psalm 51:10 Create in me a clean heart, oh God, and renew a right spirit within me.

Jer, 29:13 NIV, you will seek me and find me when you seek me with all our heart. Extraordinary plan.

Roe Jones

"But my God shall supply all your needs according to his riches in glory by Christ Jesus." Philippians 4:19

In life, we encounter love, joy, sorrow and worries among many things. It is human nature that worry dominates our thoughts when we are amidst life challenges. If left unchecked, it takes control of our daily lives, and we lose sight of the abundant blessings God has given us.

I believe in looking at things glass half full versus glass half empty. I also believe that God never gives you anything you can't handle. There are times when we face such pain and sorrow that it does not seem we can handle it. The only way to cope is to ask God for strength as you endure the trial. When I look back at those trying times, I find that the occurrence made me more resilient, resulted in a better version of me or something in my life is better as a result of it. Often the conclusion does not become clear until much later. In some instances, years later. As I look back at my life, as if it were a movie, I have confidence in knowing that God will help me overcome for He always has.

Nowadays, I start my days with a gratitude prayer. I look back in my life and recall each blessing I received from God. I recall the feeling of a prayer answered or even a realization of a blessing sometime later. I feel great awe when I realize how God orchestrated different events at separate times (even years prior) to come together in perfect harmony to result in that one blessing. It showed me that God has always looked after me. It gave me solace that I just need to focus on trusting in God and nothing else.

Theresa Jordan

Nehemiah 8:10 – "For the joy of the Lord is my strength."

On Saturday, January 15, 2022, these exact words would come out of my mouth. Lord, what do you do when your world seems turned upside down? I can recall New Year's Eve listening to my personal theme song "It's A New Season" by Israel and New Breed. Approximately four days later, I received a phone call from my uncle in New Jersey while attending the F.R.E.S.H. Book Festival given by Ms. Donna M. Gray Banks. He informed me my lovely Nana had six days to live according to her doctors and Hospice.

Prior to hearing this news, my husband Daniel had been telling me, "Reese, you need to go spend time with your Nana," Deep down inside I knew my husband was correct, but that would be acknowledging the last of the four women that assisted with raising and transforming my life would not be here anymore. I was apprehensive about going back home to Georgia, and the selfish side of me did not want to experience days without her voice, laughter, hugs, spending quality time watching TV, and lying beside my Nana when I went to visit.

However, I never realized the words expressed in "It's A New Season." would begin to manifest in my life. With tears in my eyes, I began having conversations with the Lord about the inevitable, which was the fact I knew my world would not remain the same. The Lord answered me with a distinctive voice, "You keep looking up when your world seems turned upside down, You keep trusting and believing in ME, and You keep holding onto my unchanging hand." I had to remind myself that the Joy of the Lord is my strength in every circumstance.

Deborah Juniper-Frye

"It Takes Belief and Work"

"For as the body without the spirit is dead, so faith without works is dead also." (NKJV James 2:26)

From our birth, throughout our childhood, and as an adult, God has made us in His image and LOVE is something we do so naturally. To love is to be vulnerable and easily hurt by people we love deeply and who love us just the same. It's a relationship breakup that most of the time makes you feel terrible. Did you know that a broken relationship can send your mind to a space of feeling grief? As a Grief Recovery Method Specialist, I can assure you that there are various stages to a broken relationship, which can bring you emotional strain, such as Anger, Bargaining, Depression, and Denial. Now here is an instance where we must uncover our faith and belief for a resolution. Faith Uncovered is a metaphor to expound on the fact that we must work in the measure of faith dealt to us all. "For I say, through the grace given to me, to everyone who is among you, not to think of himself more highly than he ought to think; but to think soberly, as God has dealt to each one a measure of faith." (NKJV Romans 12:3). This not only takes faith, but it also takes courage to walk your faith out.

With prayer, patience, and the power of God, what looks impossible will one day be an overcoming testimony (your true story) to help someone else use their measure of faith. Just know that whatever you are trusting God for, through working and igniting your measure of faith, anything is possible. Keep your faith at the ready and rest assured that you will receive an emergence of "Faith Uncovered."

Patricia Ann Bean-Kane

As I get older a saying I keep hearing from my elders is, "getting old is no joke." What they are referring to is the aging process which is the physical decline and decay of the body. Psalms 89, God turns people back to dust, saying, "Return to dust, you mortals! Seventy years are given to us! Some even live to eighty. But even the best years are filled with pain and trouble; soon they disappear, and we fly away. In 2 Corinthians 4:16-17 Paul gives us hope despite the aging process. Our bodies are dying, but our spirits are being renewed daily.

Unfortunately, some believe that on earth if we get enough money, notoriety, fulfillment of dreams or aspirations we will have no problems. However, in this life, we will have troubles no matter what we attain. Lasting joy comes when we realize that our present troubles are small and temporary, yet they produce for us a glory that vastly outweighs any problems we have. As believers, our body will weaken but our spirit is renewed and perfected daily.

Two Kingdom principles are developed during the aging process: dependency and humility. God treasures these within us, In the world we are taught to strive towards independence and pride. I have watched elders become more dependent on God, who uses other people to meet needs. Through dependency pride slips away while humility and gratefulness shine through. There becomes a keener awareness that earth is not home, but a training ground for eternity. Therefore, do not dwell on what is lost in this world, simply rejoice in what will be gained in eternity: a new body, rewards, a mansion, reunification with others, flesh becoming nonexistent, and perfect peace in the presence of God.

Cheryl Kehl

"May the God of hope fill you with all joy and peace as you trust in him, so that you may overflow with hope by the power of the Holy Spirit." - Romans 15:13

There are days that we may find it hard to trust in the Lord, but we must still trust Him. The Lord is not far away like it seems at times. He is right there beside you to love and guide you into everlasting joy and peace. There is something about placing your trust and hope in Jesus that is different from anything else. When I look back on all the things that have seemed to go wrong in my life, I can honestly say that the Lord was with me. The things that seemed like it was going to take me out were somehow the things that made me stronger.

I now use those very situations to stand on with assurance that God is nearby to help me. The Holy Spirit is there to remind us that the Lord hears our cries and comes to rescue us. It is not when we think the time has come, but in His time which is always the perfect time. There are times when we need things to help build up our faith and trust in the Lord. If we thought that it was in our own strength that we can make it, then we are not depending on God. He knows our future and wants it to be a bright future. If we take our minds back to where God has brought us from, we should be filled with joy. The Lord continues to have His angels surrounding us and protecting us. Allow God to fill you with His peace; it is beyond understanding. He loves you!

Reneisha Kennedy

I have always thought that joy and happiness were the same thing, but I have learned, it is not. Joy is when you can be happy even during chaos. The year 2016 was one of the worst and best years of my life. One wrong decision I made caused a domino effect of consequences that broke me mentally, emotionally, and spiritually. That decision caused me to be very depressed and suicidal. Although people closest to me reassured me that everything was going to be okay, I still wanted to die. Additionally, this was the year I found out I was pregnant. Even though this was a tough time in my life and my pregnancy was unexpected, God knew just what I needed to keep going. During my depression and thoughts of suicide, God gave me joy! The joy I experienced when I found out I was pregnant was indescribable. Yes, I was scared and still depressed but that little bit of light (joy) gave me the strength I needed to keep fighting. My daughter saved my life! God saved my life!

Happiness is fleeting and an external thing, but joy is eternal and an internal thing. Being able to feel joy during chaos and darkness is not an easy thing to do. You just must dig deep inside of yourself, find your inner strength, and try your best to pull it out. All you must do is to ask God for help. I am a living witness that God will assist you in your time of need!

In a nutshell, joy is God-sent so it is a valuable & beautiful thing!

Althea King

Therefore, when Mary came where Jesus was, she saw Him, and fell at His feet, saying to Him, "Lord, if You had been here, my brother would not have died." John 11:32 (NASB) Mary loved Jesus and whenever she was in His presence, she stopped whatever she was doing to listen to His teachings. On one occasion, her sister Martha complained to Jesus that Mary was not assisting her in the preparation needed for the guests in their home but chose to sit with Him instead of helping her. Jesus replied to Martha's concerns with a gentle reminder that what Mary chose was more important than a clean home or a gourmet meal. So, when Mary's brother Lazarus became ill, Mary sent for Jesus because she had the confidence that He loved her family, and He could heal Lazarus.

She patiently waited for her Master, but Jesus never came. He never showed up. Where was Jesus when she needed Him the most? How could He allow Lazarus to die? When Jesus finally came after the death of Lazarus and asked for Mary, she came to Jesus, but not with her starry-eyed gaze expressions from the past,. She met Him with tears, blame, and accusations. Jesus did not reproach Mary because He knew her heart and the purpose of the death of Lazarus. Out of this event was one of the shortest verses in the Bible, amazingly simple, but extremely powerful - "Jesus Wept." The answered prayer was not in Mary's timing but God's timing and for His purpose. Sometimes you may not understand what Jesus is doing in your life (Isaiah 55:8-9), but you still need to come to Him with honesty because He knew you before you were formed and knows your heart (Psalms 139). He will never forsake or turn away from you (Hebrews 13:5). He has a perfect plan and purpose for you that is greater than you can ever imagine (Jeremiah 29:11-14)

Elder Kimberly King

It is choice, not chance, which determines your destiny. Not by chance or discovery by accident but rather the unfolding of a mystery as your spirit seeks for its destiny in life. Your spirit is longing for more! The wise men of the East followed a star to their destiny. What is the star that will lead you to your destiny? You only need one star, and that is the Holy Spirit. There is a sense of urgency in the Spirit for the manifestation of God through us. Moses and Israel followed a cloud in the day and a pillar of fire at night, while Jonah was led to his destiny in a storm and in the guts of a monstrous fish.

"A person often meets his destiny on the road he took to avoid it." Let us also consider the issue of destiny and determination. "Some are destined to succeed; some are determined to succeed." But those destined to succeed without determination may never attain what is needed to be truly successful character. God needs to develop our character!

There is a difference between your purpose and your destiny. Your destiny is your ultimate election. What did God choose you to do on this Earth? What is your ultimate election? What were you elected to do before you were born? That is what your destiny is. What God created you for! What are you called to do right now in your life? Your purpose is to fulfill your present call because this could very well be the thing that catapults you into your destiny.

John 8:32 says; "Then you will know the truth and the truth shall set you free!"

Your Destiny is a Choice, not by chance or circumstance

Lindsay Kinslow

Hey there, my friend! Are you living with chronic pain? Let me tell you, it's not easy. In fact, it can be an overwhelming experience that can leave you feeling helpless and hopeless. But let me assure you, it doesn't have to define you.

I'm Lindsay, let me share with you my journey of resilience in the face of chronic pain. It's been a long and tough road, but I've never let it diminish my spirits or hinder my goals. Instead, I've found strength and guidance in my faith, turning to Psalm 46:5 whenever things feel overwhelming. "God is within her, she will not fall." This gives me the courage to push through. While faith has been a source of strength for me, I've learned that it's not enough on its own. I must put in work as well. That's why I make sure to practice self-care activities, like yoga and meditation, to take care of my body and mind. Of course, there are times when the pain feels unbearable, but I refuse to give up. I draw on my resilience and lean on the support of my loved ones to keep going, even when it seems like there's no end in sight.

May my story be a testament to the strength of the human spirit, and the power of faith, support, and self-care. Even in the face of pain and suffering, we can still find hope and comfort. We can rise above our struggles and live fulfilling lives, empowered by our resilience and the grace of God.

You're never alone, my friend. With the right mindset, support, and self-care, you can overcome any obstacle. Trust in your own strength and the support of those around you, and know that God is always within you, guiding you every step of the way

Alicia Kirschner

Anxiety comes from the spirit of fear (Isaiah 35:4) and 2 Timothy 1:7 reminds us that the Lord gives us a spirit of a sound mind. Maybe you're living in a constant state of anxiety from years of tribulations that planted seeds all over that have grown into deeply rooted trees dominating your emotional state daily causing your brain chemistry to be physically altered, or maybe you're cool as a cucumber until the storm comes and the anxiety overwhelms you and you give anxiety a foot hold (Mark 4:40). God is saying today, step out of the comfortable boat Peter, and let me show you how to walk on water.

He's reminding you to ignore your feelings (Jeremiah 17:9) and let your faith trust in me for whatever comes your way. Spend a little extra time with the Lord. Ask the Holy Spirit to reveal to you any area in your life where anxiety dwells. Trust in Jehovah Rapha (Exodus 15:26), Jehovah Jirah (Genesis 22:14). Seek in yourself the areas you have let the spirit of fear enter and pray this:

Lord, today I invite Jesus into (my finances, my marriage, my parenting, my workplace, my situation) where the spirit of fear dwelled in me, and I ask that in Jesus name he flees and Jesus dwells in that place now and forever casting out any fear or doubt not from You, my provider and my healer. In Jesus name, Amen.

Now take index cards and write verses on them about anxiety (yes, I'm giving you HW) and read them every day for at least 30 days. This will drown out the voice of the enemy in your head and invite the Holy Spirit back into your mind.

Christina Krausslach

Yahweh, your God…

will rejoice over you with joy.

He will calm you in His love.

He will rejoice over you with singing…

At that time I will bring you in…I will give you honor and praise among all the peoples of the earth…says Yahweh.

Often joy results from an occurrence as when something is given that there is a tangible afterwards, an end point of the event, of receiving something otherwise not existing and then the joy. The memory of what had happened is then often the source of the joy continuing, acknowledging the past. What I would like to suggest is that in our reality as Christians, we are brought by God to Him through salvation, yes. It is an introduction to eternity, the present and the future. All of God's works are known to Him from eternity (Acts 15:18 WEB). We are rejoiced over in relationship before all and it of His joy. It is continual because His choice is an active relationship with you which does not end.

In fact, we are rejoiced over so much that we are sung over not just spoken over or to. His words include melody. They are from the heart. He gives honor before all knowing that you are what He has made you to be and what you will continue to become. As He has His joy in rejoicing over you, your joy can be freely reciprocated knowing He is love singing over you.

…be filled with the Spirit…

By singing and making melody in your heart to the Lord; giving thanks always concerning all things in the name of our Lord Jesus Christ, to God… Eph 5:18-20 WEB

Dr. A'Londa L. Kusimo

JOY IS MEANT TO BE THE PERMANENT STATE OF EVERY CHILD OF GOD according to Philippians 4:4, we are commanded by the scriptures "Rejoice in the Lord always: and again, I say, Rejoice." Joy according to scripture is a commandment. God demands that we sustain our joy. As far as God is concerned, joy is not situation dependent. Joy is meant to be a consistent state of the spirit of man. We are told in Galatians 5:22 that one of the fruits of the regenerated spirit is joy. We are also told in Psalm 51 that one of the effects and manifestations of salvation is joy. For everyone that is a child of God, joy is a spiritual indicator. Where joy is absent, it is a pointer to something out of place in the spirit.

Joy according to God's Word is a Pointer to our salvation. Joy according to God's Word is a depletion of the regeneration of our spirit. This means there is no situation where joylessness is acceptable. There is no day that is permitted to be a joyless day, and there is no moment that is permitted to be a joyless moment. As far as God is concerned, joy is expected to be the permanent state of every child of God. Why is Joy demanded? Why is joy commanded? God's presence is our eternal guarantee for victory in every battle of life. The presence of God demands joy. If you are not going to be a victim of defeat, then you must refuse to be a victim of depression. Until you are depressed, you cannot be oppressed. The word of God tells us in Psalms 16:11 –" in the presence of God, there is fullness of joy." Until joy is present, His manifestation is absent. God's presence demands joy.

IF THE DEVIL CANNOT STEAL YOUR JOY, HE CAN NOT FRUSTRATE GOD'S PLAN FOR YOUR LIFE.

Emmanuel O. Kusimo

Thou wilt show me the path of life: in thy presence is fullness of joy; at thy right hand, there are pleasures for evermore. - Psalms 16:11

In the journey of purpose from discovery to fulfillment, joy is required. For the discovery of purpose, joy is required, and for the fulfillment of purpose, joy is required.

Joel 1:11-12

When joy dries off, the purpose dies off. According to Scripture, every believer is likened to a tree, and the purpose of a believer is likened to some fruit. That verse says the fruits perish and dries up because joy has withered from the hearts of men. If you allow your joy to dry up, your purpose will end up going out. If you are going to fulfill your purpose in life, then maintain your joy.

The devil cannot stop you when your joy is sustained. (Hebrews 12:2). The Bible says when Jesus was going through it all, one thing He never lost was joy. When your joy is in place, the plans of the devil will be frustrated. The joy cannot be successfully suppressed. No matter what is happening, never lose your joy. If he cannot steal your joy, he cannot frustrate God's plan for your life. I have good news for you: the plan of God for your life shall be fulfilled. Don't let anything steal your joy.

Almeria Lacy

A term used for years to imply the depths of a person's anger. Let's look at it in a different light. The love of God for us as 'His children.'

1 John 4:19 NIV We love, because he first loved us.

As a child I spent a lot of time in the church. Living with my grandmother was truly a blessing, as she was mother of the church, and a devout Christian. We spent so much time learning of God and His promises on Sundays, through home bible studies, vacation bible schools, speaking engagements, bible drills and so much more. By the time I was eight years old, I knew I wanted to be baptized. At an early age I understood the meaning of this, and being a spiritual child, I knew there was a calling on my life and to this day I still experiencing the love of God in my life. Today, we want everything immediately, oftentimes without having an in-depth understanding of why. We tend to lean on our own judgment, which can yield results where we find ourselves trying to fix things 'our way.' This leads us into a spiral of misfortune which can put a strain on our families, our finances, and our minds. But there is a way out. Let me encourage you, beloved. There is a way to find peace, joy and comfort, there is someone who has your best interest at heart. A personal relationship with God is so refreshing! With this fast-paced lifestyle happening around us, finding someone with time to share our disappointments, worries and grief can be difficult. Christ is an ever-present, supreme being who is waiting to hear from you. He knows what you are going through and wants to have a relationship with you! Give Him a try, for experiencing the love God will be the answer to all your prayers! ***Jeremiah 29:11 NIV***

Marnie Lacy

On February 24, 2022, I was a wreck. My son Jamal had passed away. He was my first born and my best friend, and I didn't know what I was going to do without him.

I felt weak and empty- as though my bones had slipped out of joint. My heart had melted like wax, and my emotions had all been poured out. I felt like I was not in control of my body or my mind, but in the middle of that haze, something deep within me urged me to pray. Try saying this prayer.

Dear Lord, please comfort my broken heart. Help me understand how to use this hurt for your glory and guide me as I try to figure out my path. In Jesus name Amen.

Whether you're grieving a recent loss or there's an unhealed hurt in your past that you can't move pass, just remember that God's love is big enough to heal your pain.

Latonya Lamb

I know that you've heard this saying before, the past is history, the future is a mystery, and the present is a gift. What happens when your presents don't come wrapped in pretty paper and a red bow? What happens when pain, grief, sorrow, or sickness arrives at your doorstep?

In 2017, I found out what happened. I went to sleep on New Years Eve feeling like a had a stomach bug. I woke up 5 hours later disoriented, speech slurred, face drooping, unable to walk and memories of the past 40 years vague at best. What just happened? I later discovered I had had a stroke in my sleep! At first, I cried a lot, felt sorry for myself, spent a lot of time alone, and for a while just gave up. I constantly asked God, why me. One day He finally responded, "Why not me. It was at that moment that I knew I was created for this moment. This stroke was not an accident. I knew I would never be who I was, but I could fight for who He had called me to be.

This is my story, but I know you have a story too! I want to encourage you to get up and fight! No matter the challenge is, fight. You cannot win if you don't fight. Fight with scars, fears, and especially tears. It's those unexpected turns that build our resilience. It's not easy, but I'm a witness, it is possible.

Resist the temptation to give up. You can do it! He's already fought the fight for you! Just always remember, why not me!

Daniel E. Landrum

In this life we all go through tough times and terrible situations that sometimes feel overwhelming. During those times we must reflect on our lives and put it in perspective. We know how the world has changed over the past few years. These changes provoked fear and sadness over the world, and it made a lot of people feel helpless. More now than ever we must put our trust in the Lord, keep his praises on our lips, and his joy in our hearts. Oftentimes we let situations in life determine our attitude and sometimes even our future.

But in the bible in Nehemiah 8:10 it tells us "Do not grieve, for the joy of the Lord is your strength." It also says in Isaiah 40:29 "He gives power to the weak and strength to the powerless.". So, as you go through life feeling and seeing the difficulties this life can bring, don't let anything make you feel like you can't make it through whatever situation you face.

You must remember that If joy is our strength, then sadness is our weakness. So, you must choose to keep your joy in your heart no matter what is going on around you, no matter how you feel, and no matter what the situation looks like. Continue to trust in the Lord always, keep your faith, and move forward while remembering the joy of the Lord is your strength. Thank you, Lord, for watching over us and making a way when there seems to be no way. In Jesus Name, Amen!

Mohogani Lattie

"For I know the plans I have for you, declares the Lord, plans for welfare and not for evil, to give you a future and a hope." - **Jeremiah 29:11 (ESV)**

Since God has specific plans for your future, endeavor to develop positive and hopeful aspirations in line with what His words say to you and from the promptings within your spirit because this anticipation of a better future restores joy. So, instead of being pessimistic or anxious, be optimistic for positive outcomes. *"Commit your work to the Lord, and your plans will be established."* - Proverbs 16:3 (ESV)

Expect to grow and improve by learning new skills, gaining wisdom, and becoming a better version of yourself. Expect to rise to specific positions, get promotions, or launch a successful business. Expect to build and maintain fulfilling relationships with family and friends through communication, trust, and support. Expect to maintain a certain level of physical fitness, by eating well, and managing stress effectively. Expect to deepen your spiritual understanding, find peace, and experience a stronger connection with your faith. Expect to express your creativity and share it with others, whether it's writing a book, composing music, or producing visual art. If you desire a family, set expectations for parenthood and family life. Having expectations is important because *"The plans of the diligent lead surely to abundance, but everyone who is hasty comes only to poverty."* - Proverbs 21:5 (ESV)

Still, you must balance these expectations with a healthy dose of realism and adaptability. Life can be unpredictable, and not all expectations may be met exactly as planned.

Adrianah Marie Lewis

"Honor thy father and thy mother: that thy days may be long upon the land which the Lord thy God giveth me." Exodus 20:12 (KJV)

There are many different ways to explain this scripture, but from me to you, it's about respecting and listening to your parents. Respect is the most key thing a parent would want from their children. It lets your parents know what they say to you is recognized and assures them of your obedience. Their words give you a visual of things to keep you safe and feel protected. It helps you realize that your Mother is teaching you to become independent with cleaning and cooking or even learning how to fold clothes. When listening to your mom or dad, you should do everything they tell you even if that means scrubbing the floor with a toothbrush. Everything your parents say has a purpose every time and anytime; they wouldn't make you say or do anything that's illegal or dangerous because parents care about their kids too much, so they wouldn't want to lose them. I would like to mention my Great Great Aunt, Ms. Alsie Mae Davis. She always lived up to this scripture and as the promise God mentors to all His people "that thy days may be long upon the land." As some people say, if you're pass the age of 70, the years after are your blessed ones. She was blessed + 15 years of age. God works in mysterious ways, and some don't pay it any attention. My Auntie passed away at the age of 85 years old. She outlived all her siblings and some of her nieces and nephews. Start loving your parents; they will leave someday. Use this for your references.

God loves you all!

Dr. Tina D. Lewis

"I'm here to take you to see your mom," said my neighbor as she was sitting in our living room when I got home from school. I was a confused ten-year-old. Where was my mom? Why couldn't I stay home until she got there? Once we were in ICU, I realized why. My mom was in a near fatal car accident and was in a body cast. Tears immediately began to escape my tear ducts and roll down my cheeks. After three whole months (which seemed like eternity) my mom was released. She suffered a broken jaw, broken hip, and multiple surgeries. We lost everything, including my stepdad.

My mom, my siblings and I eventually moved to the Imperial Court projects. What a culture shock?!?!

There was nothing joyous about that. I got pregnant at 18 and had my precious baby girl at 19 years old. My daughter wasn't a hindrance. No. She was a catalyst. I relocated from the projects, received a full academic scholarship to USC Keck School of Medicine and worked two or three jobs to take care of myself and my daughter.

I know this story doesn't appear to be full of joy but in retrospect, the joy is quite evident. The joy of my mom being alive, the joy of birthing a beautiful, healthy baby girl, the joy of knowing that I was meant for more and what was to come.

Today, I am an extremely successful entrepreneur with multiple streams of income. I'm the Founder of a global organization called Global Women Speakers, the #1 Platform for Women Entrepreneurs to Share their Message, Sell their Products & Services and Network with Women around the Globe. I now speak and travel the world for a living! What a joy it is!?

Dianne Lindsay

God, you are my overwhelming joy.

In you Lord, I am joyful and excited.

I have found a joy that cannot be depressed but expressed.

This joy is prosperous and contagious.

It will take you to destinations you haven't heard of

Overwhelming joy is what I have.

The joy of the Lord is my strength.

A strength so deep it goes beyond the seas.

It is my weapon of war and the fragrance I wear.

It illuminates bright as it sprinkles in the air.

God, my anchor, and the joy I received.

God, your joy strengthens me as it embraces me.

Overwhelming joy gives me life.

And it comes with no strife.

A joy so rich, it comes with great favor.

Overwhelming joy is what I have.

And that is what it shall be.

Rev. Dr. Spencer C. Lofton Sr.

1 Let not your heart be troubled: ye believe in God, believe also in me. 2 In my Father's house are many mansions: if it were not so, I would have told you. I will go to prepare a place for you. 3 And if I go and prepare a place for you, I will come again, and receive you unto myself; that where I am, there ye may be also. 4 And whither I go ye know, and the way ye know. - John 14:1-4

Anticipating the events of His death, Jesus comforts His disciples as they approach the time of His crucifixion. The anxiety and worry projected by His disciples of the unknown must have been high as it is today in our lives. Jesus, recognizing this in His disciples, decided to speak of the benefits which are to come from His crucifixion. Jesus masterfully reveals a portion of the afterlife to strengthen the faith of His disciples. We sometimes don't have the ability to look ahead and see the end product of our faith in Jesus Christ. Our fear and anxiety periodically attempt to create worry and doubt of our departure from this world and the journey into the presence of the ALL-MIGHTY God. For this reason, Jesus provides His glimpse of being in God's presence eternally. After reflecting upon the Father God and His loving grace, we realize the assurance of a new home in His presence gives us peace from our fear and anxiety. Believing in the Messiah Jesus Christ releases us from all worry and doubt for we know Jesus is the only way to our loving Father God (John 14:6). In verse three of this scripture (John 14:1-4), Jesus tells us He will return from His preparations to collect those who trust in Him. Once we place our trust in Jesus Christ, we are set free to concentrate our energies on more productive thoughts like seeking the source of the light in our new mansion (Revelations 22:5).

Kami Love

Finding joy in times of grief can be challenging but focusing on food, family, and friends can be a helpful and comforting way to cope. Here are some suggestions to make these elements bring you joy and help you get through the grieving process. Engage in cooking or baking your favorite comfort foods. The process of preparing and enjoying these dishes can provide a sense of comfort and warmth. It can also be a way to remember loved ones and the special moments shared around the table.

Spend time with your immediate family or close relatives who can offer comfort and emotional support. Sharing memories and stories about the person you're grieving can help you feel connected and less alone in your grief. If you have children, cherish the time you spend with them. Children have a way of bringing joy to the simplest of activities. Engage in activities that they enjoy, such as playing games, reading together, or doing arts and crafts. Their innocence and enthusiasm can be uplifting during challenging times.

Spending time in nature can be healing and soothing. Take walks in the park, go hiking, or have a picnic in a beautiful spot. Being surrounded by nature can bring a sense of peace and perspective. Consider joining a support group for people who are experiencing similar grief. Sharing your feelings with others who understand can be beneficial and comforting. Consider creating new traditions that honor the memory of your loved one while embracing joy. It could be as simple as having a yearly family picnic in a park, planting a tree in their honor, or organizing a charity event to give back to the community.

Tafadhali Ngwy Lubungo

Think about illuminating the path to joy through optimism. A simple grin and optimism have a tremendous capacity to make our lives happier. They bring warmth and joy into our daily lives like two shafts of sunlight piercing the heaviest of clouds. The attitude of optimism, sometimes known as the "glass-half-full" mentality, is the conviction that good things may and will occur despite adverse circumstances. When we choose it, we beckon positivity and hope into our lives. It's a way of thinking that encourages joy because it enables us to see the positive aspects of life, which reduces stress and enhances mental health. Otherwise, a smile is a sign of happiness that everyone may share. They are like contagious sparks of joy that spread from one person to another.

When we smile, we not only communicate our inner happiness but also trigger a positive response around us. A simple smile can brighten someone's day, create a connection between strangers, and melt away tensions. It's a small gesture with enormous power to create joy and foster a sense of belonging. When optimism and smiles intersect, the result is a profound amplification of joy. Optimistic individuals tend to smile more, and their positive outlook is often reflected in their cheerful demeanor. This creates a harmonious cycle: their smiles inspire joy in others, which, in turn, reinforces their optimism. They travel from one person to another like contagious joyous sparks. When we smile, we not only convey our inner enjoyment to others around us, but also elicit a good response from them. A simple grin can ease tensions between strangers and brighten someone's day. It's a simple act that has great potential to spread happiness and promote a sense of community. When optimism and smiles come together, joy is amplified profoundly.

Apostle Tamela Lucus

My soul loves Jesus for He first loved me. We say that not really understanding what it is really saying. When someone loves you, they will show you with no hesitation. You do not have to beg them to wash clothes, wash dishes, clean the house, or watch their own children. Agape love is when you don't obey God and He still forgives you and gives you another chance to do something different. We are constantly learning new things about ourselves. The best thing is we should know how much God loves us. He downloads dreams and step by step instructions to make sure we get it right the next time.

That's love. Sometimes we don't want to forgive because we want to stay mad but if we really evaluate ourselves to God's standard, we will find out that "obedience is better than sacrifice 1 Sam. 15:22." Forgiveness will free your mind, heart, and soul. You will be able to breathe and smile at the person with whom you had a disagreement or argument. Forgiveness allows us to take a sigh. Sometimes we forget that God made every single one of us regardless of how we feel about someone. Before we judge, try to pray, and ask God to reach the unreachable. Just like we are so quick to say something negative, remember someone is saying something negative about you. Words are powerful. Speak life into every situation. God is life. God is love. He loved me enough to be here. He loves you enough to be here. We are pieces of one puzzle.

Dr. Khafilah Malik

"Suffer little children, and forbid them not, to come unto me: For such is the kingdom of heaven." — Matthew 19:14

They often say that the Lord gives the biggest challenges in this life to His strongest warriors. I am not sure when God decided that I was one of His warriors, but He did. As a mother of an autistic son, there were many nights I cried *"A Bucket Full of Tears."* How does one reconcile with the pain and the inability to understand yet comprehend one's own child? It's unfathomable the pain a mother feels when she is rendered helpless.

Stop it! Stop it! I cried out for him to stop. To stop hitting me, yelling at me, screaming at me, and telling me he hated me. I cupped my hands to my face and cried out to God to help me, to deliver me from this pain. The screaming and the yelling were so loud my neighbors called the police. I was relieved that they did. I was too tired and depleted from trying to protect myself from his assaults. The knock at the door couldn't come soon enough and when it did, I felt a sigh of relief and fear at the same time. I opened the door so the routine questions would begin.

"Ma' am, are there any weapons in the house?" Ma'am is there anyone in the house in danger?" If I said yes, I knew they would take him away and if I said no, I would endure another long night of tears and abuse. As I turned around, there he stood with pain in his eyes looking confused, exhausted, and tired.

Guia Marie Marcaida

Before, I didn't know the difference between happiness and joy. All along, I thought that they had the same meaning, which talks about the feeling of enjoyment. But after believing and receiving Jesus Christ, I now have a way to differentiate the two. I realized that the happiness I felt before was only short-lived while the joy I have now will be everlasting. Just like how it was stated in the book of *Psalm 16:11, "You make known to me the path of life; in your presence there is fullness of joy; at your right hand are pleasures forevermore."* Knowing and following Christ doesn't only give us salvation but will ensure us a life that is filled with unending joy and fulfillment. I remember those times when I had no Christ in my life.

Although I can be happy and pleased with simple things, there is no fulfillment that is lasting. Some examples are when I graduated high school and celebrated my 18th birthday with friends. the first time I received my hard-earned money for the first novel that I published, those times that I celebrated Christmas and New Year's with my family. Yes, it was full of happiness and that short feeling of fulfillment when you have achieved something on your own. But then again, as I said, it was only fleeting. A temporary enjoyment that you receive or achieve will soon pass after that momentary happiness.

Fortunately, I have found my way to grasp that long-lasting joy and fulfillment. And that is by following God and having Jesus Christ in our lives. Because the fulfillment it brings isn't short but strong and permanent. Why settle for less when there's always the best way?

Jennifer Marcus

"If we endure, we will also reign with him. If we disown him, he will also disown us." 2 Timothy 2:12 (NIV)

In the crucible of life's trials, we often discover an extraordinary strength within us—a strength that endures despite the deepest wounds and darkest nights. The scripture in 2 Timothy 2:12 beautifully encapsulates this truth, and it finds resonance in the remarkable journey of a young girl who learned to endure against all odds.

At the age of 8, she was left in a strange place, her mother's words of rejection ringing in her ears, yet she chose to endure. At 10, her father made a painful choice, leaving her feeling abandoned. Still, she held on, finding the resilience to endure. By the time she was 15, she faced a horrifying ordeal, lying alone in a hospital bed, isolated from family and friends, yet she pressed on, enduring.

This young girl's story is a testament to the power of endurance, for she did not merely survive; she thrived. Through the depths of her suffering, she found a wellspring of strength that led her to a life richly blessed.

You, too, have faced trials that seemed insurmountable, moments when endurance felt like an impossible task. Remember, as children of God, we are called to endure, for it is in endurance that we discover our truest selves and draw closer to Him.

As we hold fast to our faith, even in the face of despair, we find that God's grace is sufficient. Just as this young girl rose from the ashes of adversity to live a life abundantly blessed. Through Him, we can endure, and in our endurance, we will discover the path to reigning with Him.

Dr. Angela Marshall

As a child, who could you count on keeping a promise to you? No matter what happens, you can rest assured they will always keep their promise. Now as an adult, has that same person kept their promises? The only person I know who keeps all His Promises is God. God promises never to leave or forsake us. Even when we may not see the fulfillment of those promises in front of us, we can have an assurance that by keeping the faith, our blessings are on the way. There was a woman in the Bible named Hannah. For many years she desired to have a son, but she was barren. She prayed, cried, fasted, and pleaded for a son then a vow erupted that she may return him to God for His Glory. God honored her bold and decisive cry out. Hannah emerged into a woman of faith. Are you pregnant with something, and you have not seen it come to pass?

You may be wondering if you heard God wrong because it has been years and it has not birthed yet. That birth may or may not be a child, it could be a business, a radio show, a ministry, or something else. Have you lost faith in that promise from God? After God gave you the promise, did you start to prepare to receive the blessing, or did you think it would just happen like magic? "YOU HAVE TO PUT THE WORK IN"!!! Get BOLD like Hannah by worshiping, praying, crying, fasting, and pleading with God. Hannah's voice was never heard, only her lips were moving, to the point her boldness made Eli think she was a drunken woman. God told you a promise so, are you willing to receive the blessing and be willing to give it back to God for His use and Glory? BOLD FAITH.

Lord, I thank you for your promise. Give me a boldness like Hannah. Give me childlike faith and patience to wait on your timing. AMEN.

Patricia Marston

The JOY of the Lord is our strength, and we should not forget that there is a God who wants to see us being joyful. When we have JOY within us, we see things from a beautiful and positive perspective. When we connect our spirit and soul JOY evolves. Sometimes there is pain and sorrow in our lives, but regardless of these challenges, there is always that opportunity for that ray of hope and JOY to be renewed and reactivated in our hearts. JOY brings us in closer proximity to God. There is so much JOY in heaven when souls have been won. Charles Spurgeon said, "No JOY ever visits my soul like that of knowing that Jesus is highly exalted and especially, that to him every knee shall bow, and every tongue confess that Jesus Christ is Lord to the glory of God the father."

Reading an interesting book brings JOY, watching a beautiful sunset brings us such unexplainable JOY. You cannot have JOY without Christ. In the scripture we see that JOY is one of the fruits of the Holy Spirit. JOY comes from believing in God, belonging to his Kingdom, and knowing him as Lord of our lives. *Romans 15 verse 13 says "May the God of all hope fill you with JOY and peace as you trust in him so that you may overflow with hope by the power of the Holy Spirit."*

I mourned the loss of my son, Bradley, for a while, then I received the JOY of the Lord. I realized that I could not allow this circumstance of loss to dictate my future JOY. As His child, I was no longer afraid, I decided to cast my burden on Him. He restored me, giving me JOY, and I was able to rise and go forward in HIS purpose for my life. THE JOY OF THE LORD at that moment was truly my strength.

Melsades McIntosh-Martin

During my life I have encountered many heartaches and pain, but none as profound as the recent death of my mother and the loss I experienced with the miscarriage of my first pregnancy at five months. With the loss of my baby, I felt so lost, so inadequate and I experienced a deep sense of sadness. I cried day and night; my husband nor any other family member were able to console me. I had a deep anger towards God and wanted to abandon my faith. I could not understand why such a wonderful God would let such a thing happen to me. I blamed myself for the loss, but God who restored it came through for me in a matter of months.

A year after my loss, my God restored; He had compassion on me and blessed me with a healthy baby boy. He did not stop there; I gave birth to a beautiful daughter sixteen months after my son. I also had two more beautiful daughters a few years later. He gave me double for my trouble. 1 Peter 5:10 NIV states, "And the God of all grace, who called you to his eternal glory in Christ, after you have suffered a little while, will restore you and make you strong, firm, and steadfast. "It was not all peaches and cream after I had my children. I went through many personal trials and tribulation, but I waited patiently for God's help and deliverance. Hence today the JOY that I experience when I spend time with my family, the world never gave to me, and the world cannot take it away.

"Consider it pure joy, my brothers and sisters, whenever you face trials of many kinds, because you know that the testing of your faith produces perseverance."- James 1:2-3 NIV.

Dr. Tanya F. Mattox

The word Joy conjures memories of singing the Christmas carol, "Joy to the World." This song brought smiles and the anticipation of Holiday fun. What, however, is joy? Oftentimes the word is used interchangeably with the word happy. The dictionary defines joy as: The emotion of great delight or happiness caused by something exceptionally good or satisfying, keen pleasure, elation. Happy is defined as: delighted, pleased, or glad over a particular thing. At fifteen, I committed my life to Christ and began studying the bible and found myself challenged seeking understanding of scripture that seemed contradictory. One passage was James 1:2-4 (NIV) "Consider it pure joy, my brothers, and sisters, whenever you face trials of many kinds, because you know that the testing of your faith produces perseverance.

Let perseverance finish its work so that you may be mature and complete, not lacking anything. How can trials bring Joy? Through relationships, I learned another person nor things can give you joy that will last. We should not expect another person to fill the space within us that only God has the capacity to fill. Gratitude creates space for joy. You can experience joy every day by expressing gratitude to God for every day you arise, and every breath you take. Set your intention daily to be joyful/ happy. You decide how you will experience the events of your day. Find a word, name; phrase, to serve as your grounding point. I found the Yoruba name, "Titilayo." This name translates as, "eternal happiness." Eternal happiness to me means God-given, not from external sources. I state my intention to be happy; to be joyful daily. The negative energy of others or disappointing situations will not defeat me. I choose joy. I invite you to choose joy, too.

Diane Maupin

Scripture: Isaiah 41:10 (NIV) - "So do not fear, for I am with you; do not be dismayed, for I am your God. I will strengthen you and help you; I will uphold you with my righteous right hand. "In times of uncertainty and tribulation, we often find ourselves wrestling with fear and doubt. It is in these moments that we are reminded of the steadfast promise in Isaiah 41:10. The Lord, our God, speaks directly to our hearts, reassuring us with unwavering love and support. "Do not fear, for I am with you..." These words echo through the ages, a beacon of hope for all who face trials. They remind us that we are never alone, for our Heavenly Father stands beside us, His presence a shield against the storms of life.

"Do not be dismayed, for I am your God..." When the world seems disheartening and overwhelming, remember that the Almighty God claims us as His own. He knows us intimately, and He cares for us deeply. In His care, we find solace, knowing that we are cherished beyond measure. "I will strengthen you and help you; I will uphold you with my righteous right hand." Here lies the promise of divine empowerment. God doesn't merely offer empty words of comfort; He extends His mighty hand to lift us up. In our moments of weakness, His strength fills our hearts. In our moments of despair, His righteousness upholds us.

Beloved, as you face the challenges of today and tomorrow, hold fast to this sacred assurance. Let it be an anchor for your soul, grounding you in the unshakable truth that God is with you, strengthening you, and guiding you with His righteous hand. When fear threatens to engulf you, remember that you stand in the presence of the Almighty, and in Him, you find unwavering strength and unending grace.

Melody McDaniels

Weeping May Endure for A Night, But JOY Cometh in The Morning. Psalm 30:5 (KJV)

Sometimes life hits us so hard that it's hard to find a reason to smile. I can't even begin to tell you how I've managed to find joy when life tried to knock me down literally and take me out. I went through a pandemic with a new baby, homeschooling my oldest daughter, nursing, writing my children's book, going to school, and being a caretaker to my husband, who almost died from Covid while trying to keep my health and mental health intact while helping my oldest manage her emotions, etc.

There are many seasons of life, and no one knows when it's their turn to go through a rough season. The good thing is that no matter what season we go through, God is always with us and will never leave or forsake us.

So, I encourage you to count it all JOY when life happens and it hits you hard because this, too, shall pass. It's easy to feel disappointed when things don't go as planned, but one of the greatest things we can do is rest assured that whatever we go through grows us and all things work together for good.

Everything you go through is always for someone else. Rest in His peace and find JOY despite it all.

Joy does come in the morning; it came for me, and it'll come for you.

Michelle McKenney

Never ever forget how far you've come and everything you have gone through. Remember all the times you pushed on, even when you felt like giving up. All the days you couldn't get out the bed and you wanted to call it quits, but God brought you through to see another day. Never forget how much strength you gained from the things you thought would bring you down. The pain you felt enabled you to become stronger and tackle the devil in other situations in your life. You never know how resilient you are until it is the only choice you must make. When trusting God, things are always going to get better. I wish I could tell you the exact day when that will begin. but I can't. It's gradual but you will feel lighter each day. Your heart will begin to put itself back together piece by piece. Eventually. one day you will look in the mirror and recognize yourself again. The thing that people often get wrong is time isn't your healer; Jesus is. He digs into the deepest parts of your soul and doesn't fix you. He makes you new again. So, hold onto hope that where you are is not where you'll always be. God has bigger plans for you. Be courageous and brave enough to choose and live the life you want to live. Because imagine what a terrible thing it will be to wake up one day only to realize you did not do all the things you wanted when you had the chance. Live the life God chose for you and speak your mind if anyone tries to overpower you. You are not a mat to be stepped on. You are the strength that pulls the rest of the world. In speaking with peace, raise your words, not your voice. It is rain that grows flowers, not thunder. Do not waste your time on people who treat you good one day that act like you don't exist the next.

Dr. Petrice M. McKey-Reese

"So Jesus said to them, "Because of your Unbelief; for assuredly, I say to you, if you have faith as a mustard seed, you will say to this mountain, 'Move from here to there,' and it will move; and nothing will be impossible for you. However, this kind does not go out except by prayer and fasting." Matthew 17: 20-21

In our day to day lives, we all talk with God. In our talks with God we ask for things that we need and want. Sometimes we can see those things happen right away and sometimes we can't. It's those times when we can't that we must stand on our faith. That faith for most is the size of a mustard seed. At times, human nature in us makes it difficult to do this, but we must believe in our Heavenly Father. He will never leave us nor forsake us.

This is accomplished best by prayer and fasting. This is how we can restore or strengthen our intimacy with God. Fasting helps me to rediscover my "first love" for God again and humble myself in the sight of God. Fasting can also help us become less prideful and selfish and more concerned about the needs of others. It also helps us to overcome our weaknesses and turns them into strengths. The biggest reason for fasting is so that we may hear God more clearly. When we can hear God clearly it is easier to stand on our faith.

Never stop standing and believing in your faith. Always know that God will always answer prayers right on time, not in our time, but right on time! Faith of a mustard seed is bigger than we realize

Flavya Reeves Toefield

Pain is inevitable. We all experience pain at some point in our lives. Pain comes in all different forms…physically, mentally, emotionally, and spiritually. Although the pain may seem never ending, GOD IS YOUR REFUGE. "If He allows you to come to it, He will allow you to go through it." My greatest pain is child loss. In 2015, I lost my first-born son at age 6. The pain caused me to question my faith and existence. I blamed God for it all. I was mad at Him! I began to lose myself. I grieved, non-stop. I self-sabotaged. I was spiraling downward. I didn't want to live. Still, I vowed not to allow my child loss to be in vain. I cried, I prayed, and I had to put my full trust back in God. I didn't know any other way to survive. God was my last hope.

I read Bible scriptures written on sticky notes stuck to my son's bedroom wall daily, soaked in tears on the floor. Those scriptures were of God's strength, comfort, refuge, healing, and guidance. Eventually, over time I began to gain strength and healing. I prayed for God to use me and show me purpose through it all. God began to reveal the specific ordained purpose that He placed upon my life. Through this revelation, I am the Founder/President of "Duckie's Treasure Chest." DTC is a Youth Non-Profit for disadvantaged community youth in loving memory of Jonathan "Duckie" Paul Monnet, Jr. Every time I'm able to help a child in need, I feel closer to my son. It also gives me a feeling of joy and fulfillment. God has surpassed all my expectations for my life. And I know that one day I will be with my child again in heaven.

Natalie McKinnie

"For I know the plans I have for you," declares the Lord, "plans to prosper you and not to harm you, plans to give you a hope and a future."
- Jeremiah 29:11

Life can knock you off your feet and leave you emotionally weak and unable to cope. In those times, human emotions cannot be trusted, because they will lie to you. You must believe that you are doing a perfect plan for which you have no control, and that you can make it through your devastation.

Emotions can be powerful and if not processed in healthy ways, they can leave you paralyzed. Let go of trying to grasp and understand the "what" happened, and the "why" and resolve to focus on the "who" …. not who did it, but who can fix it! Who can provide it for you at this moment? Who is sustaining you right now? Who can give you peace when there is confusion all around you? Who can give you rest in your weariness? Who can give you strength to keep going minute by minute, hour by hour, day by day?

With God's help, you can get through any devastation! God has a plan for your life. Pray and invite God into your healing journey. Surrender your feelings and lean not to your own understanding. God promises to equip you with a strength and a peace that will lead and guide you. Prayer can help you change the way you feel and adjust the way you think. Always trust God and never your emotions

Adriane M. McLeod

Trust in the Lord with all thine heart; lean not unto thine own understanding. In all thine ways acknowledge him, and he shall direct thy path. Proverbs 3:5-6

Trying to find joy in pain and sorrow may be harder to come by than we expect. In pain, we can feel every emotion imaginable and there seems to be no relief in sight. We may find ourselves kicking and screaming to get relief and it seems to be far off. We often feel the same way about God while calling out for relief and answers, yet God has left us to feel and deal on our own. God, do you hear me? God, do you see what I am going through?

There are times when you may get discouraged seeking God for answers, and He is silent. You want God to give you the exact answer to help in your situation but sometimes it's in God's silence that He wants you to trust Him. Trust God by acknowledging Him for who He is and trust that He will direct you. God never asked us to understand what we may be feeling or going through. God calls us to trust Him to lead, guide, heal and restore us.

How do we trust God? We trust God by believing His word and his promises.

In the silence is where we are still and can be guided by God in His wisdom, through His word.

Today I challenge you to lean on God for your healing, transformation, understanding and joy.

Dr. Brenda Miller

Why? Why Us? Why Now? So many emotions! Confusion, anger, denial, sadness, pain, and so many other unnamed emotions. Rick and I were married 37 years and now he is gone. God had blessed me with my soulmate. We did everything together. How would I go on? I felt the world slowly turning around me. It was as if I were outside looking in.

I retired in August 2021 and learned the following week my husband had terminal cancer. I was terrified when we received the diagnosis from the doctor. He was a matter of fact. No emotion. No one can ever be prepared to hear a death sentence.

Rick was a good and honorable man. He was kind. His life was a testimony to his character and his love for others. We had so many plans for retirement. We could finally slow down and enjoy life. We were looking forward to traveling and visiting our grandchildren. Little did we know that the next ten months would be a downward spiral resulting in my husband's death. I was devastated!

The Bible teaches us that God's ways are higher than our ways. Although I don't understand why my husband was chosen to leave so early. I know we will be reunited on the other side. That is our hope – that we will be reunited. It is there that all things will be revealed, and we will understand why terrible things happen to good people. My husband suffered here, but he has a perfect body in Heaven. My joy will be restored! We can find joy in chaos and pain. It is a matter of the heart.

Angela M. Mitchell

"Joy is prayer, joy is strength, joy is love, joy is the net by which you can catch souls" Mother Theresa

These words by Mother Teresa are a beautiful reminder that joy is an essential aspect of our lives. However, we should not seek it solely for pleasure but as a source of strength and a means to connect with others. As we grow older, we may feel like we missed opportunities to experience joy. But, as a woman who is reinventing herself at fifty, let me assure you that it's never too late to unleash your joyful spirit.

Joy is prayer because it connects us to something greater than ourselves. It's a way of expressing gratitude and acknowledging the blessings in our lives.

Joy is strength because it empowers us to overcome challenges and difficulties. When we are joyful, we approach life with a positive attitude and a resilient spirit.

Joy is love because it connects us to others. When we experience joy, we radiate positivity and attract others to us. It's a way of sharing our love and light with those around us.

Joy is about being seen and not blending into the norm of society; It's about being allowed to be unapologetically me.

Joy is the net we use to catch souls because it's contagious. So, when we experience joy, we inspire others to do the same. I encourage you to embrace bliss and unleash your joyful spirit. Let joy be your prayer, your strength, your love, and your net. May it fill your heart and overflow into the lives of those around you.

Dr. H. T. Mohair

Gratitude: A Pathway to Rediscovering Joy in God's Blessings

In the pursuit of joy and contentment, gratitude emerges as a potent ally. Rekindling joy often begins with a transformation of perspective, commencing with acknowledging and embracing gratitude in our lives.

Gratitude isn't a fleeting sentiment; it's a spiritual practice, an intentional effort to recognize and appreciate the simplest, beautiful moments bestowed upon us. It's about finding splendor in the mundane – the warmth of a morning's coffee, a shared smile, or the hues of a sunset, echoing Psalm 118:1, "Give thanks to the Lord, for he is good; his love endures forever."

A powerful way to cultivate gratitude is through a journal. This simple practice serves as a repository for our blessings, encouraging us to note daily moments of thankfulness. It may seem small, yet this act shifts our focus from hardships to the multitude of blessings adorning our lives. This daily ritual trains our minds to seek positivity amidst chaos, fostering an attitude of appreciation. It reshapes our perspective, allowing us to perceive abundance where once we saw scarcity. This shift becomes the foundation of rediscovering joy in God's grace. Gratitude transcends challenges, reframing them to offer resilience and hope amidst trials, as Romans 8:28 reassures, "And we know that in all things God works for the good of those who love him, who have been called according to his purpose." Embracing gratitude becomes more than an action; it's a spiritual lifestyle. It's a conscious choice to behold life's beauty, blessings, and miracles daily. It's the pathway back to joy, illuminated by an appreciation for God's myriad gifts in our lives.

Dr. Jacqueline Mohair

There is so much sad news in the world today. Whether it's from your TV, on the internet, within your neighborhood or even when you phone a friend. People lose jobs, some are sick, economies are dwindling, there are shooting crimes all over the place and it's all so disturbing that it could steal your joy away subtly without you knowing. Sadly, many are in despair and others have given up. However, in a world where many believers are depressed and are at the brink of suicide because of their surrounding circumstances, I came with one counsel for you today: CHOOSE JOY! Joy is a potent force, the antidote for depression. Joy heals broken hearts, brightens countenances, and helps people see only the positive side of things as they go through life. It is one of the fruits the Holy Ghost bears in us, which has nothing to do with what is happening around us, but everything to do with what is happening within. Joy is a spiritual tool which enables us to draw from the wells of salvation, that well that contains everything you would ever need in life. Do you know that both the enemy and life's troubles cannot survive in the atmosphere of joy? This is why the devil attacks your joy all the time, because he knows that when you lose your joy, the door of hope closes against you, and you lose the ability to see possibilities, thus, hopelessness sets in, and you give up. Choosing joy begins with a personal decision to never lose your joy whatever happens, regardless. Next, take your attention away from what has not happened and focus more on what God has done. Choose joy, be deliberate about your choice, and watch God turn things around for you. I chose joy today! What is your choice?

Morgan Mohair

When life gets bumpy, having a crew of friends and family is like having a superhero squad. Their support makes an enormous difference when you're feeling down. Just hanging out, chatting, and sharing laughs can turn a gloomy day around. These connections act like a safety net, giving you a cozy spot when things get tough but it's not just about having a blast together (even though that's pretty great). It's about feeling stronger because you know they're there for you. Having these friendships is like having a secret weapon against tough times. They remind us that even when everything feels upside down, there are people who care and can help us find our way back to joy.

Imagine a tough day at school or a rough competition. Having friends who cheer you on and support you no matter what is like having your own cheering squad. They make the hard stuff feel a bit lighter. Their encouragement and understanding remind us that we're not alone. Friendship isn't just about good times; it's about having a crew that has your back through it all. When life throws curveballs, these connections keep us grounded. They remind us that joy isn't far away, and with a little help from our friends, we can always find our way back to happiness.

Embrace the power of friendship, dear cheerleader! Amidst the cheers and routines, genuine connections sparkle. Devoted friends uplift your spirit, turning ordinary moments into extraordinary memories. In laughter and shared dreams, discover the magic that makes each day brighter. Friendship is your secret to rediscovering joy on and off the cheerleading mat.

Myles Mohair

When life gets tough, accepting it isn't throwing in the towel – it's about seeing things differently. It's like saying, "Okay, this is hard, but it won't beat me." Instead of focusing on the negatives, it's about hunting for the positives.

Sometimes, it's hard to spot any good when everything seems upside down. But here's the deal: every tough situation is a chance to learn. It's like finding a secret strategy in a challenging game. Those tough times? They're like tough opponents, making us stronger.

Admittedly, it's a mental workout to look at a problem differently. But when we start seeing problems as challenges to conquer, it changes the game. It's about moving the spotlight from what's going wrong to what we're gaining from it.

Strength grows from facing the hard stuff and coming out tougher. It's like finishing a grueling practice – it's tough, but it builds us up. So, finding joy in the tough moments isn't about ignoring the struggle; it's about learning from it and discovering our power through it all. Choosing to accept what we can't change and still finding joy – that's a win. It's saying, "Hey, life's hard, but I've got this." And that is the mindset? That's where the joy starts shining, even on the field.

I love playing football but, in the game, somebody must win, and somebody must lose. I keep playing and praying for the win in life and football.

<u>Cheryl Monroe</u>

In our journey of faith, we sometimes encounter trials and tribulations throughout life that shudder the foundation of our beliefs. As we navigate life, we experience different challenges, such as medical issues, professional setbacks, relationship dissension, grief, or personal struggles. It is during these times that we may find it hard to understand how joy could potentially coexist with pain and suffering.

When we embrace the concept that joy can coexist with pain, we have a different outlook on our current situation. We refocus our attention and perspective from temporary pain to eternal glory. Just as when a diamond is a crystallized carbon deposit deep within the earth subject to elevated temperature and pressure, our character and faith are shaped and strengthened through the challenges we encounter. Amid adversity, our faith is sometimes tested and refined; but by seeking God's presence, believing in his promises, and relying on his unfailing love one can experience joy. We can find joy by choosing gratitude and thankfulness, and recognizing the blessings that surround us even during hardship. As we reflect on life, joy is not dependent on our circumstances but on the unchanging character of our loving Heavenly Father. Joy is the everlasting expressions of happiness and gratitude intertwined. It is spiritual in the sense that to feel it, you simply must co-exist and be connected to your higher consciousness and understanding. While the world may experience joy from materialistic things, your spiritual self will experience joy simply because you woke up to see another day. Remember, joy comes in the morning.

Jabarrie Monsano

Life is a journey that is filled with ups and downs. It can be easy to get caught up in the challenges and struggles that we face along the way. However, it is important to remember that joy is an essential part of this journey. Joy is more than just happiness; it is a deep sense of contentment and fulfillment that comes from within.

One of the reasons why joy is so important in our journey is that it helps us to stay positive and hopeful. When we experience joy, it can help to lift our spirits and give us the energy and motivation we need to keep moving forward. It can also help us to see the good in our lives and appreciate the blessings that we have been given.

Another reason why joy is important is that it can help us to connect with others. When we are joyful, it can be contagious, and it can help to bring people together. We can share our joy with others and lift them up when they are feeling down. This can help to create a sense of community and support that can be incredibly powerful.

Finally, joy is important because it can help us to stay focused on what really matters in life. When we are joyful, we are more likely to prioritize the things that are most important to us, such as our relationships, our health, and our personal growth. This can help us to live more fulfilling and meaningful lives.

In conclusion, having joy in our journey is essential for our well-being and happiness. It can help us to stay positive, connect with others, and focus on what really matters. So, let us embrace joy in our lives and let it guide us on our journey.

Nadia Monsano

"Rejoice in the Lord always. I will say it again: Rejoice!"
- Philippians 4:4 (NIV)

In the midst of life's trials and tribulations, it is easy to lose sight of the importance of living with joy. The burdens we carry, the challenges we face, and the uncertainties that surround us can often overshadow the joy that awaits us. However, as followers of Christ, we are called to embrace joy as an essential aspect of our lives. Joy is not dependent on our circumstances; rather, it is a gift from God that springs forth from a deep-rooted relationship with Him. It is a fruit of the Holy Spirit dwelling within us, manifesting itself in our hearts and lives. Joy is not a fleeting emotion but a steadfast and unwavering assurance that God is with us, no matter what we may encounter. Living with joy does not mean we ignore or deny the pain and struggles of life. Instead, it is a conscious choice to rise above our circumstances, knowing that our hope is not found in the temporary, but in the eternal. Joy empowers us to face adversity with resilience, to find beauty during chaos, and to radiate God's love in a world desperate for hope. When we live with joy, we become beacons of light, drawing others to the transformative power of Christ. Our joy becomes contagious, encouraging and uplifting those around us. It is through our joy that we reflect the character of our Heavenly Father and demonstrate the victory we have in Jesus. Today, let us embrace the gift of joy and cultivate a heart that overflows with gratitude. As we rejoice in the Lord, let our lives bear witness to the abundant life found in Him. May our joy be a testimony of God's faithfulness and a source of inspiration for others.

<u>Venecia Monsano Thomas</u>

Life is often likened to a journey—a winding path filled with highs and lows, challenges, and victories. Along this path, it's easy to become consumed by the destinations: the goals we set, the milestones we aim to achieve, or the places we wish to reach. Yet, in our relentless pursuit of these endpoints, we might inadvertently overlook one of life's most precious gifts: joy. Joy is not just a fleeting emotion tied to favorable circumstances. It is a deep-seated sense of contentment and delight that transcends the temporary. The importance of joy in our life's journey cannot be overstated. Here is why: **Fuel for the Soul**: Just as a car needs fuel to keep moving, our spirits require joy to persevere. In moments of despair or weariness, it is joy that rekindles our passion, rejuvenates our spirit, and propels us forward with renewed vigor. **Perspective Amidst Trials**: Challenges are inevitable. However, when joy is our compass, we navigate these challenges with grace. Instead of being overwhelmed by difficulties, we find strength in joy, recognizing that every trial is but a chapter in our broader narrative.

Connection and Community: Joy is contagious. When we embrace joy in our journey, we become beacons of light for others. Our joy becomes a source of encouragement, fostering unity. **Gratitude Amplified**: A joy-filled heart is a grateful heart. By cultivating joy, we shift our focus from what we lack to the abundance that surrounds us. This attitude of gratitude enriches our journey, allowing us to savor life's simple pleasures and cherish every moment. As we traverse the winding paths of our journey, let us not only seek the destinations but also embrace the joy that lights our way.

LeTysha N. Montgomery

"Be ye strong therefore and let not your hands be weak: for your work shall be rewarded." 2 Chronicles 15:7

Sometimes you are given an assignment from God, and you aren't really sure what to do. You just know that God has told you to do something, and you are trying to figure out how to complete it. Rest assured that God will never give you an assignment that you aren't capable of completing. He knows that you have all the skills needed to be successful inside of you. All you need to do is just trust Him, follow the instructions given to you and pray!

I know that all that sounds so simple but when you are in the middle of a new assignment then it can be scary. I know that I was given a life changing assignment over two years ago. God spoke to me directly and told me to become an author to share my story with more people. First off, I didn't know anything about being an author and didn't really find my story about endometriosis that interesting. But it doesn't matter what I think. It matters what God says and what He has in store for my life. My hands were never weak because I was always sharing my story in some type of book for the first two years. Never let fear keep you from your assignment because God has something amazing in store for you!

KJ Montgomery

Rejoice in hope, be patient in tribulation, be constant in prayer.
Romans 12:12

Fibromyalgia is considered an "invisible disease." It is a challenging and painful medical condition. Your entire body hurts every day. It can be painful to sit, stand, walk, and/or remain in any position for any length of time. The severity can vary with everyone. This condition can diminish your quality of life. There is no cure, but it can be managed. With fibromyalgia (or any chronic condition) you must learn how to juggle pain management, your career, and relationships. It's not always easy, but it is achievable. *You can do it!* Unfortunately, there will be doubters. People who do not believe that fibromyalgia is a real medical condition. For any chronic condition, surround yourself with people who support you and understand your condition. *You deserve only the best!* Take the necessary steps to strive for a healthy quality of life. In addition to an exceptional support system, meditation, yoga, Pilates, walking and other forms of exercise that you can tolerate may be beneficial. These activities can help support your mind, body, and soul. You and your medical professional should work together to create a personalized treatment plan. Stay proactive, stay strong, stay positive, and never give up no matter how challenging things get! *Keep going and stay focused on taking care of yourself!* When you feel overwhelmed, find someone you trust to talk to or write your thoughts in a journal. This will help to reduce your stress level and maintain a healthy mental balance. Also, remember to pray!! Prayer is powerful as well as therapeutic. Chronic conditions do not have to consume your life.

Find Joy … Everyday!
Live your life!!
Enjoy your life!

Mary Moore

WE all have an assignment from God, all of us, and guess what? The enemy knows it. So, he has set fourth his mission. His only mission, TO KILL, STEAL, AND DESTROY! He's been on your tail, not because you're weak or worthless, but because you have a marvelous calling on your life.

The enemy seeks to steal your joy, kill your hope, and destroy your dreams.

I'm here to tell you to PRESS. It's in your darkest hour in life that your breakthrough is near. Life experiences, both good and bad, had to happen for you to gain the strength and

endurance to be the vessel God has called you to be.

Every challenge you've gone through will either change your life or help you change someone else's.

Galatians 6:9 says "do not be weary in well doing, for you shall receive a harvest if you faint not.

PRESS!

In your darkest hour, Press!

When you feel you have done all you can…. Press

Your breakthrough is on its way!

<u>Yonelle Moore Lee, Esq.</u>

Your joy is YOURS, and you have to own it and protect it. You cannot entrust it to anyone else or make them responsible for your joy. Sometimes, our struggles are where we find our greatest joy. Trying times remind us of how far we have come, what we have endured, and how resilient we are. Challenges are inevitable and there will be days choosing joy will be harder than others. There will be days when it feels like darkness inundates us on all sides and there is no escape.

In your darkest moments, when the despair seems overbearing… choose joy. Choose to believe that whatever you are going through is temporary. Choose joy. Choose to trust that you are stronger than whatever you are facing. Choose joy. Choose to understand that there are alternatives. . . that better is just around the corner or at the top of the mountain. Choose joy. Choose to accept help. Choose to know that there is always someone willing to listen and support you. Choose joy. Choose to embrace all of your learned and lived experiences that have brought you to this point. Choose joy. Choose to make better decisions, create stronger relationships, learn from past mistakes. Choose joy. Choose to model the behavior you expect from others to demonstrate that you will overcome any circumstance life throws your way. Choose joy.

Choose to reflect on how far you have come and how much you have grown. Choose joy. Choose to treasure and protect every precious moment of your life that you are blessed to experience. Choose joy. Choose to live fearlessly, authentically and without regrets. Choose joy. Choose yourself, your mental health, and your own happiness. Choose joy. Choose to support and encourage others. Choose joy. Choose to leave a legacy that can never be erased.

Latasha Morgan, M.Div., MA

"For we are his workmanship, created in Christ Jesus unto good works, which God hath before ordained that we should walk in them."
Ephesians 2:10

Masterpieces are often found in museums, art galleries, homes of the wealthy, or locked up in storage facilities because of the need to keep them safe. We look at them and admire them. Sometimes they change people's minds, bring people together, and sometimes may even divide people. Regardless of what people receive from the masterpieces created, the artist has his or her own purpose for creating the masterpiece. It's for the purpose of revealing their thoughts or souls to others without saying a word. God, the Master of all creation and the greatest artist ever, created mankind, His masterpiece, for the purpose of doing good works. It wasn't because we deserved it nor because of some great thing we've done. It was simply because He loved us. The problem is that many people don't know or believe that they were created for anything. They call themselves or allow others to call them lumps of nothing. Sadly, that's the way they perceive themselves and they stay locked up in their prison of darkness, shame, lies, and fear, while trying to stay safe. Today, God is calling you, His Masterpiece, out of the prison that you have allowed to hold you hostage. He is calling you to do the good work that He designed you for. Yes, good work. You know, those works that change lives, which require you to step out of your comfort zone, that your past can't stop, those works that you have been approved for, and that will benefit the world. You were designed for a purpose and given everything you need to complete that purpose. Now that is clear, you can walk into any room as God's Masterpiece and say, "Hello, my name is Masterpiece.

Barbara Morrison-Williams

I've had to make several decisions during this season of my life; like the decision to leave a job that had brought me so much joy but also mixed with pain. This journey has also taught me that who I am is more important than what I do. Society tends to want to define us by what we do, which is external.

But my being addresses my center, the core of who I am in Christ. And who does He say that I am? "…fearfully and wonderfully made," (Psalm 139:13-16), "But you are a chosen race, a royal priesthood, a holy nation, a people for his own possession, that you may proclaim the excellencies of him who called you out of darkness into his marvelous light." (I Peter 2:9). He calls me friend (John 15:15), a citizen (Philippians 3:30) and His workmanship (Ephesians 2:20).

So, despite the challenges during this journey, I intentionally chose joy. With the ebbs and flows, I choose joy. When I'm uncertain, I choose joy. When life takes unexpected turns, I choose joy. His joy is my strength. His joy is complete. His joy is morning glory after the darkest night. This journey is not a sprint, it is a marathon. With this knowledge, I continue to evolve into the woman of God He has designed me to be with unspeakable joy because I am His and He is mine.

Kyshone Moss

"Favor is deceitful, and beauty is vain: but a woman that feareth the LORD, she shall be praised."
Proverbs 31:30

There was a time in my life when I felt hopeless and afraid. I was paralyzed by my fears of failure and how my family would look at me after my divorce. I had to make sure I saved face when in public, even though the pain was unbearable at times. I began to strengthen my relationship with GOD and work on myself. I always knew GOD would heal my broken heart. As days went by, it got much earlier. I began to encourage others. I began to heal. I continue to love others and I continue to LIVE.

I had to realize that this was not my expected end. GOD had so much more in store for me and my family. I began to be blessed beyond measure. I gained my confidence back; I held my head up high, and I walked with no shame. I had moments when my thoughts tried to get me down, but I prayed and cast those thoughts out and started thinking positively. I began to Breathe again. While I was living my life and enjoying the fruits of my labor, GOD restored my marriage.

My Family was whole again. Life was sweet again. We must remember to be steadfast and keep the Faith.

Remember to keep your eyes on GOD, and He will Always see you through!

Michelynn Moss

But the fruit of the Spirit is love, joy, peace, forbearance, kindness, goodness, and self-control. Against such things there is no law. - Galatians 5:22-23

I've had dark and sad moments in my life, but when I looked to the sky from where my help comes, I just asked and the Lord put a pep in my step, peace in my heart, and some Joy in my Soul. What love we have! In it, we can find strength in joy, even in times of trials and tribulations. We've all had moments of sadness, hurt, pain and insecurities, but "The joy of the Lord is our strength."

Joy is a powerful force that can sustain us during troubled times, a loss of a loved one, a failed relationship or a loss of a job or of trauma. Instead, it's actually a spiritual state that we can choose to embrace. Even in the most difficult moments, we can find joy in God.

Though the sorrow may come during the night, Joy comes in the morning." Believers can experience joy because they are sons and daughters of heaven. I love the kind of joy that runs through one's soul and gives them peace. It's a divine gift and it's yours if you want it. We were made in love, and for love, by our beautiful God. I thank Him every day and I know He didn't bring me this far to leave me! So, rise up, walk in dignity, peace, and love but most of All Joy!

"There's joy in the house of the Lord... And we won't be quiet, we shout out your praise."

"God wants to make everything beautiful in His time"

Dr. Barbara Neely

Finding Joy in tough times can be a challenge, but if we keep out minds stayed on Christ, He will give peace and joy where there seems to be none. I have had so many challenges the last couple years and had to adapt and adjust to many new changes.

There were days if it had not been for God the joy would be overshadowed with grief and sadness. The Joy of the world does not measure to the joy that only God gives. Joy is a gift and should always cultivate a life of joy and contentment in all circumstances of life. We can rejoice in knowing that the joy that God in us will give us the courage to face tough times.

Evelyn Nelson

Yes, yes, yes, sing it again, "It is joy unspeakable and full of glory, and the half has never yet been told." What half has never yet been told, the half where death is staring us in the face? Or maybe it is the half of eternity awaiting us since we're eternal beings?

Romans 8:18-20

18 I consider that our present sufferings are not comparable to the glory that will be revealed in us. 19 The creation waits in eager expectation for the revelation of the sons of God. 20 For the creation was subjected to futility, not by its own will, but because of the One who subjected it, in hope...

Could it be that creation is eagerly waiting with expectation and hope of the day when the children of God will be revealed so that creation doesn't have to suffer anymore. Yes, creation was subject to futility, not of its own will as stated in the Bible, but God allowed it so. When we look at creation all around us, it speaks to us and so does God, personally! So that unexplainable joy, yes that unfailing joy, oh that effervescent joy can be and is ours to claim. No matter the weather of life, we must face it. No matter the storms in our lives or the unexpected mishaps in our lives, we can have that "joy full of glory, on earth until we get to Glory - Heaven." So let us with hope and expectation allow that glory God has given us 'on earth as it is in heaven,' share it for others to experience it too!

Shari Nichelle

"You will keep him in perfect peace, whose mind stays on You, because he trusts in You." Isaiah

At amusement parks, adventurous roller coaster riders can often be seen with their hands in the air as they faithfully navigate the twists and turns, dips and drops on the ride.

Those riders somehow muster up enough trust in the seats, seatbelts, the track, and the operator to get them through this exhilarating activity in one piece! Some of them get right back in line when it's over to do it again!

What peace they must have and what joy must follow! The concept of surrendering our will to God's way requires us to let go, much like the roller coaster rider, as we relinquish complete control of our lives to God. One of the best ways we can surrender is to acknowledge that God's ways are higher than our ways. Next, we can invite Him into our lives to use us in His will to carry out His divine design for our purpose.

No matter what you may be going through in this moment, there is perfect peace and joy everlasting to be found in surrendering all to God.

Dear Lord,

As I raise my hands in humble worship of who You are, I let go. My life, my health, my family, my finances, my soul are Yours. Thank You now for restoring my joy. Take me and use me for the edification of Your kingdom, in Jesus' name. Amen.

Dr. Thomasina D. Nicholas

Bless the Lord, O my soul, and forget none of His benefits, 3) Who pardons all your iniquities; Who heals all your diseases; 4) Who redeems your life from the pit. (NAS) **Psalm 103:2- 3**

As we wake up this morning to a new day, see the beautiful drawing of the handiwork of God. Inhale the fresh air before the smog comes, is it not clear? Listen! The birds sing ever so sweetly a song that you cannot pay for with all its notes crisp and clear. Embrace, the breeze that you feel coming from the north, south, east, and west; it is the fluttering of angel's wings. Oh, yes, they are letting us know that praise to God is essential and an important part of how He operates, decently and in order. Yes, He is our Lord and King. He did not pardon us because we are worthy,; He pardoned us because we are **NOT** worthy. Inequities in life are not based upon what is seen on the outside. When God sees us what He sees lies within our heart. Doctors can prescribe medication to begin therapy to heal us, but God specializes in redeeming all of what ails us. Jesus comes in as an attorney and God is our judge, a physician who heals all our diseases. As a timekeeper He gives back the time that palmerworm and the cankerworm have stolen from us regardless of where we have been. He crowns us, by restoring us with His loving kindness, and compassion. God restores our life despite what is known about us. Today, take a moment to breathe, sing and enjoy the sun or the rain. Praise God for your benefits and think on the positive things being done. For He has redeemed your time. Selah.

Tasha Nicole

Where challenges may cast shadows, let the radiant light of joy find its dwelling. As an unwavering Aquarius and a mother with a spirit so strong, you possess the inner resilience to overcome. In the tapestry of life, joy is a thread woven intricately, connecting moments of laughter, love, and perseverance. There are seasons when joy seems elusive, when the weight of responsibilities and the ebb of life's tides threaten to dim its brilliance. Yet, in these very moments, dear Tasha, embrace the power within you. For you are not just a go-getter; you are a beacon of strength and a custodian of joy.

In the vast expanse of your life, seek joy not as an ephemeral emotion, but as a timeless essence that flows through the core of your being. Let the laughter of your children be the melody that restores joy to your soul. As you navigate the challenges that life presents, remember that joy is not lost; it may only be momentarily misplaced.

Pause, breathe, and reconnect with the simple pleasures that make your heart dance. In the stillness, find gratitude for the love that surrounds you. Allow the strength that defines you to be the catalyst for joy's restoration. Like a phoenix rising from the ashes, let joy emerge, vibrant and resilient. As the Aquarian waters of your spirit flow, let them cleanse away any sorrow, leaving only the pure waters of joy. Embrace each day as an opportunity for joy's renewal, a canvas upon which the colors of happiness and contentment can be painted.

May your journey be adorned with moments that reignite the flame of joy within you. In the tapestry of your life, may joy be the golden thread, weaving through every experience and creating a masterpiece of love, strength, and enduring joy.

Shywanna Nock

The promise of restoration, "I will restore you to health and heal your wounds, declares the Lord (Jeremiah 30:17 NIV).

My personal journey with cancer in 2011 changed my life drastically. I went in for surgery to remove a mass and was told that I had cancer. I was diagnosed with Non-Hodgkins Lymphoma and was told that I needed chemotherapy right away. I was a young mother of three at that time and my focus was on my kids and my health.

Chemotherapy can take a toll on the body. The medicine can cause good cells to act up when it's supposed to be killing the bad cells. I can remember taking the treatment and my appearance changed after the second round of chemo. I lost all the hair on my head, eyebrows, eyelashes, and body. My appearance was different, and I wore a wig when I was out in public because this was different to me. I had to put aside what I looked like and focus on God to heal me. I started looking at healing scriptures and began speaking them over my life faithfully. My favorite one was, "But he was wounded for our transgressions, he was bruised for our iniquities: the chastisement of our peace was upon him; and with his stripes we are healed Isaiah 53:5 KJV. I also praised God with a dance during it all until he healed me.

I can honestly say that I am blessed because I have a testimony. God restored my health, and He healed me. I am a 12-year cancer survivor, and all glory belongs to Him. I am an example of: I don't look like what I've been through.

Cinderella Ochu

***Be still and know that I am God: I will be exalted among the heathen, I will be exalted in the earth.* Psalm 46:10 KJV**

You walk into a coffee shop and place your order, while you wait at your seat; your time is running out, and the attendant is taking too long. You call out to the manager or to whomever you can reach and make a complaint. One of the most difficult things to do in life is to wait.

While you wait passively at the coffee shop to be served, in the spiritual, you wait actively. What you do while waiting is as important as the wait itself. You must engage with His word and remain calm. To wait is to hope, anticipate and trust. Do not wait in doubt, fear, or anxiety, *Isaiah 41:10, Philippians 6:7, Psalm 37:7.* You wait in faith because He is more than able, *Ephesians 3:20-21.*

As a believer, waiting simply means that you surrender all to Him. You are acknowledging God's supreme authority over all things. *1 Peter, 5: 7, 1 Chronicles 29: 11.*

It can be difficult to wait, therefore, you pray for perseverance, *Isaiah 40:31*, for when it is time, He will make all things happen, *Isaiah 60:22.* Your thoughts are not His thoughts, neither are your ways His ways, *Isaiah 55:8.*

It truly pays to wait upon God. He will surely show up, and in a very big way! *Psalm 126:1*

Study also: *Psalm 125: 1, Proverbs 3:5-6, Hebrews 11:1-3, Psalm 121:1, Hebrews 13:5, 1 Peter 5:7.* Thank You Jesus for giving us strength through Your word. Amen.

Candace Okin

The most significant gift you've ever received outside the love of God, is your why. When you were born, it was with you, nestled deeply, safely within the depths of your heart. As much a part of you as your ten tiny fingers and ten toes, was your why. It was with you then, and it is with you now.

Ready for you. Waiting for you.

Filling you with purpose and potential.

You know what it is. It is the gift that is yours that you willingly and joyfully give away. It is a gift that you can never run out of. It is what makes you the Master Creator's greatest creation. You see, many may have the color of your eyes. They may share your hobbies, even some of your talents and interests, but NO ONE ELSE has your why. Not like you do. It is immense in its power, and with your activation, is limitless in its impact.

Yet in all its magnificence, it must be handled with intentionality and care, because this life constantly influences you to do otherwise. It influences you to neglect it, to misrepresent it. At times, you may even abandon it. But I'm here to encourage you to remember.

Remember your why.

Your why is your mission? It is your reason for being. It is your calling. It is an extension of God's unfailing and infinite love; it is a reminder of His unbreakable promises. It is the light of the world; the city on the hill that cannot be hidden.

You don't have to look hard to find it, because it is within you. It IS you. Sit in silence and remember. Let it awaken and ignite your spirit. Then go forward, and never forget.

Adeola Oladele

Isaiah 43:2; When you pass through the waters, I will be with you; and when you pass through the rivers, they will not sweep over you. When you walk through the fire, you will not be burned; the flames will not set you ablaze.

For the last two years, I have been praying to God to show me His love, show me He is always on my side and always with me especially on those days when it feels lonely even in a crowd. And I always hear Him say, I am always with you. Whether you see it or not; but as a human I wanted proof.

At the same time, it just constantly felt like everything I asked God for, He wasn't doing it, so I stopped asking and went along with the attitude of whatever you want to do just do it.

Around that same time, a friend would call me randomly and tell me, "Adeola, you know that you are very loved right" and I'd just smile because deep down I wasn't believing what she would say to me. And then, someone else would send me a text telling me how much God loves me, and how much God is doing for me. I looked at them with so much doubt.

Towards the end of last year, another of my friends would call me and say, "I miss your smile. Stop feeling like you are alone because you are not. God loves you."

This year, I have accepted that God is always with me, and He loves me. So even though you might not see immediately, never doubt that God is ALWAYS with you no matter what the situation is. He will never leave you. God loves you!

Issata Oluwadare

I've been thinking lately — how peaceful children can only come from a peaceful home. Happy children can only come from a happy home. I've been thinking how much of who I am, and how I move through the world impacts the moods, attitudes, and behaviors of my own children.

More specifically, I watch as my infant take his cues from me. He scans my facial expressions each morning to see what type of day it's going to be. That is a lot of responsibility. While scary, it's caused me to become more thoughtful and intentional about what I allow in my heart, who I allow in my space, how I behave and what I'll tolerate.

I would never want to feed my child poisonous thoughts, behaviors, or ways of being. And so, I must choose joy. I must find my happiness. Finding my happiness looks like taking girl trips, date night with my husband, staycations, and finding quiet' moments to be alone with God. It means meditating on the promises of His word, even when they are delayed. It is choosing people who love me to my fullest while encouraging me to become a brighter, more vibrant me. Joy means acknowledging your pain, your circumstances, and still deciding to thank God for another day. Choose joy, today. Your children and those who love you the most deserve a healthy and whole you.

Arletha Orr

A lot of times when things happen in our life, we think it is the end. We think our life has ended. It seems as if every time we advance in life and begin to have the freedom to live, something comes and snatches it away. Another bill is due. Someone gets sick. We must fix something on our vehicle. They're giving us a hard time on the job. Or the children won't obey. This list can be limitless.

The amazing part about life is when it knocks you down, you can bounce back and put the pieces where they go.

In 2016, I thought my world was over. I lost my only husband and only two children in a train accident. Truly, I didn't see that coming. I thought my life was over. I thought God had forsaken me. I felt isolated and betrayed. Although I thought it was the end, it was just the beginning.

After the accident, God gave me a word that changed my life forever…LIVE! Just as He gave me hope to make it through, you too can make it through.

I don't care what it looks like or how hard it may get, know that God has you covered and has your best interest at heart. It may seem like your world is crashing, but it's all part of the process. Trust the journey. Trust the process…and watch God work in your life.

Sharone Pack

"No discipline seems pleasant at the time, but painful. Later, however it produces a harvest of righteousness and peace for those who have been trained by it." **Hebrews 12:11**

I know discipline is not one of your favorite words nor is it mine. However, when I need some personal encouragement to never give up, this is the scripture that I lean on. When I feel like I want to quit because something isn't as easy as I thought it would be, I remind myself to keep going because of what will be produced in the end. Discipline is necessary in all areas of our lives. Wouldn't it be nice to get in shape without ever having to exercise? Of course, it would! However, that's not the case, for most of us anyway. Discipline helps you build muscle. It strengthens your mental muscles allowing your mind to think positively. It strengthens your spiritual muscles when we're in constant fellowship with our Creator, our financial muscles when we are disciplined in our spending, and our emotional muscles when we are in touch with ourselves. Being disciplined doesn't happen overnight. It takes time, preparation, sacrifice, and courage. Self-discipline is a form of loving yourself. Loving yourself enough to prioritize your life. Loving yourself enough to be brave and have faith that your dreams are going to come to fruition. We may have to say no to certain people, places and/or things to stay focused on a goal of yours. And guess what? That's okay. I had to learn this more and more myself. And I still haven't arrived, but I am making progress. So, let us not view discipline as a bad word, but as a guiding light towards a harvest of righteousness, peace, and the realization of our full potential.

Jeremy O. Peagler

Bless the Lord, O my soul, and forget not his benefits.
Psalm 103:2 (KJV)

My wife and I were driving recently and at some point, during our trip, we began to discuss how good God has been to us. We told each other story after story, each one building momentum on the heels of the one that came before. Just by talking, our faith was stirred! I remember at some point during the conversation, we both fell silent, and just rested in the moment. Not out of sadness or disappointment, but rather, in awe of God's goodness. We could see the hand of God woven throughout the fabric of our lives. In every moment, in every breath, He is there.

One of the most powerful gifts we possess is the ability to recall. Something beautiful and sacred happens within when we intentionally remember God. I don't know about you, but I get encouraged when I think about who God is and what He's done in my life. How He chose me, how He transformed me, how He forgives me, how He walks with me, how He speaks to me, how He chooses to use me for His glory, and how He has intricately planned every moment of my life. Every time you recall something God has done for you, you "forget not." I encourage you today to "forget not." Remind yourself often of who God has been in your life and how His promises never fail. My Friend, forget not!

Tikita Peagler

But the hair of his head began to grow again...
Judges 16:22 ESV

One of my favorite stories in the Bible is that of Samson. Samson was uniquely strong and given the gift of physical strength from God. Before he was born, God told his parents that Samson was special and that his life purpose was to save Israel from the Philistines; therefore, he must abstain from alcohol and never cut his hair because his strength was contingent on it. Well, life happened, Samson made bad decisions, his hair was cut, and consequently, he lost his dignity, strength, and joy. I recall the time in my life, after suffering many miscarriages, we received news that we were pregnant with twins. We were overwhelmed with joy and believed God had given us double for our trouble. Unfortunately, I miscarried after three months. I was broken and silently questioned God's faithfulness. My joy and faith were at an all-time low. I resolved that I no longer wanted children and proceeded with life quietly broken. Surprisingly, and seemingly supernaturally, my faith and joy were restored without any effort on my part. As a faithful Father, God gently healed my heart. When Samson disobeyed God, he found himself bald, bound, and without strength. Yet, God hadn't forgotten about Samson, and without personal effort, his hair began to grow back. With the growth, his strength returned, and he was able to break free and defeat the Philistines as destined. After my joy and faith were restored, I later found out we were pregnant with a son. Following his birth, I became pregnant again and delivered a second son that same year! God didn't forget about Samson, nor me, and He hasn't forgotten about you either. Hold on, your joy is coming!

Monique Pearson

Song of Solomon 4:7: You are altogether beautiful, my darling, there is no flaw in you."

Sometimes you may feel like an old penny; worthless, dirty, and of little value. That is what the enemy will have you to believe. I come to share with you that you are worth more than gold, you are renewed and clean as pure white snow. The price tag on your life says priceless.

You are more than what you have been through. You are not a victim, you are thriving. From broken to brilliance you have taken the shards of your life and the splinters and turned them into a Van Gough. Your standing strength turns your pain into your power which makes you an everyday hero. You're a living witness that joy does come in the morning, and that pain does not last always. You are walking in the greatest season of your life because you did not let the lowest season take you out. Many see the penny as low value but continue to show them how one penny can lead to riches beyond their imagination.

T.K. Peoples

Romans 12:19 Do not take revenge, my dear friends, but leave room for God's wrath, for it is written: It is mine to avenge; I will repay,"
says the lord.

Today, reflect on Romans 12:19. Let the words resonate deeply within your heart and soul. It is tough to resist the urge to make someone pay for what they have done to you. But remember, "Do not take revenge, my dear friends, but leave room for God's wrath, for it is written: 'It is mine to avenge; I will repay,' says the Lord." We live in a world where people will deliberately harm others simply out of spite, jealousy, and internal anger in which they suffer. However, we must consciously decide to release all feelings and actions of vengeance. Instead, we must trust in the higher power; we must trust in God.

In moments of personal offense or injustice, it is natural to seek retaliation, to right the wrongs with our own hands. However, God reminds us in this verse to choose a different path of surrender and faith. This verse pleads with us to release our grievances into the hands of God, acknowledging His power over the affairs of humanity. I have struggled with forgiveness but learned that forgiveness is for my benefit. Holding on to anger will only destroy us from the inside out. Release that burden unto God. Invite a spirit of compassion, be able to extend mercy to even the most undeserving, and trust that God's justice will rise above and surpass any retribution we could envision. Today, choose to heed the wisdom of Romans 12:19 and allow God to be your avenger. Strive to leave room for God's divine justice in your heart and actions and walk the path of forgiveness and grace.

Jada Perteet

      In the pursuit of joy, mindfulness stands as a guiding light, revealing the beauty of the present moment. Psalm 118:24 reminds us, "This is the day that the Lord has made; let us rejoice and be glad in it." For single moms like me, mindfulness isn't merely a practice; it's a lifeline, a gentle pull from life's whirlwind. Engaging in mindful activities—be it meditation, deep breathing, or a serene walk—helps heighten our awareness of the present. Philippians 4:6-7 urges, "Do not be anxious about anything, but in everything by prayer and supplication with thanksgiving let your requests be made known to God. And the peace of God, which surpasses all understanding, will guard your hearts and your minds in Christ Jesus." Mindfulness is a master at decluttering the mind. It carves space for joy by erasing regrets and uncertainties, much like Isaiah 26:3 reassures, "You keep him in perfect peace whose mind stays on you because he trusts in you." For us, mindfulness is a reminder that joy isn't reserved for some distant future; it's woven into our everyday moments. Amidst the challenges, it serves as a beacon of hope. James 1:2-4 encourages, "Count it all joy, my brothers, when you meet trials of various kinds, for you know that the testing of your faith produces steadfastness. And let steadfastness have its full effect, that you may be perfect and complete, lacking in nothing." So, to all the single moms out there, mindfulness isn't just a buzzword; it's our sanctuary, our way to navigate life's complexities. It reminds us that despite the struggles, joy is within reach, nestled in the folds of the present moment where God's grace abounds.

The Israelites had come out of Egypt and were on their way to the Promised Land. Moses sent twelve men ahead of them to spy out the land.

One leader was chosen from each of the twelve tribes to go ahead into the land. They spent forty days walking through the land and then they came back with their report. The report they brought back is given to us in Numbers 13:26-28: "And they [the twelve spies] went and came to Moses and said 'We came unto the land whither thou sent us, and surely it floweth with milk and honey; and this is the fruit of it. Nevertheless, the people are strong that dwell in the land, and the cities are walled, and very great: and moreover, we saw the children of Anak [the giants] there.'"

Two of the spies, however, Caleb and Joshua, refused to go along with this negative attitude. In Numbers 13:30-31, we read this: "And Caleb stilled the people before Moses, and said, 'Let us go up at once, and possess it; for we are well able to overcome it.'"

The impact of the negative report of ten of the twelve spies had a disastrous result. Because of their fears the entire nation of Israel refused to go into the land, thereby forfeiting God's promises to them!

The only two people out of that entire generation who saw the Promised Land were the two men who gave a positive report, Joshua, and Caleb.

No matter what sort of "giants" we are confronted with in life we must move forward by our faith not our fears.

Pastor Sharita Phillip

"My brethren, count it all joy when you fall into various trials"
James 1:2

Yes, you can count on all Joy! Often, when we are faced with tough times in our life, it's hard to imagine being joyful, let alone seeing how the Joy of the Lord can be our strength when all we feel is sadness or defeat. However, what if I told you that there is an inner Joy that you can possess that doesn't matter what is going on around you, whether good or bad? I am reminded of Paul when he shared that, yes, he is perplexed and crushed on every side with trouble, but we are not lost or abandoned by God. Three significant people in my life have passed: my younger sister, my mother, who was also my Pastor, and my dad. Their deaths brought normal grief, but the timing of these events was also profound. October is my eldest daughter's birthday. All three deaths occurred on and around her birthday. My family and I had started dreading the month of October. Although it is the month we should have joy as we prepare to celebrate the birth of my daughter, it has become a month of sadness, a month that crushed our spirits. The reality is that we could have chosen to accept the sadness, but instead, as we prepare to welcome the month of October each year, we have chosen to lean closer to God by praying and fasting. We decided to celebrate my daughter's birthday and reflect and celebrate each birthday that her aunt, grandmother, and grandfather were allowed to celebrate with her. We decided to count it all joy each year. Let's face it, we all have experienced trials and tribulations, but it's your decision how you go through the experience, Choose to Count it all, Joy!

Constance Phillips

During times of despair is when God is working his hardest. He knows our minds and our hearts. With His hands on our lives, we can only fall as low as He allows. There are times on this journey where you will fall into a rut. The rut could be a multitude of things such as divorce, death, or mental illness. With determination and prayer, you will slowly but surely come out of the sunken place.

Psalms 121; I will lift my eyes unto the hills, From whence cometh my help. Psalms 91:2 I will say of the Lord, He is my refuge and my fortress: My God; in him will I trust. The scriptures let me know that God will never leave or forsake me even in my toughest hour. He is my advocate. Psalms 91:7 Though a thousand fall at your side, though ten thousand are dying around you, these evils will not touch you.

SheAir Phillips

"Weeping may endure in the night but Joy cometh in the morning."
Psalms 30:5 NIV.

The Brokenness started to feel normal until the morning came and it didn't. I remember one day standing in the exact spot where I broke down just months before. I felt relief and contentment.

Bare feet in the grass, connecting with the earth and God in the most natural way.

Twenty-twenty was the year everyone was excited for. There was a saying "2020 Clear Vision." People were ready to execute plans, but little did the world know there were many lessons that truly needed to be learned. I called that year my Self-love tour. The blindness of having a baby and becoming a wife was lifted from my eyes and I realized I did not know how to separate myself from those roles and I felt lost in who I was as an individual. Maturity and Faith were key to my healing. I was grieving the life I thought I was supposed to live but God has destined a life for me that I am unaware of and although time may feel unbearable, impossible, long lasting, it's not always.

All the "Help me God" moments, summarized to that very moment standing after the brokenness. I could now say, thank you Lord for helping me through the pain, anger, fear, sadness, and hurt. Although, I am not 100%, Every day, I thank God for blessing me through each obstacle that felt like it would have taken me out. I knew I had to seek God as my source and provider.

Julia Pierre

Psalm 16:11 KJV
Thou wilt shew me the path of life: In thy presence is fulness of joy; At
thy right hand there are pleasures for evermore.

Permission to shine is the journey to divine purpose. We are up for the task of being the reflection of our illuminating self. God will keep moving in love, wisdom, and authority for those that have allowed themselves to experience the fullness of God's joy. Joyful is a laugh in a unique universal world that is united in Christ and on one accord. Bring the life applicable Word of God knowing that nothing is impossible for those that trust in the Lord. We have permission to shine in our authentic core living the purpose.

God has blessed us with joy. We are trained and processed to full throttle into the work and assignments of our life's purpose. We are locked and loaded for the World shift, sharing in a Kingdom mindset ready for fellowship to increase in our hearts, mind, and valued efforts. We are encouraging our inner wisdom, passion, and drive for living, loving, and learning. We are seeking and living a Kingdom lifestyle, sharing and caring with intentionally applied Kingdom principles in our lives through faith, grace, and vision. We are focused on a journey to divine purpose and a spirit filled connection that resonates with the truth of the Good News that takes the masses in a manifested life vision to be a wealth of holistic wellness.

Davonte Pinkney

In times of uncertainty and when the burdens of life seem heavy, it's easy to lose sight of the joy that resides within us. Yet I want to remind you that joy can be restored even during your job search. The journey to finding employment can be challenging, but it is also an opportunity to deepen your faith and trust in the divine plan for your life.

Remember that joy is not dependent on external circumstances. It is a gift from God waiting to be uncovered within your heart. In the book of Psalms, we are reminded, Weeping may endure for a night, but Joy comes in the morning. Psalm 30:5 Your current situation is but a season, and with faith, perseverance, and trust, your morning of Joy will arrive. When the weight of uncertainty presses upon you, turn to meditation. Seek solace in the assurance that a greater plan is unfolding, one that holds a fulfilling job for you. In those quiet moments find joy in the uncertainty that your needs will be met, as it is written in Philippians 4:19, And my God will meet all your needs according to the riches of his Glory in Christ Jesus."

Additionally use this time to cultivate your skills, expand your network and remain open to opportunities. Sometimes blessings come in unexpected forms and your diligence and perseverance will be rewarded.

May this period of your Job search become a season of spiritual growth and an opportunity for your faith to flourish. Trust in the restoration of your Joy and know that the Almighty is guiding your path. In this process remember that joy is not a destination but a journey and may you find it anew as you seek a fulfilling job and career.

Bernadette Plummer

As an avid person who works in community service, I have a restored vision of humanity. People amaze me as they come out and selfishly give themselves, so others may have a small glimmer of hope in their lives.

A small act of community service is valuable. A person may not know what impact that might have on several generations to come. When people give genuinely from their heart to others who are less fortunate, I believe that there is not a vessel that can hold what you get in return.

People who come just to be able to help another person cannot sometime understand the magnitude of that generosity. We teach children how to garden, plant trees, shrubs, and vegetables, to bring food from the farm to the table in their household within a Food desert. With this small act, we teach a child how to feed his family and the generations to come. We are instilling in the future generations to grow produce in order to sustain their lives without having to go to the supermarket.

The small act of just spending time to teach someone a new skill is immeasurable.

Felicia Pouncil

In the quiet moments of reflection, I find myself marveling at how caregiving for my parents for a decade transformed me. It was a journey of love, sacrifice, and discovery—a journey that has taught me profound lessons about life's blessings.

As I cared for my mother and father, I learned that life is a tapestry of moments, each woven with threads of joy, pain, and resilience. During the challenges, I discovered an inner strength I never knew existed. The sleepless nights and the overwhelming responsibilities pushed me to my limits, but they also unveiled a wellspring of patience and compassion within me.

Through my journey of caregiving, I've come to appreciate the simplest of pleasures—the warmth of a gentle smile, the comfort of a shared laugh, or the beauty of a quiet sunrise. Life's true treasures aren't found in material possessions, but in the relationships we nurture and the moments we cherish. Caregiving showed me the power of gratitude. Each day, I'm reminded to be thankful for the gift of life, for the ability to make a difference in someone's world, and for the love that binds us all together. During my trials, I found a deep sense of purpose and fulfillment.

To those who are on a similar journey, I offer you these words of encouragement. Embrace the challenges, for they are opportunities for growth and self-discovery. Lean on your support network, for you are not alone in this journey. And remember, the act of caregiving, though demanding, is a noble and loving endeavor. May you uncover the hidden blessings that lie within the journey, and may you be reminded of the profound love that connects us all.

Kaidynce Pugh

Psalm 31:24 - Be of good courage, and he shall strengthen your heart, all ye that hope in the Lord.

In a world where challenges often test our resolve, I stand as a beacon of inspiration. I am Miss Kaidynce, a young soul who defies the odds and soars beyond the confines of my life's struggles.

Born prematurely at just 28 weeks, I faced a turbulent start to life, battling both physical and psychological obstacles. Yet, with unwavering determination, I emerged as a true warrior, equipped with a determined spirit.

Now, on the cusp of high school, I embody the essence of a consummate student-athlete. Excelling both academically and athletically, I strike the perfect balance between commitment and passion. However, beneath my achievements, a hidden struggle persists—the challenge of confidence. From education to social settings and communication, I struggle with self-doubt. Despite my lack of confidence, I refuse to let it define me. I recognize that confidence is a skill that can be developed and nurtured over time. With each setback, I view it as an opportunity for growth and learning, refusing to be held back by my doubts.

Having witnessed the power of God's intervention in my life during moments of uncertainty and weakness, I draw my strength from a deep-rooted faith. My belief that God will provide everything I need to conquer any obstacle sets me on a path of courage and hope. Let my story serve as a reminder that no matter the challenges we face, we have the strength within us to rise above adversity and find empowerment and joy in every single day.

Patrick Purcell

Have you ever heard the saying, "I think I can?" Well, even if we all can't remember the cartoon character that made these words legendary, the irony in this is that thinking, in reality, isn't actually doing. As a man thinks in his heart so he is, but how do we extract what's in the heart and put it into motion with our life and faith?

There is one character in the Bible who, if we would take a closer look at her life experience, we would discover that what's in the heart needs confirmation by active faith. God said, "Let us make man in our image and likeness." His thinking required motion and touch!

Luke's gospel gives an account of a woman with the issue of blood who thought within herself she could be healed if what she determined in her heart would become active in motion. She understood, according to the customs of the land, that if she was recognized she would have to offer an apology and maybe even suffer grave consequences.

However, there are times you seek that must become unapologetic. When she touched Jesus, He said, "Who touched me?" Why? Because virtue left His body, but offense never entered His heart.

I can imagine Jesus' thinking, "Finally someone has extracted from me that they could receive by faith without having to be instructed!" Jesus says to the woman, "Go! Thou faith has made thee whole!"

No apology needed! Your search is complete!

Tiffany Quinn

Life is full of challenges and hardships, but amidst the struggles, there are also moments of joy, delight, contentment, jubilation, and love that can bring a smile to our faces and fill our hearts with happiness. When we focus on these moments, we can find the strength and resilience to face whatever difficulties come our way.

As we go about our daily lives, let us not forget to appreciate the good things that come our way. The warmth of the sun on our skin, the sound of birds singing in the trees, the taste of our favorite food, the feeling of a hug from a loved one - these are all moments that can fill us with delight and contentment. It's important to remember that it's not just the big moments that matter, but also the small, everyday things that make life worth living. A smile from a stranger, a kind word from a neighbor, a moment of quiet reflection - these are all moments that can bring us closer to a sense of jubilation and love.

One motivational scripture that can help us appreciate life's blessings is found in the book of Psalms. In Psalm 118:24, it says, "This is the day that the Lord has made; let us rejoice and be glad in it." This verse reminds us that each day is a gift from God and that we should find joy in it. Let's take a moment today to appreciate the smiles in our lives - both the ones we give and the ones we receive. Let's look for the moments of enjoyment, delight, contentment, jubilation, and love that are all around us, and let them fill ourselves with gratitude and joy. May we find the strength and resilience to face life's challenges with a smile, and may we always remember to appreciate the beauty and goodness that surrounds us.

Demowah Quoiyan

1 Samuel 15:22 – Samuel said, "Hath the Lord as great delight in burnt offerings and sacrifices as in obeying the voice of the Lord? Behold, to follow is better than sacrifice and to hearken than the fat of rams.

The Lord is pleased when we obey Him. It pleases Him when we listen to His commandments and instructions. Obedience is an act of worship, and God rewards obedient people. Stepping outside the will of God can create unnecessary stress and hardship in our lives. When we walk in disobedience, we disrespect God's word, which is sinful. Exodus 19:5 say, now if you obey me fully and keep my covenant, then out of all nations you will be my treasured possession. However, the whole earth is mine. As God's treasured possession, there is a covenant established with Him. He specifically chose you for a purpose. Often, we wonder why things are not working the way they should. We wonder, hopelessly searching for an answer or solution. We fail to realize that when we obey God, He gives us the answer and clarity we seek. We find peace, fulfillment and experience the joy of the Lord. Stop trying to make things work on your own. Seek the Lord and His guidance. He will direct your path and order your steps in His word. He is an all-knowing God and wants the best for us. Guess what? There is still good news for you. It is not too late to walk in obedience to God's word. There is still time to turn your life around. Your adherence to God will make you prosperous. He will bless you and your children, and everything you touch will prosper. Your way will be bright and clear. There will be no lack in your home or family. -Amen

Dr. Latasha Ramsey-Cyprian

"For we walk by faith, not by sight." 2 Corinthians 5:7

We serve an amazing God. A God that loves us despite our shortcomings. A God that is always there and will guide us through any storms we go through in our lives. It can be hard to maintain our faith during challenging times. It can be tough to trust in the good when everything in your life seems to be going bad. However, the tough times are when our faith is most important. Our faith can always be restored if we are willing to seek it out. Even though we don't see God working, we have to trust and believe that He's preparing us for a blessing from what we are experiencing.

Faith is about trusting God so deeply that it affects the way you live. Walking by faith is not the same as walking without planning. Walking by faith means you are walking with Jesus and living today according to God's promises. There will be times when you will feel alone and misunderstood. It will require strength, courage, and it's a journey that is exciting and life changing. The journey will allow you to witness and experience God.

Dear Father,

Give me the strength to navigate in the world solely on trusting in you and on your belief of the unknown and unseen. Even though I might not be able to see where I'm going, I will keep moving and l will look to you as my guide. I will listen to your voice and heed your direction for my good and your glory. I will speak boldly and confidently as if any situation I face has already been resolved in a positive way. I will rejoice and praise you through the hard times because I know that you are in control. Amen.

Dr. Catovia Rayner

2 Timothy 1:7 KJV: For God hath not given us the spirit of fear; but of power, and of love, and of a sound mind.

Give me a moment of your time. Today I give you permission to do something wonderful and amazing for yourself. Take a deep breath and think about what you need to do to restore your mental and physical health. Make the appointment, clear your day, ask for family support, and spend a day treating yourself to rest, joy, and happiness.

Have you ever noticed how you feel when you do something for yourself, like buying a new outfit, a nice piece of jewelry, or getting a newer car? Then you take a moment and look around, expecting loved ones and friends to support your decision. Instead, you feel the total guilt for taking care of yourself.

Often, we spend too much time taking care of everyone else but ourselves. At times, we avoid that ache or pain until the point of emergency. Then, you realize that you deserve to treat yourself.

Well, starting today I give you permission to ignite the spark within yourselves that is full of Self Care and Love. There is absolutely no reason why we can't celebrate self-worth and value. Now is the time to live in the moment, free from fear and regret. Being able to show yourself love and worth is most important in these ever-changing times.

Coach Raynor

Mighty God of the universe, blazing the trail for sinful humanity, as I come in your presence have mercy on me. Jesus, thank you for becoming the lifeline for drowning sinners, even though millions have not realized; you are the best thing that could ever happen to us. God in your mercy, spare me I pray, for you know how wretched and blind I once was and did not recognize it. Father, please look down upon our rebellious nations who spitefully hate you and have mercy. There! without beholding the crimson red blood dripping from Christ hands, amid the unbearable pain still He did it for you and me. Seeing His nail-pierced feet ripped beneath a naked tattered stained bloody garment, with his coiling, body stretching to the ground. Friends, this picture serves as a reminder from here to eternity of God's unfailing love. Seeing His blood forming a fountain at the people's feet depicts his compassion through His amazing grace. Such redeeming transaction supersedes the cost of the world's merchandise in goods, giving us as children heavenly liberty in heaven and on earth. Lord, thank you for the exchange, in such relationship for knowing Christ. It is not about religion but a relationship. This freedom from sin activates our God given abilities with expectation to step into our abundance in Christ to populate heaven and earth for God's glory. Christ freed me from sin and He can do the same for you. Repentance is asking God's forgiveness of sins, inviting Christ into your sinful heart, trusting the word, knowing sinners cannot enter the Pearly Gate. Christ told us, to love the Lord your God with all your heart, body, soul, and mind and our neighbor as ourselves. People these two commands can transform our lives in abundance, building relationship on earth with God for eternity.

Pastor Beverly J. Renford

Mark and I were both born on a Monday in August of 1958; he was in New York and I in Michigan. We met at church in the early 'eighties, married, and began "This Our Life, Our Beginning." General Motors hired him in August. At twenty-nine, with five jobs between us, we purchased our home and began replenishing the earth. Years later, our fourth daughter was born in August. Cognizant of these facts, we realized that August, which means "consecrated" or "venerable" was significant to our family. In addition, "respected" and "impressive" represent our birth month; it is the eighth month of the year, and we are the blessed parents of eight adults.

In 2008, President George W. Bush approved a bailout, loaning billions of dollars to GM and Chrysler to avoid an auto industry collapse, but many of us GM hourly workers did not fare as well. We were served foreclosure papers, and the children were forbidden to attend their private schools. Feeling desperately helpless, we sought a feasible means for ten people to survive; therefore, we decided to fight for what we had.

We chose Chapter 7, as it allowed for restructuring and full repayment. We were in a bind, and our children were watching our every move. Using the principles of faith, tithing, and arduous work, our prayer life went into overdrive. We quoted scriptures telling of God's promises and sure blessings and spoke positivity although overwhelming negativity was our reality.

Days turned into nights, and weeks into months. Joyfully, it has been more than eight years since making the final mortgage payment, and one of our daughters receiving a full-ride scholarship.

Alicia Rengel

In the realm of Christian faith, the concept of "the Joy of the Lord" is a powerful and transformative idea. It goes beyond mere happiness; it is a deep, abiding sense of joy that comes from knowing and serving God. This joy is not dependent on external circumstances but is rooted in our relationship with the Almighty. One day in Bible class, I shared a simple message on a kitchen towel that read, "Grow where you are planted." Little did I know that this message would become a profound reminder of God's intention for our lives.

The Bible provides us with numerous verses that illustrate the essence of finding joy in the Lord and growing where we are planted. In Philippians 4:4, the apostle Paul encourages believers, saying, "Rejoice in the Lord always; again, I will say, rejoice."

The act of giving away the kitchen towels with the message "Grow where you are planted" to my sisters in Christ was a simple gesture, but it carried a profound truth. We are called to find joy in our current circumstances and to trust that God has placed us where we are for a purpose. Romans 8:28 reminds us of this, saying, "And we know that in all things God works for the good of those who love him, who have been called according to his purpose." In conclusion, the Joy of the Lord is a treasure that surpasses all understanding, and it is found by embracing the concept of growing where you are planted. As we anchor our joy in our relationship with God and trust in His divine plan, we can find contentment and purpose in every season of life. So, let us continue to share this message of joy and encouragement with others, and inspire one another to cultivate a deep and abiding joy in the Lord.

Charlissa Rice

What does living free consist of? Freedom of your thoughts, feelings, emotions? Freedom to be whatever and whoever you want to be? To me… living free is the power to live your life by your rules.

You have the freedom to control your destiny. This mindset didn't come into my life while I was younger. I grew up being a "people pleaser," however, as I got older and became wiser, living free is consistent in my life. I decided that I will not let society clip my "freedom wings' and that I will fly amongst the sky of opportunities. I want you to love, I want you to grow, I want you to be the best version of yourself possible. I want you to live, I want you to live FREELY. Not every day will be a good day, however, living free depends upon us. How will you choose to live freely?

Harriet Rice

My JOY is spread over my family and friends, also the people I interact with daily. Seeing a young child dancing and laughing gives me JOY. A beautiful sunrise or sunset gives me immense JOY, not to mention the birds chirping in the morning. When we become sick, we should not dwell on being sick, but think positively about getting well. A joyful and energetic person usually sends out positive vibrations, and they in return usually have that experience of JOY reflecting on them. A good movie, having conversations with my nephew, his wife and his children who are 4 years and 71/2 years give me so much JOY. Reading an interesting book gives me JOY. When my beloved husband (A Blessed memory), and I used to walk in the park, we held hands, we rode our bikes, sometimes we just sat in the park reading books to each other. I would listen to his lovely voice while he sang to me. Doing that brought me great JOY. After my husband died, my JOY depleted. I grieved for a long time. It would hurt my heart seeing couples holding hands on a Saturday or Sunday evening when I was out shopping. I stopped going out on the weekends for a while, especially on Sundays. I felt so alone. One day an idea came to me. I decided to do some volunteer work as a Psychiatric Social Worker on the Chemotherapy floor of a New York Hospital. I started to play the piano again and the sound of the music restored my JOY. I used to play the piano at home.

1. Mozart Piano concerto in 'D' minor No. 20

2. Beethoven Piano concerto in 'G' minor No. 4, and

3. Schuman Symphony for 4 hands

I am sending JOY to everyone reading my page.

Barry Stephens Ricoma

Late one night while staring at my reflection... I asked. ME: Mirror, why do you show me my unfulfilled hopes and dreams? Do you enjoy seeing the pain I suffer after a fall? You like to count my scars from the day's crawl. You enjoy seeing my weary face suffering through the long night. knowing the next day is going to be a longer fight!

MIRROR: NO friend!!...I am showing you what could be... a better place. LOVE, HAPPINESS & ABUNDANCE awaits you if you keep your faith and embrace GOD'S grace.

ME: Mirror, mirror on the wall I am unsure I can answer this call.

MIRROR: Fear not, for you have the strength to continue to STAND tall. No matter what the new dawn brings, I will be here reminding you to fight for your dreams! You just must take the first step on this path. The request I ask of you is small but know this…

GOD WILL NOT LET YOU FALL!

According to 1 Corinthians 13:12

For now we see only a reflection as in a mirror; then we shall see face to face. Now I know in part; then I shall know fully, even as I am fully known. And 2 Corinthians 3:18 (ESV)

And we all, with unveiled faces, beholding the glory of the Lord, are being transformed into the same image from one degree of glory to another. For this comes from the Lord who is the Spirit.

Evg. Dr. Debra Riddlespriger

The enemy comes to kill, steal, and destroy, but I come that you may have life and that more abundantly. John 10:10b

Spirit, mind, and body, we are created by God to do good. Ephesians 2:10.

We are not created to be or have anything less than what God created us to be or have. Period! Phil. 1:6

Through Christ, we have access to all that's needed to complete our purpose. It doesn't matter how challenging it may be, He is our help. Isaiah 50:7

Our Heavenly Father provided the blueprint for all who love Him and are called to do His works. Romans 8:28 Therefore, every situation we endure will end perfectly well, because God is always at work on our behalf. Psalms 138:8.

What does this have to do with having joy? Everything! We have joy and hope in God's Word and trust in His Promises. This gives us the privilege and opportunity to choose God's way when faced with afflictions. Ponder, Pray & Pencil it:

1) What has GOD BROUGHT you THROUGH?

2) In your current situation(s) and God's ability to handle it. WHAT DO YOU BELIEVE? 3) In your current situation(s): WHAT Will YOU CHOOSE?

IT'S YOUR CHOICE. Will you enjoy it, or struggle with it? When trusting God, there are no gray areas. We either give Him all or carry the burden ourselves. Matthew 11:28-30

I encourage you to CHOOSE JOY because in it, you will find strength to walk victoriously in your God-given purpose!

Dr. Sophronia Winn Riley

Taste and see that the Lord is good; Psalm 34:8

I remember reading this passage as a child, "Taste and see that the Lord is good." The first thing I thought was, how can a person taste the Lord? It was not until my sophomore year of college that the passage became real. It meant "experience" the Lord and see that the Lord is good. I had to experience Jesus Christ for myself when times were becoming difficult as a young adult. I explain it this way: If I had a handful of grapes, and I could illustrate the sweetness of those grapes with the most eloquent of words, which would make you long for the pleasure of tasting the sweetness of those grapes. You can see the beauty of that cluster of grapes and that they are a luscious portrait of the most pristine grapes you have ever seen. In your mind, you have conjured up a sweetness you have never experienced before; you were listening to words that made you want to eat just one of those grapes. The grapes filled your nostrils with a sweet, sweet aroma you will never forget. However, to know the authentic, delectable sweetness of that grape, you must taste it or, better yet experience the deliciousness of it.

Then someone freely gave you a grape, and you took a slow, loving bite of it and wanted more of that sweet nectar that filled your heart and mind with sheer pleasure—same thing with God. My grandmother taught me about God and His Son Jesus, who so freely gave His life for me. It did not make sense to me until I had the pleasure of experiencing God's grace and mercy for myself, and then I knew that my God is good. I can see his goodness daily in me and in my family's lives. I want everyone to experience the love of God for themselves and know He is good.

Dr. Tina Riley

"If you abide in My word, you are My disciples indeed. And you shall know the truth and the truth will make you free." (John 8:31-32 NKJ)

To activate God's promises…my words and my actions must agree with His word. I realized God's truth after having been in a health storm; diagnosed with diabetes. My thoughts were, I have Jesus in my life, faith of a mustard seed, and walking the narrow path, and it could be worse.

A month earlier, I had been to Hawaii with my love, yet I was fatigued and had blurred vision. However, a week prior to vacation, I shared in family Bible study to remember to praise God and thank God… not only when things are great but during adversity, during trials, and the storms. Still, God is faithful to see us…through, over, under, and around our problems; we must trust and believe Him. As I trusted and believed God through diabetes, He revealed He was there. God revealed the Truth and freed me from not knowing. The first was when my doctor touched my arm and in a quiet voice said to me "this is important. Go to the emergency room, and I love you." Secondly, God revealed Truth in the emergency room when the nurse said, "Oh Honey, God wanted you to be here." Lastly, the Truth of the Matter was God revealed that I abided in His Word, and I am His, therefore, this disease is a testimony. In three months, my numbers were back to normal.

God gets all the glory, honor, and praise. He never left me, and He kept me. The Truth of the Matter is…God is real and my Light in the Darkness makes me free indeed!

Michele Roach

I can recall when testimonies were shared freely during church service. They were testimonies that touched lives, and uplifted those who needed to know that they were not alone in their battle. Throughout every storm, trust in God. Stand on His promises.

From living in my car, experiencing electric shock, memory loss, therapy, seclusion, stuttering, excuse after excuse, distractions, procrastination, God finally sat me down. He provided everything that was needed to restore my faith. His Word, answered prayers, provided peace in His word, my family, finances, and my voice.

Through it all, I've come to realize that God sitting me down was the perfect timing for me to listen, pray, and rebuild my faith. I found peace in knowing that it is not over when I think it is over. Joy is knowing when others walk away, God is with you and me.

Own your voice! Your testimony deserves to be heard. Your walk with God is at the heart of your testimony, the tears that God wiped from your face, and the peace you found in His word. Someone needs to hear your testimony. Your walk with God. Encourage all to own their voice and share their testimony. Testimonies change lives.

"Give praise to the Lord, proclaim his name; make known among the nations what he has done."

"Consider it pure joy, my brothers and sisters, whenever you face trials of many kinds," - James☐

Dr. Darcele Marie Cole-Robinson

Have you defined what failure means? Do you let failure define you? Have you shifted your perspective? Will you have to accept failure for what it is? Do you know that you are not alone? Are you willingly able to try to forgive yourself? I am sure you will need to let out all your frustration. Always understand that great ideas take time and patience. You must lose your fear of failure. Failure is a part of the process. People who never fail, never try.

You need to get it wrong, before you can get it right. You learn nothing from winning; you only learn from your failures. Don't give up! Keep on trying to work harder. Failure makes us stronger because it often continues to make us strive to achieve our goals with greater determination than ever before. Sometimes, failure prompts us to shut down. I believe it's a good thing; because it gives us time to process our pain that has been created. God wants us to keep on striving, keep on trying, and to keep trying to reach our goals. Never give up.

We must stay focused, and secondly, we must press on. Be encouraged, forget the past, and advance forward. It is part of God's perfect plan. God makes no mistakes. He knows the beginning and the ending of our destiny. God silently plans for us in love, plans allowing for our failures. He knows that we are going to fail. Failure causes many to lose that gleam in their eyes, to give up on their dreams and drop their hands in the middle of the fight. Confront the spirit of failure and allow God to show you that the VICTORY is yet attainable.

Jaden Robinson

Look on the bright side. That's what people say when something goes wrong, when you want to give up, when nothing seems to be working. Look on the bright side. Or look at the joy. Look at the good that is to come and not the darkness of today. When we think of joy, we think of rainbows, and smiley faces. But that isn't all that joy is. Joy is dancing in the rain because life has felt like a huge drought.

Joy is telling a stranger 'Good morning' because you woke up that day.

Joy is spreading love, and peace, and kindness to those who seem like they just need a little extra sunshine in their life, even when you need some yourself. To be joyous, or full of joy, does not always look like being happy, or even feeling it.

Joy can frown, joy can cry, joy can have its good days and its bad. What makes joy who it is, is its ability to uplift others even when it's down. So, look on the bright side. Look at those around you and be their joy.

Be their bright side and be yours too.

Dea. Kenneth Eric Robinson Sr.

What would you ask for if you knew God would give you anything you wanted? Would you request money, a long life, or some kind of prominent position? When God appeared to Solomon and allowed him to ask for whatever he wanted, Solomon asked for wisdom. God was so pleased with his request that He not only made him the wisest person who ever lived apart from Jesus, He also made him the richest person. This set-in motion a principle that we need to be aware of in dealing with our finances: Wisdom always precedes wealth. There are over 200 verses in the book of Proverbs that deal with money, and each of them falls into one of seven categories. Proverbs 9:1 says, "Wisdom has built her house she has hewn out her seven pillars." *1 Timothy 6:10 says, for the love of money is the root of all evil. This is one of the verses about wealth that is often misquoted.*

The answer to this is when we allow it to become an idol in our lives. The most prosperous people are those who get wealth and keep it. They are teachable concerning financial matters. Some people will not accept advice because they think they know it all or because they are afraid of looking foolish. They go broke then get help. It is much better to seek counsel from a financially successful person than it is to keep reproducing costly mistakes. Be financially faithful and avoid get-rich-quick schemes. Closing the Wealth Gap, Income Gap and EMPOWERING individuals and families to create a financial legacy is a noble cause we will continue to achieve. Now is your time to step out on faith and do it for you and your family. Let me know when you are READY.

Coach Vuyanzi Rodman

Joy can be a tricky thing.

We find joy in what we do, who we love, and sometimes what we possess, but what happens when those things elude us?

Our joy is lost.

If we hold on to the outside world to give us joy, we become a roller coaster of feelings and emotions. Today, I encourage you to restore the joy that already is inside of you,

no matter how much you have felt its absence. Your joy has always been there.

Your joy, that feeling of great pleasure and happiness, is deep within you, in a state or dormancy as it waits for you to experience it through your own exhibit of interpretation of the God that lives inside of you.

Thus, it is time for you to restore your joy, the joy you never lost…

Restore joy in what you do because it is the outward expression of who you are…

Restore joy in who you love because it is the divine expression of your love within

Restore joy in what you possess because it is the material expression of what you possess spiritually….

Let your joy be a well-spring of the divine happiness you were meant to have.

Latrice D. Rogers

Have you ever been told, "Don't cry," or "Stop crying?" If you have, these commands may have been well-intenended (to make you feel better) or deliberate (to silence you). In either case, crying is a response to some emotion—sadness, anger, frustration, excitement, joy—and is meant to be experienced. Regardless of the emotion triggering the tears, tears are necessary. Tears are a form of release.

Tears are meant to water your spirit. Water is my nature element. It cleanses, takes shape and shapes. It's gentle and powerful, from quiet ripples to roaring waves. It's both calming and challenging, from sounds of a babbling brook to a surging storm. Water is transformative. Whenever emotions cause us to cry, we should experience those tears knowing that our spirit is being watered. When we are watered, we change, we grow. Take tears as an opportunity to reflect and think about life lessons. What are tears revealing for you? If tears are in response to a negative emotion, we should see them to release, cleanse, renew. If tears are in response to a positive emotion, we should see them to celebrate and express gratitude. In the journey to be the best version of myself each day, I'm evolving. I have emotions that make me cry. I realize it's okay to sit with those emotions and not turn them off. I'm learning to let my tears transform me and propel me to move through life with a clearer path to walk in my purpose.

So, emote—don't stop crying, changing, growing. Think about the promises of God. Your purpose is planted in you. Water your spirit and embrace the *"weeping [that] may endure for a night, but [the] JOY [that] cometh in the morning." Psalm 30: 5*

Dr. Patricia Rogers

You might ask, how does "visibility" bring you joy? To be visible as an entrepreneur, you must attract as much attention from as many people as possible.

I worked twenty-nine years in the corporate arena, and my skills and determination to excel in my career kept me in the limelight. People will try to stop you from achieving your goals, but with a determination to succeed, you will win. I was passed over three separate times in my career for a promotion. I persevered through each challenge and received the promotions I deserved. After retiring, I invested in coaches who could show me how to discover my gifts and talents so that I could live my life on my terms. I desired to be a public speaker and provide a platform for other entrepreneurs to be seen and heard while promoting their products and services. I started in my backyard, and I was doing it for free. Having a coach taught me how to monetize my gift of bringing people together. I started hosting annual in-person conferences in hotels in 2014, providing a platform for entrepreneurs to speak and promote products and services and connect with other inspiring entrepreneurs so that they could gain more clients.

Using my social media skills and promoting the events across social media platforms gave me global exposure. Entrepreneurs flew from around the world to speak at the conferences. The pandemic allowed me to pivot on a dime to virtual events. Unity In Service, Inc., hosts quarterly *virtual* events. My zone of genius is setting up speaking platforms and showing entrepreneurs how to show up professionally, build relationships on social platforms, and increase their bottom line by being more visible on social media.

Nataylia Roni

God's Creation is:

I wake up early in the morning to see the SUN and it knows I see it come
out in all its splendor and glows. Showing itself, to those who blow kisses in
mid-air Taking photos, click, and then share.
Bright red iridescent colors, took over the sky Blaring Blazing Blissfully for a
moment ...then sigh. Ahhhhhhh
Gasps for breath fill the atmosphere. Then in a moment the sun retreats.
Rotating to a distant beat. Leaving behind feelings of what was
Shadows Shape shades float from above. Whispered echoes from those in love.

I wake up early in the morning to see the SUN and it knows I see it come out in
all its splendor and glows Showing itself, to those who blow kisses in mid-air.
Taking photos, click, and then share. Bright red iridescent colors,
take over the sky.
Blaring Blazing Blissfully for a moment ... then sigh. Ahhhhhhh

God's creation God wants you to shine.
God wants you to rise. Once we step into our throne, the sky is just on the cusp
of what he desires for you. Holding onto that grateful spirit. Knowing in all things. JOY
comes in the morning.

To enable every seed that is planted in you to grow and take root. This requires
us to look into the mirror and see God's promises for tomorrow. Holding onto and giving
birth to greatness.
Enabling us to be at peace with who we are ordained to be.
Enjoying the moment and living truthfully.

The best you can do is be. Then every day is a WIN-WIN situation. For God will
shine his light on you and through you. You are Loved. You are enough.
You are God's Creation..

Dr. Radiance Rose

1 Corinthians 15:10 (KJV) - But by the grace of God I am what I am: and his grace which was bestowed upon me was not in vain; but I labored more abundantly than they all: yet not I, but the grace of God which was with me.

Gratitude and grace are two of the most powerful forces in the universe. Gratitude is giving thanks for all the good things in our lives. It is a recognition that everything we have is a gift and that we are blessed beyond measure. When we're grateful, we focus on what we have rather than our lack. This shift in perspective changes our attitude and behavior. Instead of feeling anxious, depressed, or stressed about our circumstances, we feel content, hopeful, and at peace. We recognize that we have everything we need to live a prosperous life. Grace is the unmerited favor of God. It is a gift that we receive because He loves us. We are a perfect, hand-crafted blend of body and spirit, having an imperfect human experience. When we operate in God's grace, the spiritual bridges of reconciliation, justification, and sanctification are established.

In conclusion, gratitude and grace are a gateway to greater heights in our lives. Gratitude attracts divine blessings. When we embrace that we're right where we should be, we let go of the need to be in control, and we trust that everything will work out for our highest good. God's grace is mighty and sufficient. It's time to let go of our fears and allow God to guide and guard our lives, enabling us to receive abundant joy 365 days a year. Today, be the face of gratitude and grace.

Follow Me
Instagram:@therealcoachrai
Website: vivicole.com
Email: rr@vivicole.com

Dr. Felicia Russell

The weight of the world is on their shoulders, and it tends to be too much, and there is fear they are about to fall on their faces. We prayed and the wait for the trusting prayers are delayed, but we know they are not denied. They gossip about you and lie to you, and you doubted your worth. The hurt and the unjust pain is unbearable. Your ears have heard enough of the opinions. The doors that were knocked on didn't open. The next level is unfamiliar and seems uncertain. You've been judged and misunderstood. You gave access to people that didn't deserve it. Your feet are tired from going in the wrong direction. But God!

It is in this hour to trust God; He is shifting the atmosphere. God will open doors that you didn't even knock on. The God that we serve is not an ordinary God. The truth is in God and His word which will not come back void. If we continue to lean on God's word and fight the good fight of faith, we will understand that we were chosen on purpose with a purpose. We cannot become a better version of her or him without God. We are chosen to break generational curses. We are chosen to be a better woman/man than we were yesterday. We were chosen to go through those trials and tribulations so that the world can see the works of God can be manifested through you. I am here to remind you of something today: while becoming her, I realized I am God's chosen one. As Pastor Suprenna Ward said, "we belong to God not people." We are no surprise to God. Becoming Her, The Chosen One.

Dr. Alvina Ryan

Ebullient is the word that comes to mind when I think of joy. In fact, ebullient means exceedingly joyful. This year let us pledge to embark on 365 days of ebullience. May we radiate positivity, cultivate gratitude, and spread kindness wherever we go. Together let us create a symphony of joy that resonates not only within us, but also in the hearts of those we touch.

As we journey through the coming months, let love be our guiding force. What type of love? Love for ourselves, for those around us, and for the world we inhabit. Acts of kindness, both big and small, have the power to create a tapestry of interconnected joy, weaving a fabric of compassion that combines us together. Let us recognize the power of a smile. A heartfelt smile can transform not only our own outlook but also creates a ripple effect of positivity that touches everyone we encounter. Every day offers a fresh start and a chance to embrace new beginnings. Choose to find joy in the little things. Laughter, the universal language of joy, shall be our constant companion. Let us commit to embracing life's treasures daily and show our appreciation by journaling end-of-day messages of heartfelt gratitude.

I decree and declare that your year will be filled with exuberance and zest for life. You will live a life that will inspire and uplift everyone you meet. You will embrace the positive energy that surrounds you. Cheers to finding new ways daily to celebrate and spread positivity to everyone. As you cultivate a spirit of ebullience, make each moment count. Here's to a year of ebullience, a year of boundless joy and endless possibilities. Cheers to embracing life with open arms and hearts.

Brenda Sawyer

This joy that I have, the world didn't give it and the world can't take it away. (John 14:27) I am so glad this joy I have is not predicated on material things of the world, but on the joy that only God can give me. Having this joy is where my true strength lies, because I can do all things through Christ who daily strengthens me.

When God allows me the privilege of seeing a brand-new day, I rejoice, and I become glad in it. I never want to take my waking up for granted, because it's another day I didn't have to wake up to see. I like to think of it as being my lifeline to unspeakable joy. All I must do is think about how many did not get a chance to wake up to see a new day. This thought makes me feel more joyful and thankful that God allowed me this blessing.

In today's world full of chaos and confusion, who couldn't use a little more joy? I know I can. With this joy, I will be more intentional to infectiously share and spread it to others, so I can be the change that I want to see in the world today.

The Scripture I want to leave with yu is, Nehemiah 8:10 (KJV)

"Then he said unto them, go your way, eat the fat, and drink the sweet, and send portions unto them for whom nothing is prepared: for this day is holy unto our LORD: neither be ye sorry; for the joy of the LORD is your strength."

Amenna Scott

This is the day my brother/cousin died; his birthday is June 12th and mine is March 12th. On the day he passed away, I was in denial and in belief, I didn't have anybody to protect me. Our big brother took it badly as well because our cousin passed away in his arms. I went to college for business and had to write this paper called "The Meaning of Life," but I didn't write it. When I spoke it everybody in the classroom was crying. People wanted to hug me, but I wasn't receiving them. My classmate and I went to Chill's and that was the day I was going to take my life. Soaked in depression, I missed four or five days of dialysis. My heart felt like a heavy brick and I can actually visualize my heart in my hand beating and saying help me, but I allowed my depression/pain to ignore all the warning signs, but God didn't give up on me.

Jesus sent my aunt and my cousin to come to the house and I knew it was God that sent them. They gave us a ride to Georgetown Hospital and by the time I got there I could not walk. I went into cardiac arrest and I died. I saw my mommy holding my hand calling me MeMe and I had to go back in my body because Jesus was not ready for me, and I am not going to lie, I was mad at God for putting me back into that body. One day my big sister asks me to go to Church with her and finally I said yes, and my other big sister grabbed my hand and ran me up to the prayer line. When my Pastor prayed for me it changed me. I felt something so pure, and loving come through my body. I never looked back again, and I gave my whole life to Jesus. I love Him so much and that was the day Jesus saved me…

Dotty Scott

In the intricate dance of life, amidst the symphony of our triumphs and trials, there exists a profound truth, often veiled by the complexities of our experiences - joy is a choice. It is not a passive reaction to the favorable winds of fortune, nor do the stormy seas of adversity extinguish it. In its purest form, joy is an intentional decision to embrace the light, even when darkness seeks to prevail.

Every soul, in its journey through the temporal landscape of life, encounters moments of exaltation and depths of despair. These oscillating experiences, though diverse, offer us a singular, transformative opportunity - the choice of joy.

The scriptures impart a pearl of profound wisdom, *"Consider it pure joy, my brothers and sisters, whenever you face trials of many kinds"* (James 1:2). This divine counsel beckons us to elevate our perspective, to view our tribulations not as insurmountable obstacles, but as gateways to a deeper, more profound experience of joy. It is a joy that is not contingent upon the external but is rooted in the eternal, an unyielding fortress that stands resolute amidst the changing tides of time.

As we navigate the multifaceted journey of life, may we remember that joy is not merely a spontaneous emotion but a deliberate choice. It is a sacred commitment to seek the light, to embrace hope, and to dance to the eternal melody of divine love, even when the echoes of despair seek to drown it out. In every moment, with every breath, we are endowed with the empowering choice to live in joy.

Do you choose Joy?

Shari Sears

"So, encourage each other and build each other up,
just as you are already doing."

1 Thessalonians 5:11 (NLT) We sometimes think that doing charitable deeds are seasonal; we were taught to be especially nice during the holidays. Thanksgiving and Christmas are times when we tend to show more kindness; we are more grateful, we are more thankful, and we are more compassionate because of the holiday season.

Why are these acts so important during the holiday season? These acts of being kind, grateful, thankful, and compassionate should not be seasonal. Could you imagine us serving a seasonal God or if God treated us like we treat others? That would be interesting to say the least. It is funny when you think about it because we want to hear from God immediately; we do not want to wait.

Practice, being kind, grateful, thankful, and compassionate, not just at certain times or a certain occasion of the year. We need these things all year round so why make others wait? Give them what they need right now. To put forth an effort is free, and it does not require a lot of time either. Remember, it is nice to be nice because you never know when it may be your turn. So, I challenge you to be kind, to be grateful, to be thankful and to encourage others every day, not just because it is a special day but because it is a new day.

Dr. Angela Seay

Splendor and majesty are before him, strength and joy are in his place.
(1 Chronicles 16:27 NIV)

Joy is a powerful source of energy. Joy is gladness not based on circumstances. God is joy. We are created by joy and sustained by joy. Joy is a birthright from God; therefore, joy is within. It is a part of the body structure. Identify and embrace it! Claim it! Own it! Once you acknowledge and embrace your power of joy, share it! The more joy you have, the more you will give. The more you give, the more you will help others find joy because joy is meant to be shared to uplift others.

The powerful source of joy is radiant; it glows, it illuminates love and happiness. I own my power of joy. If by chance yours is not radiating, I share my energy with you as a spark to your spirit. I challenge you to be intentional to spread joy, share love with a focus on making the world a better place. Never underestimate the power of joy. When joy is a way of life, love is a reflex.

Remember, keep smiling for it is one of your greatest assets. Make it a grand day on purpose. You have the power to do so!

Dr. Erica Sheffield

In despair, I emerged as a survivor, my life burdened by emotional bondage, suicidal attempts, the pain of an abortion, the fracture of divorce, the suffocating grip of depression, the endless maze of self-doubt, and the heart-wrenching loss of a 7-week-old daughter. My story is not one of tragedy but of transformation and triumph, a testament to the power of faith and resilience. Amidst my struggles, I discovered one profound verse that illuminated my path. The verse, Romans 8:28, proclaimed, "And we know that in all things God works for the good of those who love him, who have been called according to his purpose." Through my journey, I learned that life's challenges were not endpoints but steppingstones, each one leading me closer to my true purpose.

My tribulations, once seen as insurmountable obstacles, became the very building blocks of my transformation. In my darkest moments, when I stood at the precipice of despair, I found solace in the unwavering presence of God. This gave me hope! Today, I stand as a mentor, guiding others through their own trials. I inspire them to shed their masks of pain and insecurity, reminding them that God's strength is made perfect in weakness. My life bears witness to the truth that challenges are not meant to break us but to mold us into vessels of strength and compassion. As you reflect on my story, consider your own challenges. Are they roadblocks or steppingstones? Can you, like me, find solace in the verses that sustained me? Let my journey challenge you to embrace your own destiny, knowing that God's presence and purpose are ever-present, even in the face of life's greatest trials.

Choyce Simmons

Within the intricate fabrics of life, we often embark on a profound odyssey, a journey that takes us from the depths of pain to the pinnacle of wholeness—an existence filled with completeness and purpose. Along this winding path, we encounter loss, pain, setbacks, and moments that make us question our worthiness. It's amidst the fragments of our past, the scars we carry, and the test of trials that we may, at times, feel as though we are nothing more than shattered pieces of a once-cherished mosaic. But let me tell you this: Your worthiness isn't determined by the cracks in your armor or past mistakes.

Your worthiness runs deeper; it's a precious gift woven into your very being by a Creator who crafts masterpieces with love and intention. You are a masterpiece carefully sculpted with purpose and plan. Just as a skilled artist lovingly crafts a work of art, so, too, have you been crafted by the hands of a loving Creator. In moments of turmoil, when your heart is heavy with hurt and doubts loom large, it's all too easy to lose sight of your worthiness, to question your very essence. Yet, even in these moments of shadow, I implore you to remember this: You are deserving of love, joy, and healing. Beloved, the Creator sees your worthiness, even when you fail to recognize it within yourself. Today, declare with resounding clarity: You are enough, just as you are, with all your imperfections and scars. You are a work of art, wonderfully made. Each new day offers an opportunity to embrace yourself, to grant grace upon yourself, and to revel in the fullness of God's boundless love. Stand tall, for you are a living testament to resilience, destined for the brilliance of wholeness once more.

Kim Simmon

The Checks Are in the Mail.

Philippians 4:19 KJV

God will supply all my needs according to his riches in glory this…. Scripture is a pivotal part of my daily existence it Resonates in my heart and soul. God has and continuously. Supplies the needs of my family, my finances, and in my personal life.

In my early thirties, I became a parent for the first and final time. Parentage is one of the most rewarding. Life-changing, at the time challenging experiences One could face children are typically brought.

Into the world with two parents, and the hope is Both will be supportive and work as a cohesive unit In the upbringing of their child… unfortunately this Was not my fate! I was a single parent. God knows what we need before we do, I have a Plethora of testimonies of financial blessings God Has granted me the role of a single parent. I've received it. Unexpected, found money, on occasions and God gave me financial favor through people. Acts 10:28 34-35 KJV God is not a respecter of persons. He will provide every person with the opportunity to receive blessings.

One morning I petitioned God for $60 my prayer, was answered the next day! Wait on God he Will meet your needs, I'm a living witness, He loves us all the same! My child is now twenty-something. A college graduate and working in a thriving career. Trust God He will never fail! He loves and is concerned about you.

Paulette Simmons

Living a life of transparency requires a commitment to ethical behavior and a willingness to be accountable for your actions. It means being willing to admit your mistakes, take responsibility, and face the consequences. In the same vein requiring the same from others. It's being real with yourself when you're not "okay" with situations or circumstances. To live a life of transparency, it is important to cultivate self-awareness and honesty with oneself so that you can be honest and open with others. Living a transparent life can be challenging, as it requires vulnerability and a willingness to be judged by others at times. However, it can also be incredibly rewarding, as it can lead to greater trust and stronger relationships. It can also help you to make better decisions, build boundaries, restore trust in others, and cause you to pay attention to how others respond or handle you.

Living a life of transparency involves clarity in your goals, values, beliefs, and communicating openly with others when appropriate. It is living a life with no guilt, shame, or regrets. It is living a life with a sense of freedom in integrity and people are drawn to authenticity. When others feel that you are honest and genuine, they begin to build trust, and this can lead to deeper connections that can be life changing.

As you see, living a life of transparency can be beneficial in many ways, including being truthful and upfront about who you are and what you stand for. Overall, living a life of transparency involves being true to yourself so that you can live your life out loud and freely without barriers, hidden agendas, while striving to act with integrity and honesty in all aspects of your life. You are worth it!

Amber Sims

"To appoint unto them that mourn in Zion, to give unto them beauty for ashes, the oil of joy for mourning, the garment of praise for the spirit of heaviness; that they might be called trees of righteousness, the planting of the LORD, that he might be glorified." Isaiah 61:3 KJV

NJ born, living in KS, I wasn't ready to be a single mom to two kids with no support, so I decided to go the adoption route. As the days grew closer, I just couldn't go through with it. I went into preterm labor, and not even a month later he passed away due to complications. I was numb for months, forgetting that I had a daughter living; I wanted to give up on everything. Fast forward to 2017- my daughter, then 5 years old, went into cardiac arrest and was put into an induced coma for 3 months. During these few months, life just stood still. I kept pinching myself to wake up from this nightmare I was living. I couldn't help but think about the tragic death of my son, and just prayed that I wouldn't have to bury another child. I had no one to comfort me in those last hours, but my daughter was surrounded by love every day. Days, weeks, and months went by. The doctors woke her up and we began the healing and recovery process. It was a long, hard road; she had to relearn everything, but she also taught me so much. Even now she continues to help me see God's amazing Grace. My son may have only been on this earth for 25 days, but I made sure he was loved, and his purpose was fulfilled. We may not know the plans that God has for our lives but there is always a reason for everything. I may not have my baby boy here with me anymore, but God has blessed me with another beautiful baby girl, that has healed my heart and allowed me to love again.

Coach Teon Singletary

Have you ever asked God for something, and when He presented you with the opportunity, you had second thoughts? That's not you. However, this was the story for one. During one of their prayer times, this individual asked God to help them with empathy and to make better choices in life. They wanted to add more value to others. Now, why did they ask for that? God made sure this prayer was answered. Their mother had to go into surgery during New Year's Day. For this to happen, she had to come in a day prior for preparation. Yes, on New Year's Eve. The father wasn't available during that time due to work. The brother and sister were either out of town or had work-related issues. Now, this individual, on the other hand, was given three choices. Attend the scheduled business event, attend the New Year's Eve party they were invited to, or spend the night at the hospital with the mother.

Being reminded of the prayer submitted to God, they became aware of what must be done. The choice was made to serve the mother when she needed it the most. Guess what? That individual was me. And the peace I had after making that choice was overwhelming and changed my life forever. Five years ago, I would not have made that choice. Because of the change that was working within me, I made the right choice this time around. Reflection: We all have the power of choice. Depending on how we exercise that power will determine the outcome of our future. Live today to grow yourself and make better choices. It doesn't matter how big or small; each one counts. First, list the things you will choose to do differently. Next, all you must do now is execute those choices. If it's hard for you to take action, pray and meditate on them daily. You have the power of choice. So, choose for today.

Demaryl Roberts-Singleton

Being kind and generous is my forte'; it's the essence of true beauty and a reflection of our Creator. Beauty is cultivated in our hearts and often overflows with generosity and kindness. Generosity and kindness have made a humongous difference in my life. Generosity and kindness are beautiful because they show how God has loved and blessed me despite my challenges. I have been through the rain and storm, and God helped me weather the storms. I have had many challenges, but I take comfort in knowing that God continues to give me the love, willpower, and strength to help the less fortunate. In the late 80s, in Colorado Springs, CO, I had a friend who traveled from California with five kids, including an infant. This individual fell on tough times and was on his way to the Midwest to get help from his mom.

Although I struggled as a single parent during that time, I opened my home to that individual and the children. I provided them with food and shelter after they drove approximately 1,300 miles. To this day, that individual has done very well in life and has been blessed with intelligent adult children. God has been generous to me with his resources; despite my life challenges and difficulties, God has taught me never to give up on people in need. Those who continue to be generous, and kind will be enriched. Generosity and kindness have improved my spiritual, physical, and mental well-being. Being kind and generous over the years has improved my self-confidence, self-awareness, self-esteem, and self-love. Generosity and kindness have made me feel part of something greater than myself.

Dr. Angela Sinkfield-Gray

After this I beheld, and, Lo, a great multitude which no man could number of all nations and kindreds, and people, and tongues, stood before the throne, and before the Lam, clothed with white robes, and palms in their hands. -Revelation 7:9 KJV

John saw a great multitude, a number that no man could number around the throne. I believe he saw me; I believe he saw you also.

Many times, on our daily journey the situations, circumstances, trials, and tribulations of our daily walk can become heavy and hard to bear. The velocity of them seems to come so swift that they knock the very breath of life out of us, and many times the lie that the enemy tells is that these things will never change, that everything will stay the same. But that is so far from the truth.

Everything on earth is temporal, everything shall pass away, even the trials and tribulations. Every believer has a promise that we will overcome this world because Jesus Christ overcame and then He gave us His victory.

We have promise of eternal victory. The fire of the trials you are feeling are real, but so is the glory that you are producing in the earth realm; therefore, set your eyes toward heaven. One day Jesus will wipe every tear away. When it's all over, we are going to have a time when we get around the throne of God; we are going to have a time.

Zariya Skai

Sometimes we have bad days, and sometimes we have okay days. But we should all be kind on all the days.

I remember my school had kindness week, and we sang a song. I like music because I love helping people.

"Kindness, Kindness, oh, whenever you try this, you will find the world a better place."

I learned that we do not know what type of day someone has, and just a little bit of kindness can help their day a lot.

I think of things that add a little joy to my life so I can continue to be kind to others. I think of things like eating my favorite fruit, playing, watching a fun movie, and snuggling with someone I love or my pets. Sometimes, I look to the skies and pray or ask for a hug. It's okay for you to do the same. And if you can't do those things, talk to your angels; they are with you every day.

I promise! Be kind; it will add a little joy to your cloudy day and someone else's day too.

Darlene Smith

In our journey through life, we often encounter moments of darkness and despair. These trials can steal our joy, leaving us feeling lost and disconnected from the happiness we once knew. However, just as the sun rises after the darkest night, joy can be restored even in the most challenging circumstances.

The Bible teaches us about the concept of joy restoration. Psalm 30:5 says, "Weeping may endure for a night, but joy comes in the morning." This verse reminds us that even in our most trying times, joy is not lost forever. It may be hidden momentarily, but it can be found again.

Restoring joy begins with a shift in perspective. Instead of focusing solely on our troubles, we must turn our gaze toward God's promises. Philippians 4:4 encourages us to "Rejoice in the Lord always." Our joy is not dependent on our circumstances but on our relationship with God. When we choose to rejoice in Him, even during trials, we open the door to joy restoration.

Additionally, joy is often renewed through gratitude. When we take time to count our blessings, we discover that there is still much to be thankful for. Gratitude has the power to turn our hearts away from despair and towards joy.

Joy restoration often involves community. Sharing our burdens with others and finding support in our faith community can provide the encouragement and love needed to mend our broken spirits.

In conclusion, joy restoration is not a one-time event but a journey. It requires a shift in perspective, an attitude of gratitude, and the support of a loving community.

Nakiea Smith

When God said, I knew you before I formed you in your mother's womb and I can count every strand of hair on your head; this was God's way of letting us know that He is a God of details and that He sees things from a macro level. We only see things from a micro level because we are operating from our human desires. God is operating from heavenly ways. Our own expectations of how we think life should go can sometimes interfere with God's plan. We must let go of what we deem as just good enough, and accept what God is doing in our lives. He has given everyone God-given gifts and talents. However, it is our responsibility to cultivate those gifts and talents. Once they are cultivated, then we can present them to the world to contribute and make a positive impact.

The fruit of the Spirit lives within all of us. You must be honest with yourself in every way. Forgive yourself and others. Love yourself and others unconditionally. You must understand that everyone has a path and journey, including you. God has given you the tools and resources to become your authentic self. You do this through Love. God is Love. You must let go and let God. Once you love yourself everything you need will be supplied to you.

Prayer Jehovah,

I am coming to you asking that you continue to guide me in the right direction, even if it does not make sense to others. I am learning that the opinions of others do not determine anything. I have faith that all things are working towards my greatest good, no matter the circumstances. I understand that in this season, God will continue to show up for me when others cannot. I am grateful for the support system. God I am thankful that You continue to show up for me. Thank You for loving me unconditionally with no strings attached!

Terrence Smith

In a world full of challenges and distractions, finding your purpose and a deeper connection with your faith can be a guiding light on your journey. As a 15-year-old, you have an opportunity to embrace your individuality and explore your spirituality. ***Embracing Your Uniqueness. Scripture: Psalm 139:14 - "I praise you because I am fearfully and wonderfully made; your works are wonderful; I know that full well."*** Your name is a testament to your individuality. God created you uniquely, just as He intended. Embrace your differences and recognize that you are wonderfully made.

When faced with life's uncertainties, turn to prayer. Seek guidance and strength in your conversations with God. Let your faith be your compass, guiding you through the difficulties of adolescence and helping you find your purpose.

Building Healthy Relationships. Scripture: Proverbs 13:20 - "Walk with the wise and become wise, for a companion of fools suffers harm." Surround yourself with positive influences who share your values and encourage your spiritual growth. Building healthy relationships is essential in your journey to finding purpose and connection with your faith. "Each of you should use whatever gift you have received to serve others, as faithful stewards of God's grace in its various forms. "Take time to explore your talents and gifts. Whether it's music, sports, art, or academics, discover how you can use these gifts to serve others and bring glory to God. Navigating Challenges is part of life's journey. Instead of avoiding them, embrace them as opportunities for growth and endurance. Your faith will strengthen as you overcome obstacles.

Dr. Theresa A. Smith

I am Blessed to know my "why" and purpose in this life. Each of us is given a gift embodied within us. Rather than just going through the motions, knowing your why gives you a reason to get out of bed each morning. It gives you clarity on what you want out of life – and what you need to do to get there – allowing you to set meaningful goals and crush them like a boss.

When you have a clearly defined sense of purpose, it boosts your self-confidence and allows you to pursue your dreams unapologetically. When you're focused on something that sets your soul on fire, your commitment to your goals and dreams becomes unwavering. Instead of being intimidated by things that are challenging, you find the will to roll up your sleeves and get it done.

You have the energy to reach for more, and you won't settle until you crush your goals, regardless of the obstacles that are thrown your way. If you're trying to find your why, remember that this isn't supposed to be easy. It will require a lot of intentional thought and action to figure out what your THING is, but once you find it, the sky really is the limit.

Try not to get overwhelmed and frustrated and trust that you will find your why. It may not come to you today, tomorrow, next week, or next month, but you will eventually have what Oprah so eloquently refers to as an 'a-ha moment.' And the rest, as they say, will be history. My "Why" is helping others. I LOVE people and I thrive when I see others succeed. Do you know why?

Dalton Spence

The JOY of the Lord is truly our strength. Without Christ we will never have real JOY. It is one of the most impactful, positive, and powerful emotions we as human beings will experience in our lifetime. This job I am currently doing I believe was specifically chosen by God for me to do. I teach music to the poorest of children in my community. Their parents are sometimes unemployed, working part-time, single parents doing the best for their children on meager incomes. Sometimes, because of their economic status, the children are deprived of improving themselves academically; I have received JOY from setting goals for these children, and for myself too. When I do this, my own skills and talents will, no doubt, take us to places that will amaze those with whom we associate. I am using music as a tool to teach the students life coping skills. By excelling in music, they will learn resilience, and independence. They will also learn time management and be responsible people, taking their respective place in society. I love to see the JOY on their faces when we, as a musical group, attain first place in a music competition. I receive JOY from knowing that I have created the opportunity for them to be successful in music. All my thirty years of experience in teaching comes into play in doing this job. I am also a comedian part time and making people laugh brings me JOY. There is an amazing natural high that I get when I perform, and people are laughing their hearts out. The feeling I get is unexplainable. I seize every opportunity to celebrate people who have accomplished wonderful things after overcoming adversities. They inspire and motivate which gives me tremendous JOY. I have found JOY on my Journey of life. You too, can just seize the opportunity!

Jaya Suganya Srinivasan

"God has rescued us from the dominion of darkness and brought us into the kingdom of the Son he loves," Colossians 1:13

"Identity" is every person's need in Life. It is something everyone strives to attain. Knowing your Identity in Jesus Christ is being aware of who you are in HIM and consciously living in that reality. It is not based on your Education or Social status or your Net worth. Your identity in Christ depends on your relationship with Him. Although the World and Satan try to define your identity, it is what God says about You that Matters. Isn't that amazing!!! So never allow the world or anybody to define who you are. There is constant pressure for you to model and live in the identity that the world gives. But you do not have to succumb to this pressure if you know that the God who made you has blessed you with a Glorious Identity. Knowing your identity in Christ impacts the way you think and behave. The Bible says .... You are now a new creation.

You are a Child of God. You are Blessed.

You are Redeemed. You are a Royal priesthood.

You are a Chosen generation. You are Set free.

You are Forgiven. You are Precious. You are Loved.

The more you know who you are in Christ,

The better your character and behavior will reflect the Christ in You. Your whole outlook on life will change for the better.

Let us learn to live and walk in this Glorious Identity.

Colossians 1:13 Assures that Jesus has rescued us from the rule and influence of the World and led us into realm of Love Abundant, Joy Unspeakable and Peace Undeniable.

Dr. Saundra E. Stancil

Do you know you were purposely born in the right place, born in the right family, born in the right time? You are Not a mistake! Yes, go ahead, and smile! SMILE brightly and brilliantly and feel it! There was a time when you were broken, down, felt defeated; or you may be down right now as you read this devotion. Here's what I want you to do…take a deep breath…and inhale, now exhale. Do these two more times. Do you feel calmer with this exercise?

Now walk over to your mirror. Look into that magnificent image (of You)! Release the thoughts that you are ugly, not good, feel ridiculous, unimportant, a disgrace, and any other thoughts stealing Your Greatness, Your High Value, Your Joy.

And repeat after me… (and complete these statements):

-I am glad that you..._____.

-I am proud that I.... _____.

-I am worthy because…_____.

Next, pray this prayer with me–out loud. And if you don't feel like it, do it anyway–silently–as I pray out loud with and for you. And when you pray, feel it in your spirit, in your chest, and keep that feeling there, hold it, and know that I am praying with you… "Thank you, Lord God, for your gifts, Your Trusts, and Your Patience with me. Teach me so I learn all that You have for me this moment that I am the blessing and that Your Will is done. In Jesus Name, Amen."

Now, that is the start of your day. You can make this a part of your routine every evening before you go to bed, every morning, or even midday before and after lunch. You are magnificent, and you will see and feel the difference. And, let me know how you are doing.

Gina Stockdall

As a child, no one anticipates their parents divorcing when they turn nineteen. No one pictures a long-term relationship becoming abusive. No one wants their friends to side with said abuser when they need them the most. No one dreams of getting academically suspended from college. No one visualizes being twenty-two and living on their mother's couch. However, one day I woke up and I found that all of these things were my reality. I turned to alcohol, partying, and meaningless relationships to try to fill the void I had in my soul. I was angry, disappointed, depressed and broken. I became a shell of the person I once was.

Psalm 126:5 says, "Those who sow in tears, shall reap in joy." (NKJV) This verse holds a special place in my heart because it helps me reflect on how far God has brought me. One Sunday after I moved back in, my mother invited me to church. I ended up going and attending a Bible study that evening. It was in that class that I started having a relationship with Jesus. I knew that my life was broken at that moment, but somehow, everything would be okay. Since devoting myself to the Lord, I have completed two degrees, started a business, been in a healthy marriage since 2019, had two beautiful children, found my place in church leadership and been sober since December 31, 2016.

We live in a broken world where pain is inevitable. However, the tears you cry today are seeds being planted that will grow to a bountiful harvest of thankfulness and joy tomorrow. Life without God is scary. Life with God is full of restoration and unconditional love. What God-given joy can you find in your life today?

Pastor Annette Sunday

"Now Faith is the substance of things hoped for, the evidence of things not seen." - Hebrews 11:1 (KJV)

When a person has faith in God, that faith is sincere from the heart and full of love, trust, and confidence in God. When we trust God there is no room for doubt. Doubt can be a hindrance that will affect your ability to trust God completely. We can show our faith in God, by reading and listening to His Holy Word. God is always worthy of our faith and trust in Him.

Growing up in Alabama as a child there was an old hymn that people in the South used to sing about faith. One part of the hymn would say, "Ninety-Nine and a Half Won't Do, I Know It Won't Do." Today as I remember that hymn, I can relate to its concept because it's true. Sometimes we will say that we have faith in God and that we trust Him for everything. Let's talk about the word "trust." We cannot say I have trust in God, "but…." When we connect the word "but" to our trust, this is not real trust in God. The enemy uses the word "but" to cloud and affect our minds by planting seeds of doubt. When we have doubts, we are not sure about what we are saying. So yes, ninety-nine and a half won't do! Faith is an action word which will teach us to have trust and hope in God. So yes, we need to have 100% trust in God to activate our level of Faith.

Dear Lord, please strengthen and increase our Faith as we strive to learn about and get closer to You. In Jesus Name I pray. Amen

Pastor Marcallus Sunday

Philippians 4:4-8 (KJV) Each day we should start our day by rejoicing in times like these; you may ask, how do I do that? First by thanking God for waking you up this morning. Seeing things happening in your life that's less extreme such as the price of food and gas that keeps going up.

We can't control that, but we can control how we spend. Families are being torn apart, wars and violence are all over the world. We experience school shootings, police brutality and even churches are not going beyond the sanctuary. These are some of the things that cause us to be anxious.

The Bible tells us to rejoice because now is the time to pray and not get caught up in the world's affairs that cause us anxiety. We should think of things that are good, pure, lovely, and honest. Remember today is the first day of the rest of your life; decide today how you want your first day to go and it will have a tremendous impact on the rest of your life.

Can you imagine someone in prison or in the hospital, someone on their death bed telling you to rejoice? If you are reading this, you have so much to be thankful for. The passage says, if you can be happy about anything in your life, think about these things; don't worry about what's going on in the world, but pray about it. Let the world see God in you. Remember the God of peace is with you, no matter what you are going through.

Dr. Natasha Sunday Clarke

Trust is the foundation of any strong relationship. A Wright State University article titled "Building and Repairing Trust" states that trust is one of those unusual qualities that is time-dependent -- meaning the longer you know someone, and the more trustworthiness has been demonstrated, the easier it becomes to trust that person.

When we read Proverbs 3:5, trust in the Lord with ALL your heart and lean not to your own understanding, we should be thinking about the relationship we have with God.

God is asking us to trust Him with Everything and lean not to our own understanding. God is saying I don't need your help <u>fill in the blank with your name</u>. You asked me to take care of you, you asked me for a job, you asked me for children, you said Lord bring me a Godly spouse. Oftentimes, we as believers only want to trust Him when we think we need Him.

Proverbs 3: 6 says, in all your ways acknowledge Him and He shall direct your path. This means the good, the bad, and the I am not so sure ways. In all my ways He will direct my paths if I continue to acknowledge Him.

TRUST is an action verb, it can't be taken lightly, especially when we say in good and bad times--in sickness and in health--for richer or poor. When we are following the GPS, the signs are posted everywhere. If we are traveling on an unfamiliar road, we need to proceed with caution, and have patience. The process of building trust is going to require time and patience.

God wants us to trust him with EVERYTHING. Not some things some of the time, but ALL things All of the time.

Angela Sunday Cobb

II Corinthians 5:7 and Proverbs 3:5-6
Walk by Faith, not by Sight.

Everything I do, I pray and ask God for guidance. I was 16 years old, pregnant, and confused, and lost on what to do. God spoke to me and said, "My child, you can handle this, Walk by Faith." When I decided to leave North Carolina to move to Texas, I asked God, "should I do it," and He referred me to II Corinthians 5:7.

Everything in my life has always been me Walking by Faith even though the sight may have seemed blurry. There may be times in your life where you need to make a decision and you're confused about what to do. The answer is to seek God and ask for guidance just as we learn in Proverbs 3:5-6, Trust in the Lord with All thine heart and lean not unto thine own understanding, in all thy ways acknowledge Him and He will direct your path.

When I wanted to quit my full-time job and start my own childcare center, God said, "Trust in me and I will direct your path." These two scriptures are the head of my life and all decision making. I pray they become yours as well. God Bless.

Rosa Sylvester

"From the end of the earth will I cry unto thee, when my heart is overwhelmed: lead me to the rock that is higher than I."
Psalm 61:2 (KJV)

As we go through life it becomes hard to find joy in our situation or even within ourselves. We may search for things to entertain us, distract us, or numb us. But none of that gets to the root of the matter. "We need Jesus!" He is the "rock in a weary land." He is the unchangeable one. Forever I AM. "The Word made flesh." He is everything we need Him to be and more. When we go to Him first, we can bypass the nonsense, it leads us around in circles, getting us nowhere or further into trouble. The Bible says, "lead me to the rock that is higher than I." We need to get above those things that drag us down. Climb upon the rock of His Word, the Bible.

We can read the Bible out loud or have it read to us (there are several apps for this). This way, we can hear the joy and gladness coming from our Father's heart. He wants us to know that His love for us supersedes everything. He is love. He is our source – our foundation. When we need our joy restored, let us go to the One who gave it to us in the first place. Let us fill up with God's truth so that He may restore our joy today.

Karen Sztendel

The easiest thing for human beings is to maintain joy and happiness when everything is going well. It is easy to pray, easy to study the Bible and even talk about God's promises then. But... When can we really put into practice everything we have received in good times? When can we really show what we are made of? When can we really understand God's promises? In difficult moments, it is when I can understand what God left in His word for our life: in hard moments His word is medicine, in dark moments it is light, in loneliness it is our Father who hugs us, and He tells us not to be afraid. These days were personally a moment where I was able to really put my faith into practice and when joy in my life has been a decision more than anything else. I feel like I'm in a test, where God wants to teach me. He wants to test me, and He wants to see what's inside me in a practical way.

These days I had no joy, everything around me was discouragement, but the promises of God echoed inside me and told me repeatedly that everything would be fine. What I experienced was not easy; in a single week, I lost someone very important in my family and very dear to me and in the same week my nation, Israel, entered an unjust war. We experienced a Massacre on October 07, 2023, the most painful after the Holocaust. During this time, I learned that my situation does not define me. HIS PROMISES define me, and I am what God says I am, not what the world says I am! We are alive today, amid war and mourning. This Joy is a supernatural gift! Nothing was extraordinary. I was willing to seek and put into practice the true Joy that comes from Him.

Antonía Taylor

I was what one would consider a "joyful" person. I had NO IDEA that the enemy was coming to try and rob me of the joy God intended for me. I was a 7-year-old who thought joy was cabbage patch dolls, dogs, and pink sparkly things. It was all fun, until I was raped and all the joy a little girl is supposed to have, was darkened. It was like the light was sucked out of me. It would be nice to tell you that suddenly I got my joy back, but that was not the case. I would go on to endure several other abusive situations over the years, including being raped by a pastor's husband; They were my spiritual parents at the time.

It was detrimental for me, a 17-year-old striving to be who God had called me to be. The flesh side of me was angry and hurt. I felt abandoned and I told God I didn't want anything to do with church again. My spirit was fighting to keep the faith in God and keep me from committing suicide. I struggled daily because believing God during what seems like hell, was hard. However, when I turned to God and gave Him the pain, He began to restore my joy in ways that only He could. He uses my testimony to free and bring joy to others, which in turn brings me joy. The point? Don't let anyone or anything keep you from believing in God, the Source of Joy. When you feel discouraged, abandoned, hurt, abused, etc., think of the previous things God has done for you. Gratitude helps you find joy in the present moment. There is a plan for your life that includes you being full of God's joy. Just remember when times get rough, the JOY comes from fellowship with God (Psalm 16:11).

Felisha Taylor

"That same day, when the evening came, He said to them, "Let us cross to the other side." - Mark 4: 35

We are going to the other side. Do you know that place beyond your hurt and pain? It's the place where joy and hope are renewed after a storm in life. How do you get to the other side? The only path to it is through sorrow, frustration, and difficult emotions.

Shortly after my divorce, the words "other side" were expressed to me as I expressed my fears and sadness regarding my marriage of 23 years ending abruptly. As I made updates to my benefits, I was comforted by the lady on the phone. She shared her experience with divorce and kindly said, "you know, it's better on the other side of it." Those words sprouted hope in my despair. Words are seeds. Something always grows from them. This is why the Bible tell us, "Let your words be seasoned with grace" and "power of life and death are in the tongue."

It blossomed into a book, I penned and titled, "The Other Side." God wants us to give what we have been given. What better way to give encouragement to others going through similar circumstances than a book? The need for encouragement is likely why you have this very book in your hand. It's the loss of a job, loved one, or another life crisis that leaves you feeling despair.

Let today's devotional remind you that you will get through this, and you are not alone. We are going together to the other side one step at a time. Come on, let's get going!

Dr. Tschanna Taylor

We, as a people, are facing so much adversity since the pandemic. Anywhere from broken relationships, failed marriages, desire to be married, bankruptcy, depression, physical/emotional/mental/sexual abuse and so much more. But how do we pick ourselves back up and keep going? How do we trust that God has a plan for our life? How do we love ourselves back to life? Together we will awaken our innate wisdom and inspire each other to heal and blossom in safe and nurturing ways. We will gather for spiritual and physical restoration, learning, sharing and community building.

One of the most powerful things you can do as a man or woman is to CHOOSE to be happy while living life on your terms, no matter what. You get to choose new thoughts, new beliefs, and new values. You get to choose that you were meant for more. Make your happiness a priority by freeing yourself of any lingering stress or negativity. Take inventory of your emotions and start creating the joyous life you deserve! Make connections and find the inspiration to move forward in your life in a way that brings you true fulfillment and joy. You were made for more joy & happiness...

You were made for more of the life that God has for you.

What are YOU choosing to believe about what's possible for you?

Evangelist Maria Terry

2 Corinthians 12:10 (New International Version)
That is why, for Christ's sake, I delight in weaknesses, in difficulties.
For when I am weak, then I am strong.

God is a flipper, what the enemy meant for evil God turned it, He flipped it for my good.

What God gives you is not what He intends for you to have. He intended for you to flip. Flip IT ...you are going to win in the end, not because you avoided it, not even because you overcame it. You can't flip it until God FLIPS YOU! There is a YOU that YOU haven't met yet. You have no idea how strong you are until you had to face adversity. God does things big and fast. God isn't just a God of steps; He's a God of leaps. He is the only one who will take you to school when you didn't even know you were in a classroom.

There is a whole nation waiting for your strength, your push, your get up, your FLIP. What you think is your weakness is someone else's strength. Show them that it may look impossible, but there is a flipside to the divorce, there is a flipside to losing out of the new job, there is a brighter side to having a child out of wedlock. God can flip that situation and make it look good. There is always a flip to the madness if you do not lean to your own understanding. When I look weak, my praise is louder. When I sound weak my hallelujah is louder. Weeping may endure for just one night, but guess what, morning is coming and my JOY is coming because God is on the FLIP side of my situation. Ask me how I know.... glad you ask. Because I'm still here.

Joyan Thomas

My beloved sisters and brothers, my name is JOYAN yes JOYan , so I feel encouraged to encourage you today to have JOY in your lives, no matter what your circumstances are. "For the Joy of the Lord is my Strength." Nehemiah 8:10

The biblical root of the word JOY means to rejoice and make glad. We have with full authority in Jesus' name to rejoice because the Lord is a forgiving God, gracious and compassionate always! What does a joy filled life look like? In today's world, when we talk about the pursuit of happiness and success, those are dependent on a condition of our outward lives, but the JOY of the LORD is something the spirit grows within us. HAPPiness only gets experienced temporally when something HAPPens, however, true JOY comes from the Lord. It is something we must choose that is already within us. At 28 years young with my whole life in front of me, I was diagnosed with a brain tumor and the only chance for a long life was surgery. There was an 80 % chance of dying and a 20 % chance of living. Even while on the surgery table, I had a heart attack and survived. I decided to believe what the Lord says about me and what my parents named me and that was to have JOY despite my circumstances!

Having a JOY filled state of mind is the only way for the Lord to give us His strength to go through circumstances. As a survivor, I spend my days putting JOY in others

Jesus first

Others second

Yourselves last

Vera Thomas

I have joy with no restraint.

No matter what I may go through.

I stand on His Word that always holds true.

As a vessel to be used by God

Nothing can destroy my peace or my joy.

Even during heartache and pain

I thank God for everything.

Praise is what brings the joy I claim.

The joy of the Lord helps me sustainA feeling of great pleasure and happiness.

The joy comes from knowing I am truly blessed.

Life is full of many trials and tests.

I must confess that joy within

Comes from Jesus, my provider, my friend.

I pray for strength today to handle whatever comes my way. I choose to let the joy of the Lord be my strength and wisdom to react according to His Word and purpose for my life. My joy comes from being thankful, no matter what. Even in sickness, I can have joy, knowing "He was wounded for our transgressions, bruised for my iniquities; the chastisement of my peace was upon Him, and with His stripes, I am healed." (Isaiah 53:5 KJV) In trouble, I can cry out to the Lord, and He will deliver me (Psalm 107:6 KJV). The joy of the Lord is my strength because His Word is a light to my path. (Psalm 119:105 KJV)

Darlene Thorne MDiv.

In the gentle whispers of Jeremiah 31:25, God extends a divine promise: "I will refresh the weary and satisfy the faint." Imagine the embrace of this covenant, where God's love is eternally inscribed within our hearts, offering a sanctuary for the weary soul. This assurance signifies a covenant beyond external laws, a pact where God inscribes His law within, fostering a new nature within believers.

Identifying Weariness - As we recognize the weight of weariness, let's delve into our own experiences. Recognizing signs of spiritual, emotional, and physical fatigue is the first step. During life's trials, let us acknowledge the moments when our spirits felt fatigued and our hearts heavy with the burdens of the journey.

Claiming God's Promise - Trust blooms in the soil of God's faithfulness. Embrace this promise not merely as words on a page but as a living covenant of love. Let the everlasting love of the Lord be a balm to wounds and a light in moments of darkness.

Practical Steps for Refreshment - Picture a sacred space of prayer and meditation, where you commune with the Father. Establish a regular time for prayer and meditation to deepen your connection with God. Seek the warmth of a faith community, a gathering of hearts pursuing the same promise. In unity, find the strength to weather life's storms.

Satisfying the Faint - Amid weariness, cultivate a garden of gratitude. As you nurture a mindset of contentment, witness how God not only satisfies but overflows with abundance. It's a promise fulfilled in every moment of need.

Shawntia Thorpe

Joy is a heartfelt positive emotion that is expressed through inner peace, happiness, satisfaction, fulfillment, and gratefulness. It is deeper than pleasure (which is temporary) and is triggered by spiritual experiences. It is a state of mind that can be developed. It could be that because of the sad experiences you have had, your mind is clouded by depressive and painful thoughts. However, you should remember that what you focus your mind on is what rules you. Why not turn your focus on the word of God? Why not replace those daunting thoughts with what the loving God says to His children? *"This book of the law shall not depart from your mouth. You shall meditate on it day and night..."* (Joshua 1:8). This is the best way to transform your mind and align it towards joyfulness. It is the way to restore the joy of the Lord that you have lost in those stormy days. You will find that the more you stay in God's word, the more joy wells up in your heart because of the truth written concerning you. The word of God is the surest catalyst for transforming your mind because it is full of promises and truths that can bring joy to your heart (Psalm 119:105). As such, *"... let God transform you into a new person by changing the way you think. Then you will learn to know God's will for you, which is good, pleasing, and perfect."* (Romans 12:2 NLT). This scripture explains why you must put your mind, attention and focus on it. Bear in mind that joy is a fetcher of good things (Isaiah 12:3). This is why you must find and protect your joy!

Shanee Tinnin

You carry burdens. The weight of past experiences, disappointments, and pain can be overwhelming, but during it all, know that you are seen, valued, and loved unconditionally. In this sacred space, let us embark on a journey of healing and renewal. Release your baggage, for it does not define you. Embrace the truth that you are more than the scars you bear. You possess a resilience and strength that knows no bounds. As you lay down your burdens, invite forgiveness into your heart. Forgive yourself for the mistakes and shortcomings of the past. Embrace the power to heal and grow, knowing that each step forward is a step towards liberation. Let go of self-judgment and allow grace to envelop your spirit. In the embrace of divine love, find solace and comfort. Know that you are worthy of love and belonging, regardless of your past. The unconditional love of God is a balm Let it wash over you, bringing forth restoration and renewal. As you journey forward, gather strength from the stories of remarkable women who have overcome adversity. In the process of healing, tend to your own well-being. Nurture your body, mind, and spirit. Prioritize self-care, for it is not selfish but a necessary act of self-love. Surround yourself with a community of like-hearted individuals who uplift and encourage you. Together, we can carry one another's burdens, fostering an environment of compassion, understanding, and support. As you continue, never forget the depth of your worth. Your experiences have shaped you, but they do not limit you. You have the power to transform your pain into purpose. May you find strength during your struggles and may the Lord guide you towards healing and wholeness. As you release your baggage, may you embrace the freedom and joy that await you. For you are a woman of remarkable strength, resilience, and beauty, Get up You Got this!

Nikkia Tisaby

I remember in high school my first boyfriend shared intimate details about our relationship with his friends after we broke up. Soon those details were repeated, and the rumor mill started. Many of the rumors were far-fetched; however, I did give myself to someone I thought loved me and that fact couldn't be denied. The entire experience left me feeling defeated, heartbroken, and insecure. Battling those negative emotions and the constant taunting opened the door to depression.

Forgiveness is the intentional and voluntary process by which one who may at first feel victimized, undergoes a change in feelings regarding the offense and overcomes negative emotions such as resentment and vengeance.

Colossians 3:13 says: "Bear with each other and forgive one another if any of you has a grievance against someone. Forgive as the Lord forgave you." Although he hurt me, I found the strength to forgive my ex-boyfriend, however. I found it difficult to forgive myself. I had a terrible internal voice that constantly kept my head down. Eventually I realized I was seeing myself based on others' perceptions of me and not God's. The Divine says: "If you seek forgiveness, know that I have forgiven you. You've always been forgiven."

Yes, I was bruised…but not broken! I realized I wasn't damaged goods and through the renewal of my mind, I accepted myself as God accepts me. Your mistakes, no matter how bad they seem, give you a badge of experience. There is no advancement in life without being uncomfortable. Forgiving yourself can be hard, however, it is your right…not an option. Remember no one can break what they didn't build.

Viviana Torres

"God, why haven't you answered my prayer?" When prayers go unanswered it leaves us in doubt. This is exactly what the enemy wants. The enemy's goal is that we lose hope in the Lord and remain ignorant in our understanding. This feeds the enemy or "beast" in our life. So, why? Why do our prayers go unanswered? One, it's God's timing, not ours. Psalm 27:14 reminds us to wait on the Lord.

Second, there *is* power in prayers. Don't pray hoping it will happen. When it aligns with God's will, believe that it <u>will happen</u>. Third, God needs us sharp in spiritual warfare. Yes, there is pain that comes along in our lives. This is how God teaches us spiritual endurance. We rejoice in the Lord even through suffering. In Judges 3:12-30, Ehud pierced a double-edged sword through the fat belly of king Eglon who kept the Israelites in bondage. The blade went so deep the handle disappeared into the fat. Imagine your prayer is God's message to the enemy. A double-edged sword of the Spirit, the word of God cutting right into the fat.

Have faith our prayers are penetrating the belly of the beast that has grown very fat from your pain, fear, anxiety, depression, oppression, poverty (etc. you fill in the blank). Hebrews 4:12 tells us that His word is sharper than any two-edged sword; it can cut through spirit and bone. Believe that our prayers will be answered, and they will infiltrate any attack the enemy has over our life keeping us in bondage or iniquities. Fourth, in Matthew 17:21 NKJV, Yeshua reminds us of some demons that require prayer *and fasting*.

Lastly, remember what Yeshua has done for us at the cross, so that our trial may seem miniscule in comparison.

Elyzon Tosin

After losing him to Brain Cancer, I discovered I was pregnant. I walked down the streets of Lagos with tears welling up in my eyes, wondering if life was worth living at all and how I would fend for this unborn child. From the Chaos of being the first child with siblings and parent's dependent on me, I couldn't bear the thought of returning home to become dependent on those I once provided for. I cried myself to sleep most nights out of fear, pain, loss, and frustration, not knowing what to do next or where to start. How could the person I love the most fade before my eyes? How would I survive without him, and how would I nurture an unborn child? I wasn't sure how to navigate this phase and the stigma of being a young widow, so I decided I wouldn't ask for help or reach out to anyone. I would be happy regardless, travel, focus on myself, love myself, and care for my child regardless of what anyone felt or thought. I refused to be labeled or defined by the predicament life threw at me. I decided it was time to redefine the course my life would take from there on out. First, I had to find joy. Then, I picked myself up from the rubble and charted the next course on a quest to make meaning and find purpose.

Lamentations 3:25-39 MSG

Who am I?

What do I want?

How do I want to be addressed

How do I provide for myself and my child?

Do I pursue my passion or work a job that just pays my bills?

We will never be fully aware of what we can accomplish if we let fear keep us back. Indeed, life isn't fair, but I have learned to maintain my joy amid chaos and life's uncertainties.

Dr. Gloria Trueh

The Bible says we are to "let all bitterness, wrath, anger, clamor, and slander be put away from you, with all malice. Be kind to one another, tenderhearted, forgiving one another, as God in Christ forgave you." (Eph 4:31-32)

Forgiveness brings freedom to both parties, while unforgiveness breeds bitterness, resentment, anger, hatred, and division. When we confront those who've sinned against us, not in malice or vengeance but in gentleness and reconciliation, we give them the opportunity to confess, repent, and seek forgiveness. Jesus said in, (Matt.18:15) "If your brother sins against you, go, and tell him about his fault between you and him alone. If he hears you, you have gained your brother. Do not let unforgiveness and bitterness keep you in bondage. Receive what God has promise you!

Release that person! Be free. (Meditate here)

In the Lord's prayer forgiveness is mentioned about forgiving our debtors, meaning we must forgive those that have done us wrong no matter how hard it is to do. Peter asks Jesus, how many times should I forgive my brother who sinned against me? Jesus said to him, I do not say to you, up to seven times, but up to seventy-times seven. (Matt. 18:21-22)

Unforgiveness is deadly, in many ways. Researchers have found that unforgiving people have higher-rates of stress, sickness, divorce, sleeplessness, cardiovascular disease, lower immune-system…. Pray and ask the Holy Spirit to bring to your mind all the people you need to forgive and the events you need to forgive them for, then say their names out loud, "I forgive you!" God will answer your Prayer!

Let's Pray: Heavenly Father, I am sorry for not forgiving (-), I release (-) from my heart today! I receive my healing and peace now. Amen!

Suzette Tubi

One thing I have learned in life is that not every tear I've cried is a tear of sorrow, but also blessings. After experiencing some traumatic times in my life, I turned to the One and only who is the giver and Creator of joy. God gave me joy and I fight daily to maintain it. I was born with joy; Joy to the world Suzette has come! But life happened. My joy became unrecognizable. Eventually lost & stolen after being unutilized. John 10:10 (NCV) says, "The thief comes to steal, kill and destroy; but I came to give life - life in all fullness [fullness of joy]."

After much prayer and time spent studying the Bible, I discovered that joy is a weapon. I started waking that weapon by declaring Nehemiah 8:10, "The Joy of the Lord is my strength." Joy is our strength, but not without the Lord. Romans 15:13 tells us that joy fills us with hope. Galatians 5:22 says joy is a fruit of the Spirit, not happiness. Joy is meant to be eternal. Happiness is temporary. Joy is God- given, and happiness is people given. Joy is not circumstantial, happiness is. Like James 1:2 - a servant of Jesus Christ said, "Count it all joy, my brothers and sisters when you meet trials of various kinds." I decree and declare I will now utilize my God-given divine weapon of joy by ensuring I stay "contagious" and infect everyone around me.

Caren Tunget

" So now the case is closed. There remains no accusing voice of condemnation against those who are joined in life-union with Jesus, the Anointed One." Romans 8:1. When I was a new mother, I did the unthinkable. I clinched my son tightly in my arms one day, afraid to surrender his life (and therefore, mine) completely to the Lord. I know…gasp! I had an Abraham moment, and I failed. Mind you, at least three mothers in my church had recently lost a child suddenly from unexpected accidents, and because a previous illness and subsequent miscarriage gnawed on my suspicion that I may never have another, I allowed a spirit of fear to overshadow my faith. Afterward, the weight I carried from my lack of trust was always with me.

I felt unlovable, especially by a holy God, triggering an old insecurity from my childhood. The enemy loves to use our past failures and heap such a heavy burden of guilt upon us that we believe the lie he whispers in our ears, "You are not worthy of God's love." I knew God 's unconditional love and forgiveness, but I didn't really believe it. I thought I believed, but my actions proved otherwise. I allowed condemnation to rule over me. I tried to prove my worth through achievement and self-improvement but found it all left me empty and lonely. Oh friends, God's love doesn't waver when we waffle. His grace is sufficient for our guilt. Total surrender of every area of our lives is not a one-time act, but the lifelong journey of sanctification. Let go of the lie, and begin to live in freedom and peace, knowing you are fully loved and accepted by the One who willingly chose to pay your debt in full.

Rhonda Turner

Why does God have me where I am Today? What is my purpose? Jeremiah 29:11 says, "For I know the plans I have for you, declares the Lord, plans for welfare and not for evil, to give you a future and a hope." Many times, we step over God and ask others for our purpose. We value their opinion more than God's. As He allows us to experience struggles, they are meant to help teach and grow us… remember we all will have a TEST so we can give a TESTIMONY.

God loves you enough to let you grow into your divine potential and strengths. All the bad things that may happen to us in this world may feel consuming, but they are teachable moments in this thing called life. Everything that feels unfair in this life will be made right by understanding the true joy of God's plan for your purpose. Focus more on "being" than on "doing." It is important for you to find your calling from God to fulfill your life's purpose. Remember God has formed you in His image to prepare you to play a unique role in each step of your life's story. You have a destiny that will bring glory to God, share the grace of God, and extend the reign of God.

Ephesians 2:8-10: "For by grace you have been saved through faith, and this is not your own doing; it is the gift of God—not the result of works, so that no one may boast. For we are what he has made us, created in Christ Jesus for good works, which God prepared beforehand to be our way of life."

Tierra Turner

In the tapestry of life, we all encounter moments of hardship and pain. These moments can leave us feeling lost, wounded, and in need of healing. The journey to healing is a deeply personal voyage that requires patience, self-compassion, and self-discovery. Here is your guide to embarking on a transformative "Journey to Healing." Begin by creating a sacred space for yourself, free from distractions. Over the course, take time each day to reflect upon your emotions, experiences, and the wounds that need healing. Journey through your thoughts without judgment. This process of self-reflection will help you acknowledge the pain you carry within. Identify the roots of your pain.

What memories or experiences are connected to your wounds? Allow yourself to express anger, sadness, and fear. These emotions, when released, pave the way for healing. Healing begins with self-compassion. Acknowledge that it's okay to feel hurt. Practice daily self-affirmations to reinforce your worth and strength. Forgiveness is a powerful tool for healing. Start by forgiving those who have caused you pain. Remember, forgiveness doesn't condone their actions; it frees you from the burden of holding onto resentment. Equally important, forgive yourself for any self-blame or guilt you may carry. Healing doesn't have to be a solitary journey. Reach out to trusted friends, family members, or a therapist. Share your experiences, allowing their support to bolster your healing process. As you progress on your journey, engage in activities that bring you joy and fulfillment. Reconnecting with hobbies, passions, and moments of happiness reminds you of the beauty and resilience within you. The journey to healing is also a journey of self-discovery.

Betty Tyler

Are there periods in your life where you've searched for something—but never seem to find it? You've tried to medicate the emptiness with people, places and things that in the end just didn't satisfy. In turn, your void and emptiness grew deeper, but with more stuff. Why not let God fill your emptiness and hunger? There is a place in your inner being, your soul that only God can fill. That place is for Him to dwell and commune with you. We were created by God and for God. He is waiting to fill the void in each of us. When we allow God to fill the emptiness within us, our souls are fulfilled and at rest.

When we try to fill our souls with other things, we are restless and remain empty. God put a longing inside of us that is intended to lead us back to Him. He is our heavenly Father and He wants to share an intimate relationship with His children. Throughout the bible, God filled the lonely and broken hearted. Just a few examples, (1) in the book of Genesis chapter 29, God filled Leah. She pressed into God as He showed faithfulness towards her; (2) Miriam who was Moses' sister is another notable example.

She was alone and vulnerable, but God filled her (Exodus 2); (3) God showed David favor. David spent time in the wilderness being lonely and hiding from King Saul, but God filled him (1 Samuel 16). Don't let emptiness live in you or overtake you. Connect with your local church for a sense of community; read your bible daily and let it seep into your bones. Quote God's promises for your life. Seek a Christian accountability partner or mentor that can walk with you through your process to a healthier you. Then rejoice in the everlasting God for filling your void.

Tralyne Usry

Have you ever been in the middle of a trial and said to God, "This is not what you promised?" I have! In the middle of IT ALL, where God was processing me, I disregarded His promises. The process stole the promises right from under me. My very foundation was "rocked!" I wondered if God was really God! Peace stolen. Peace of Mind stolen and so much more. The culprit, PROCESS! How, so you may be asking?

Welcome to this brief "Testimony Service!" We are overcome by the words of our testimony. (Rev. 12:11).

I was diagnosed with MS (multiple sclerosis) and my entire world changed. I lost so much; my classroom, my apartment, my income, my independence and most of all, MY JOY! I stopped smiling. This was so far from who I was as a person! I was the very "life of the party" and the delight of my kindergarten classroom. Before. Afterwards, I wanted to die, and suicide was a frequent suggestion. My joy was gone. Little did I know, it was a process. Through this trial, I learned God is a healer! I read the scriptures before and knew them in my mind. I could quote all the scriptures on healing, but I hadn't experienced it. BUT NOW, I have more than head knowledge. I HAVE EXPERIENTIAL KNOWLEDGE which CAN'T EVER BE TAKEN FROM ME! I GOT MY JOY BACK! God's promises were ALWAYS true but because the process was so hard, I allowed the enemy to steal!

Don't Let the Process Talk You Out of the Promise.

Don't be a VICTIM! Catch the thief! Know that what God has for you is ALWAYS good! Experiencing bad? It's NOT His promise!

CHALLENGE: RECEIVE YOUR JOY BACK!

Debra Valentine

Years ago, I was consumed by life investments. As a young wife and working mother of two, I had the day-to-day routines to keep my family on track, whether through homework, basketball practices, or supporting my husband as he traveled up and down the highways to support his parishioners. Unfortunately, migraine headaches pushed me to be first in line. For months, the headaches emerged twice weekly.

On one specific Sunday morning, my family left for church and allowed me an opportunity to move about at a slower pace. After a hot shower, I felt ready to go. Following the usual route to church, I hopped on I-65 N. Traffic was low, yet some strange, uneasy feelings began to emerge. I felt assured that my husband and children had passed this area unharmed, but I immediately prayed for protection and understanding over this feeling. Within my surroundings, it looked like the road and concrete barriers were seamless, therefore, should a driver need to pull over, he wouldn't know the designated area. Furthermore, I was amazed that every car I saw was either gray, black, or white. I wanted so much to see a red or yellow truck, even a traffic light, but neither availed themselves. I made it to church, enjoying a wonderful day of worship and fellowship. However, in subsequent months, several medical evaluations showed I had indeed experienced a stroke at some point. I was also diagnosed with Cone Dystrophy, a degeneration of the retina of the eye. But God! I can still see colors. I haven't experienced a migraine headache in years! Furthermore, evidence of a stroke was only a spot on the brain scan. OH Yes, I Have Great Joy!!!

Carlica Villines

As a mother living far away from her family, the desire to return home can weigh heavily on your heart. Separation can be challenging, and at times, it feels like a piece of your soul is missing. But remember, joy can be restored even amid distance and longing.

The journey back home is not just a physical one; it's a spiritual and emotional one too. In these moments of longing, turn to the source of your strength, your faith, and your love. Begin your day with a prayer of gratitude for the family you love so dearly. Thank God for the moments you've shared and for the promise of being together again. In your current surroundings, seek out the beauty that surrounds you. Whether it's the smile of a new friend, the beauty of nature, or the warmth of a community, cherish these moments.

Modern technology can be a blessing. Use it to stay connected with your loved ones. A video call or a heartfelt message can bridge the gap between your hearts. Instead of focusing solely on the destination, find joy in the journey itself. Each step brings you closer to reuniting with your family. Remember that everything happens in God's timing. Have faith that when the time is right, you'll be reunited with your family.

Use this time of separation to serve others with love and kindness. Helping those in your current community can bring a sense of fulfillment and joy.

As you walk this path, may your heart find peace, knowing that the desire to return home is a testament to the love you hold for your family. Your journey is not in vain, for in it, you can find the restoration of joy, the strengthening of faith, and the deepening of love.

Chiquita Villines

A child is the most precious thing to this world. Unfortunately, some kids don't have the choice to stay that way. As a child, we are taught that adults are there to protect us, but when I was twelve, my protection ran out when a person close to me introduced me to adult behaviors early. I knew what he was doing was wrong. I did just what was told of me. I stopped looking for excuses for his behavior and started to live in my truth. I would always say "God's gone handle him, because that wasn't nothing but the devil." After all the pain and tears, I tried to go on with my life and be around my mama.

I tried to stay gone if she was home or be asleep by the time she came back. I shut down; I just became isolated. I remember my teacher Mrs. P asked me what was wrong with me. I just told her "I hurt myself on my cousin's bike." Making up excuses for him hurt me the most because he was the one to cause me harm. I remember moving in with my aunt, on my dad's side. It was a different environment for me. For the first time, I felt safe enough to openly tell someone the trauma I experienced. When I spoke my truth, I felt so relieved. I didn't feel small about myself anymore. I felt like I finally stood up for myself. I was determined not to become that stereotype. I always had a clear understanding that it was not my fault. I often see individuals that this has happened to be taken over by their inner thoughts thinking it was their fault. My first step was accepting it, identifying it, and immediately starting to work on those changes. I am blessed because my outcome could've been worse. Finally, I let it all go and wrote a letter to release all the negative energy traits that had burdened me.

Kenecia Villines

"You make known to me the path of life; in your presence there is fullness of joy; at your right hand are pleasures forevermore."

Psalm 16:11

Joyfulness is driven from the spiritual and emotional aspects of our lives. The knowledge of truth ties them together as it directs our spiritual journey and emotional reactions to what happens and, as such, determines our joy restoration.

The knowledge of the promises of God that He will never leave you nor forsake you (Hebrews 13:5[b]) among other promises, informs your faith in God. Joy then becomes a byproduct no matter the situation, especially when your joy seems lost. With this knowledge, as you engage in prayer, you do not focus on just speaking, you listen as well because He may be saying something to you through His Holy Spirit in you. Paul's prayer for you; *"May the God of hope fill you with all joy and peace in believing, so that by the power of the Holy Spirit you may abound in hope."* - Romans 15:13 (ESV) stems from knowledge that God is the source of true joy.

Joy is not merely fleeting happiness, but a deeper and more profound sense of contentment and well-being. The knowledge that what goes on in your mind contributes to your emotional well-being, makes you deliberately think only on *"whatsoever things are true… honest… just… pure… lovely… of good report and virtuous…"* (Philippians 4:8) even when situations say otherwise.

Dr. Dorn J.B. Walker

At age 23, I was trapped in a grief whirlwind when my husband, sister, and uncle suddenly died. God's comfort brought me through. I remarried and lived a joyous life for twenty years. Then, grief returned when seven more family members died. God reminded me to "Show up" for my life despite the pain. They were gone, but I was still here! Isaiah 61:3 instructed me to exchange pain for wholeness. Seek Beauty (God's presence) instead of ashes. Put on the Oil of Joy (God's healing balm) instead of mourning, and exchange heaviness for God's garment of praise. When grief repeats, it's like avalanches rolling.

Constant heartaches and tears that continue streaming Down the cheeks with roaring cries beneath a dark sky

With scars upon scars unhealed and frayed nerves that's fried. Without continuous trust, without continuous hope

Without continuous love, the detour to comfort has no road.

In You, Lord Jesus, I rest. In you, Lord Jesus, I seek peace.

My constant quest for You rescues me when grief repeats.

When grief repeats, I repeat my quest for the One I know.

And rise from the miry clay and from beneath the darkest shadow proclaiming I must "show up" because I still breathe life. I have Purpose and Destiny that's still alive.

With mustard seed faith, I press through repeated pain.

With strength renewed and all hope regained.

Repeating Grace never runs. It flows from our Savior God meets our every need with His repeating Name Jesus, Yahweh, Healer, whatever I need! His Grace unchanged!

Apostle John Walker, Th.D.

"I have told you these things so that My joy and delight may be in you, and that your joy may be made full and complete and overflowing."—John 15:11

Have you ever desired something from someone, be it a parent, sibling, husband, wife, or even a co-worker and 'that person' – simply could not give you what you desired. Have you ever had a longing to connect with a peer that was intellectually mature but found that there was a disconnect and you found yourself all alone? This was my position toward my earthly dad. God created us that His joy and delight might be in us and that our joy may be full, complete, and overflowing lacking nothing. My Dad was adopted at an early age, and he had some irreconcilable issues with his biological Father. As the oldest Son, I always reached out to spend time with him, but he did not have a mutual longing for me. There were deeper conversations and experiences that I wanted to have with my dad. So, one evening after I left his apartment, I had a conversation with God and expressed the above sentiments – and much to my surprise, God said "what you desire from your dad, He cannot give you." God was saying at this time, your dad doesn't have the capacity to give you what you desire. I began to weep --and at that moment, God the Holy Spirit said, "but I am Here." God was saying "My joy and delight will fill you that your joy may be full, complete, overflowing – lacking nothing" The Lord was saying you're chasing something that only I can fill. "I am Here" - I am your Joy! I experienced the fullness of Joy in Him.

Lisa Walton

"Count it all joy, my brothers and sisters, when you meet trials of various kinds." - James 1:2 (ESV)

Sometimes, life's storms in the form of personal struggles, health issues, financial problems, relationship difficulties, and others can be relentless and intense, much like a storm that refuses to pass quickly. They make us feel overwhelmed and distressed as they test our resilience, making it hard to see any light at the end of the tunnel.

Be comforted that Joy can still be found amidst the downpour.

I know you're wondering how. It is by the "art" of learning to shift your perspective and mindset to focus on the positive. 1 Thessalonians 5:16-18 (ESV): *"Rejoice always, pray without ceasing, give thanks in all circumstances; for this is the will of God in Christ Jesus for you."* It is by finding a way to celebrate life, recognizing the positive aspects, small victories, or the moments of grace that are present even in insane situations.

In Philippians 4:4 (ESV) *"Rejoice in the Lord always; again, I will say, rejoice",* we are commanded to develop resilience and faith, instead of dwelling on difficulties.

You can choose to focus on personal growth, inner strength, and the potential for positive change that can emerge from these trials. You can realize that storms eventually pass as it can be your opportunity for deepening your appreciation for the beauty of life just as is pointed out to us in Romans 5:3-4 (ESV): *"More than that, we rejoice in our sufferings, knowing that suffering produces endurance, and endurance produces character, and character produces hope."*

Lisa Washington

"Do not be anxious about anything, but in every situation, by prayer and petition, with thanksgiving, present your requests to God." Philippians 4:6

Whether it was preparing to send my son off to college or preparing my daughter to be a wife and have her first child, I used to always carry feelings of anxiety and stress. I worried about how things would go. Would my son be ok on his own? Is my daughter ready to be a wife and mom? Had I done enough as a parent to lead them in the right direction? I questioned everything and assumed the worst, but why? I could have just as easily thought about all the goodness that was being given to my family and be thankful for the experience. But many times, we allow our minds to take us to spaces where peace never lives, and what does that do? It steals our joy. My mother used to always ask me, "Why do you always think the worst of everything?" I didn't understand the power of prayer and the importance of trusting in the Lord and being thankful for his blessings. How dare I be so ungrateful for all that He had done for me and my family. I was missing the blessings and the lessons that the Lord had so graciously shared. In Acts 27:35, Apostle Paul shares an act of thankfulness amidst a storm at sea. Instead of being anxious and stressed about what might happen, Paul prayed a prayer of gratitude and thanksgiving and encouraged those around him, which serves as a reminder that even amid a storm, be thankful for everything.

"Give thanks in all circumstances; for this is God's will for you in Christ Jesus." 1 Thessalonians 5:18 NIV

Andrea Waters

Do you wake up excited about going in to your 9-5, or whatever it is you do for work? Most of us take work for granted, complain about Mondays, and spend all week pining for the weekend. I encourage you – no, I challenge you – to change your perspective from drudgery to joy. Why? I'm glad you asked.

No matter your occupation – blue, white collar, no collar at all – God created you with unique skills and talents. This expression of our skills is our God-given GIFT. It's called work, and one of the many ways we fulfill our purpose here on earth. When you think about your contribution to society – be it bus driver, accountant, doctor, stay at home parent – what you do matters. HOW you do it matters even more.

Does this mean you'll be skipping work every day, feeling 100% satisfied with every aspect of your job or career? Of course not. That's not what it means to find joy in what you do. Joy comes when you see beyond the mundane. Joy comes when you recognize how your work impacts others, and how it's preparing you for where you're going. Let's connect the dots here. The GIFT of work that God has given you…done to the best of your ability and with JOY….is preparing you for your Next Level of service to God's people. This next level could very well be out of your comfort zone and into your greater purpose. It all starts with the work of your hands. Find joy in it!

Dr. Melinda Watts

¹ I will extol thee, my God, O king; and I will bless thy name for ever and ever.

² Every day will I bless thee; and I will praise thy name for ever and ever.

³ Great is the LORD, and to be praised; and his greatness is unsearchable.

⁴ One generation shall praise thy works to another and shall declare thy mighty acts.

⁵ I will speak of the glorious honor of thy majesty, and of thy wondrous works.

⁶ And men shall speak of the might of thy terrible acts: and I will declare thy greatness.

⁷ They shall abundantly utter the memory of thy great goodness and shall sing of thy righteousness.

⁸ The LORD is gracious, and full of compassion; slow to anger, and of great mercy.

⁹ The LORD is good to all: and his tender mercies are over all his works.

¹⁰ All thy works shall praise thee, O LORD; and thy saints shall bless thee.
*** - Psalms 145:1-10***

When the struggle is real, just chill!

There will be days when we struggle. We struggle to read, we struggle with life uncertainties, we struggle to pray yet through our struggles praise Him anyway!

Do not be dismayed, you just praise Him anyway!

When the struggle is real, I learn to praise Him anyway. Make the Lord larger than your struggles. The joy of the Lord is our strength, and our praise is a weapon that confuses the enemy. Make the exchange. Use your weapon of praise during the struggle and watch the Lord brighten your day.

AGAIN, I SAY PRAISE HIM ANYWAY!

Cynthia Waugh

I had no energy, no strength, after the passing of my husband (a Blessed memory) who left this earth to be with our Heavenly Father. JOY disappeared from my heart. I felt so sad, and so alone. Vinroy was my best friend, my confidant, and my loving husband for over 40 years. I thank God for giving me the strength to care for him during his last days when he was incapacitated. I was by his side cushioning his discomfort, making sure he was in no pain with the assistance of prescribed pain relief medications. After my husband was laid to rest, it took me a while to renew my JOY. I missed hearing his voice calling me from the bedroom, Merks!

Merks! I missed the sound of *music* being played by him, I missed seeing his *smiles*. I missed his *gentle touch*. The day came when I had a new routine, and that was collecting my grandsons Ameer and Akoi from school. My JOY was restored as they are always happy whenever they see me. They share jokes with me, making me feel like a kid again, they assist me with tech problems, and they spend their afternoons at my home where they do their homework and relax while having their snacks. Whenever I am at a function hosted by a family member, I get immense JOY in seeing and interacting with my nieces and nephews. The JOY I receive in hearing and learning about their achievements in their chosen vocation is unexplainable. I am so proud of them. The purest form of JOY is bringing happiness into someone's life. I am so grateful for my niece, Dania, and my nephew, Morton, for bringing me so much JOY. Wishing for them, an abundance of JOY in their lives, and the lives of their children and their significant others.

Joann Weathersby

God will not always save us from the fire; but He most definitely fashions and perfects us there. God's purpose for permitting adversities is to bring us forth as mature vessels for the master's use. In the natural world, precious metals such as silver and gold are processed by intense heat. Gold is placed in the furnace to remove a substance called dross. Silver is likewise purified by fire. Scripture says that if you take away dross from the silver, there shall come forth a vessel for the finer (Proverbs 25:4). This passage is truly relevant as I take a panoramic view of my life. What I see is that the greatest pains of my life produce the greatest spiritual gains. Pain is a pusher but where I ended up was my choice. Pain propelled me into the presence of the only one who could perfect me.

To mature my faith, God had to take me through the fire. I was in the furnace of heartbreak, betrayal, rejection, mourning, marital issues, and job loss. My faith was stretched, but it was also strengthened and stabilized. God used what happened to me to perfect His will for me. The fire was necessary, and the fire is necessary; it was the fire that illuminated God's call on my life to preach His gospel. The same fire fixed my focus on the peace and comfort of God's will and His word.

To you I say, be encouraged. God is the fire in the furnace. He controls the time and the temperature of all trails. Be comforted by Romans 8:28 "and we know that all things work together for good to them that love God, to them who are the called according to his purpose."

Keith West

As a retired owner-operator, author, and certified life coach, my journey into the realm of prayer is a deep personal and spiritually enriching experience. Each day, the presence of the Holy Spirit is clear, guiding my path.

Like any journey, there are always challenges, but as I persist, the Holy Spirit takes over, and God's divine guidance becomes evident. This journey reaffirms my belief that prayer is a vehicle for change. Through prayer, I spoke life into my own existence, a lesson I learned from a youthful age.

Growing up attending church alone, I was instilled with the importance of trusting God. To tutor our children, we must exemplify a life grounded in prayer, demonstrating that God is our guiding force. We cannot impose our faith on others, but we can play our part in building God's kingdom.

My hope is for people to recognize that we all possess testimonies and affirmations, but the common thread among us is the ever-present nature of God. No matter the circumstances, God remains a constant presence in our lives.

Prayer is filled with incredible power. It strengthens our connection with God and empowers us to face life's tribulations. In my role as a life coach, I incorporate prayer as a source of strength. My favorite quote, "REMEMBER TO TAKE GOD WITH YOU IN ALL YOU DO IN YOUR LIFE."

Prayer is not a mere ritual; it is a vibrant and transformative force. It has enriched my life. Let God be the compass guiding your life and watch the magnificent transformation it brings.

Trish West

     What is beauty? Beauty is defined as *"a combination of qualities, such as shape, color, or form, that pleases the aesthetic senses, especially the sight."* Society often places undue emphasis on external appearances and material possessions. The perspective of beauty has become deeply ingrained and has manifested in the way people judge others based on their appearance, possessions, and socioeconomic status. Beauty has become what pleases the eye. I used to think the same thing. I used to question my own beauty. As a former full-sized woman, I often questioned if I am beautiful enough for someone to love me. My thoughts on beauty impacted my self-esteem and my self-worth. Society had taught me that in order to be beautiful, you needed to be a certain size, certain complexion, especially as an African American woman. Society taught me I needed to have certain possessions to make me even more beautiful. I needed to drive the right car, live in the right neighborhood, make a certain amount of money. Then I realized, that is not what true beauty is. Beauty goes beyond appearances and material possessions. It encompasses one's inner qualities, self-belief, and faith. True beauty lies in knowing and embracing oneself, fostering self-confidence, and finding love and acceptance from within. The statement, *"It's okay to not be okay,"* is a crucial message that counters the societal pressure to always appear perfect. It acknowledges the struggles many individuals face in their pursuit of societal beauty standards. My journey from questioning my own beauty to realizing that true beauty is rooted in self-acceptance, self-belief, and faith is a powerful message. As a mental health professional, I have used my journey to encourage others to prioritize their inner beauty (their mental health), as they embrace their outer beauty. Remember: YOU ARE BEAUTIFUL!

C. Duane Wheeler

It felt as if I were floating.

In a pool if living water

Gentle wave after wave, washing.

Not over me, nor under me, but through me.

And nothing could stand in its way or resist it.

Not garment, not flesh, not even nagging little depressed feelings.

that haunt, longing and obsessed, as they lurk for crevices in,
here now of no consequence.

No, not even my natural joy,
distractor for hopelessness could approach it,

Nothing could resist this assertive positive flow.

It came in a single awareness, of hope and joy,
that they do exist, even for me.

I was bathing in the pleasure of this reality, with no regret the
manifestation was not yet.

The relief from the belief, satisfaction can be mine
flowed from my pores and fingertips.

I know now, for certain, and in an all-new way, desperation can be
overcome, and joy becomes.

To choose to stand my ground, profess my desire
and never shrink back until my miracle day is.

A Psalm of Duane.

Dr. Jenaya White

"May the God of hope fill you with all joy and peace as you trust in him, so that you may overflow with hope by the power of the Holy Spirit." - Romans 15:13 NKJV

As we journey through life, we will experience peaks and valleys but one thing that will always remain constant is the love that God has for us. During times of adversity, we naturally feel overwhelmed and anxious. However, as believers, we have a powerful source of comfort and guidance- our faith in God. Trusting God is not just about relying on Him to solve all our problems, but it is about having faith in His plan for our lives.

When we trust God, we surrender our worries, fears, and anxieties to Him. Having trust in God is acknowledging that we cannot do it alone, and we need His help. This is not a sign of weakness, but rather a sign of strength, as it takes a lot of courage to let go of our need for control and place our trust in God.

It's never easy to choose joy during challenging life circumstances, but with God, it is possible. The process of restoring joy requires time and patience. Be gentle with yourself and take these small steps each day. Turning to God's word is the first step. The Bible is full of promises that can uplift your spirits and renew your faith. Second, there is prayer. In prayer, we can connect with God and share our hearts. The third step to finding joy is to serve others. Serving others can give us a sense of purpose and remind us of the power of love and compassion. Fourth, surround yourself with supportive family and friends that will encourage you. May God bless you and give you the strength to trust in Him in all things and renew unspeakable joy in your life.

Stephanie White

Always remember that helping hurts. Stay contagious with positivity when others want to bring shade to your shine. Keep thriving; every small effort pays off, no matter the day or the time.

Own up, fix your mistakes, and always remember tomorrow will be better than today with your progress. Always remember to stay focused and stay on the course.

Keep your strength and stay encouraged with patience when you have been mistreated. Endure the test, learn from the mistakes, and prevent them from happening again.

If we do our best, we can always have room for improvement and growth.

Every day is a challenge for taking care of family, maintaining a business, or facing obstacles that come our way in life.

Points of view and expressions may be different, but that doesn't mean that they are wrong. Others can be passionate, while others can move at a faster or slower pace. It's ok! It's all in God's timing. Always remember God's timing is the best. We all have different personalities and different ways of doing things and getting things done. If you are a leader, you guide, not expel, anyone from their potential to be great or even greater than you. Always remember the sky is big enough for all birds to fly!

Dr. Angela White-Stephens

The Lord is good to those who wait for Him. To the soul who seeks Him, it is good that one should wait quietly for the salvation of the lord. It is good for a man that he bears the Lord in his youth. ~Lamentations 3:25-27~ This is something amazing- to be in a place or state or being able to genuinely rest and wait on God. To wait on God is to place all your hope in Him, to seek and trust that God is the one and only who can deliver you. Your entire confidence rests on and in Him. We should always wait upon the Lord because He is God, and we are not. We tend to think sometimes that if God is not right there showing up instantly in our time of need or trouble, we need to do things to help Him out.

Well as we all should know, He does not need our help! We are not doing anything, God is. However, seeking and waiting is one of the greatest gifts of our Christian faith. When we trust God and put all our hope in Him, it demonstrates confidence that He is indeed in control. I have come to realize that waiting can become a very uncomfortable place. This is the time that God shapes and defines us the most, and this is one of the reasons why Lamentation 3:27 says it is good for a man that he bears the yoke in his youth. To learn the value of waiting early on in life is a beautiful gift. In our time of waiting, why not completely give God control of your life and say God, I don't know what you are doing or why, but I am willing to wait on you and Lord, I know that it will be worth the wait. Amen

Tammi Whittman

"The Lord is close to the brokenhearted and saves those who are crushed in spirit." Psalm 34:18

There are times when the spirit of depression and anxiety enters our lives or the lives of our loved ones. When we are faced with constant harsh criticism, rejection, and just day to day disappointments, this can become overwhelming for anyone. Some have experienced the loss of loved ones and the world they once knew no longer exists. In the midst of this, they become more isolated and tend to sink further into depression. . . . Suffering in silence while clutching their broken hearts.

The good news is, although we may feel the pressures of life, we are not alone because God is always present. Just as the enemy knows when we are at our weakest, God is right there waiting with open arms to lift us up. We must learn to trust "Him" and trust "His" process. "His" words are our good news! Although we will encounter dark days, it is such a relief to know that leaning on our heavenly Father will bring us comfort and joy.

So, give thanks unto the Lord for not only being near the broken hearted and close to all who are crushed in spirit but give thanks to our Lord for saving us from ourselves. Most of all, give thanks for the joy that is on the horizon. Don't give up and don't quit! Stand firm in your faith…for your joy is on the way.

Danyell Winkey-Smith

I was truly able to find My Joy through the power of forgiving. Forgiving others for the way they treated me over the years gifted me with an abundance of joy and peace. But first, I had to give all my worries and fears to God, learning to trust Him all over again. It's human to sometimes question or blame God for our misfortunes, especially our losses including death, unhealthy relationships, and failed careers. However, once we understand the true meaning of having faith and allowing God to lead us, then and only then, will we have peace. Being joyful is finding your happy place and space. Remember that it is not the responsibility of others to make us happy. We are responsible for learning what truly makes us happy.

My first joy is that God blesses me and wakes me up every morning to enjoy whatever He has planned for me, including the hurdles, obstacles, hurt/pain, along with the blessings. And every night before I close my eyes, I pray thanking Him for another day to experience what was meant for me and to be blessed to start all over again. My joy has been sustained because I was able to defy the odds and change the trajectory of what society stated I was supposed to be. Refusing to be a victim, I decided to be a game-changer, dispelling myths of my unfortunate circumstances. I am joyful for life, love, new beginnings, my husband, children, grandchildren, family, friends, Sorors, good health, the gift to be myself at the expense of being judged and to love unconditionally. Surviving and living to experience God's blessings and forgiveness are the key elements to happiness and Joy!

Ivy Wilcox

"The LORD is close to the brokenheart d and saves those who are crushed in spirit." Psalm 34:18 NIV

Have you ever been in so much pain that you did not know when you would heal? The wounds that were caused by the choices made, self-inflected or of no fault of your own dispel the myth that pain is not real. Your flesh told you to give up, but the small voice within, whispered, "Hold on." That was the voice of God letting you know that He is close to those who are brokenhearted and when your spirit is crushed within, you will be safe with Him.

Just as there are four seasons of nature, there are seasons in our natural lives too. The season of pain will dissolve when you decide to make a change. It's when we turn our eyes away from our disappointments and look to His wider purpose and plan, we then discover that His mercies never fail or come to an end. For they are new every morning- great is thy faithfulness. The pain that you are feeling is necessary for your growth. The pain you are not willing to transform- you will transmit to others. Transmitted pain, anger, discouragement, and putting on a fake facade will be transmitted to others when you fail to be vulnerable and seek help. Leave the shame of your pain at the altar and allow God to heal you from within. Trust me, God never fails. Pay attention to the light of Christ in your life. Though it may be dim right now, as you move forward in faith- Allow Christ to take residence in your pain; that is when true healing will begin. Joy is coming in the morning.

Annette Wiley

"These things I have spoken to you, that my joy may be in you, and that your joy may be full." John 15:11 (ESV)

Feeling drained, defeated, and searching for comfort? Then, it's important to recognize the divine promise of joy for strength and solace. *"Do not grieve for the joy of the Lord is your strength."* - Nehemiah 8:10[b] (NIV). The joy promised by God is a wellspring of strength that can sustain you and give you refreshment in your darkest moments if you can simply open your heart and yield.

Psalm 30:5 (ESV), *"Weeping may tarry for the night, but joy comes with the morning."* This beautiful metaphor assures us that even in our darkest moments, joy is on the way, just as surely as dawn follows the night.

Understanding this divine promise is the first step but realizing this promise in your life through the power of prayer, faith, trust in God's plan and expressing heartfelt gratitude, even in difficult times is the key to help unlock the promised joy. Additionally, the wisdom of spiritual mentors, and a heart open to receiving God's love can all be instrumental in realizing the divine promise of joy.

Joy and rejoicing are an integral part of God's plan and creation. This is why Isaiah 55:12 (NIV) says: *"You will go out in joy and be led forth in peace; the mountains and hills will burst into song before you, and all the trees of the field will clap their hands."* Embrace these as your reality!

Belinda Wiley

Psalm 71:23, 24 (NIV)
23 "My lips will shout for joy when I sing praise to you—I whom you have delivered."

A song writer says, "when I think of the goodness of Jesus and all he has done for me, my very soul shall shout hallelujah, praise God for saving me."

Many times, we focus so much on all the negative things we have had to experience. How about you cast your mind back on the good things God did for you even in those troubled days? You will more than likely pinpoint those times when you had it bad, but you were rescued. You'll recall those times when you were at the end of yourself and were about to give up, but somehow, salvation came for you.

Now, allow your mind to remain on those thoughts. Allow your mind to drink in the feeling of being loved by a big awesome God (Ps. 103:1-5). Then, let the gratitude that wells up in your heart spread. You will find that songs of Praise and worship are forming within you, allowing these to flow out like rivers cascading gently down the hills. Sing those songs of Praise and worship to God. Praise Him with a dance if your feet can take it. Praise Him with sounds and cymbals and other instruments you can lay your hands on (If you know how to play). Praise the Lord! Praise Him the best way you can. Don't stop! Keep praising! As you go, you'll find unspeakable joy bubbling from the inside out. It is because; *"out of your belly shall flow rivers of living waters"* (John 7:38). Sometimes, this joy may push you to tears. Let it flow.

Maurice Wiley

In the journey of life, we often find ourselves lost in the pursuit of purpose, identity, and meaning. For some, this search spans a lifetime, as they navigate the twists and turns of existence, seeking to understand who they truly are. Today, we reflect on the profound story of a man who, after fifty years of searching, found solace and restoration in the loving embrace of God.

My journey is a testament to the human spirit's resilience, and my surrender to God is a celebration of the enduring power of faith and divine grace. For half a century, I pursued various paths and endeavors, hoping to find my purpose and identity. Yet, it was only when I humbly submitted myself to God that I discovered the profound truth: my identity, my very essence, was inextricably linked to his Creator.

Joy is a profound emotion that transcends circumstances. It's a deep, abiding sense of contentment that can only be fully realized when we rest in God's love. This man's story is a testament to the transformative power of faith in restoring lost joy. His years of searching were not in vain, for they ultimately led him to the source of all joy.

As we contemplate my journey, may we be inspired to surrender our own lives to God, trusting that in Him, we can find our identity and experience the profound joy that comes from being in harmony with our Creator. Joy restoration begins with submitting to God and allowing His love to define our true selves.

Let us pray: Heavenly Father, we thank You for the story of this man's journey and the joy he found in surrendering to You. Help us to trust in Your plan for our lives and find our identity in You. Amen.

Francine Williams

As far back as I can remember there was always someone telling me what was right and what was wrong. Even though as a child, I didn't always agree.

All that I was told was right in the eyes of the person that was doing the telling. Despite the voices, I heard everything I was taught from the age of five, and I knew I was in my Heavenly Father's Hands.

When I could look up to the Heavens, I would see God in the form of clouds. I would see Him in the wind, The sun shining on my face was God's blessing to me, When God blessed me with the gift to discern the spirits in people, it was His way of protecting me from many things.

I would see the image of animals in them letting me know the character of good and bad.

As I got older, looking back in hindsight, God never allowed me to be in a gang, become an alcoholic, drug addict or a prostitute, but the opportunities were there.

God had Angels to block the enemy of my soul.

Why He allowed me to be molested, raped, and beaten by my Mother and put away in a State Institution, I didn't understand then, but what I know now is that God delivered me. He bought me out to be a shiny testimony of His Glory. One thing I do know is that I have always been in His hands.

Tanya Butler Williams

I am deaf and hard of hearing. For many years I believed I was broken, ugly and unloved. So, I hid my hearing loss.

A strange woman stopped me and said" God asked, "Are you hearing me." Then another said God wants you to hear Him. I wondered why God would send such a message to me.

What I learned in Psalm 85:8 when God speaks of hearing, it doesn't always mean in the audible ability to receive a message. God speaking about the ability to hear is admonished by scripture to walk in the way of peace . . . His words are "Are you hearing me? If the decision or idea does not establish a sense of peace within you, it may not be God.

So, when you "hear," it must be in the form of "peace." Peace is not outward (audible) Peace is inward (inside of you). Listen closely, not just by the audible intaking of the message being given. Listening closely is about discerning what is being said. Mark 4:24 says "in all thy getting, get understanding." Getting understanding is a way of hearing what someone is saying to you. Another way God speaks to us is out of Love. When you understand what someone is saying to you, then you can respond out of knowledge and love for that person.

If you love that person, then what matters to them, matters to you and you won't continue to behave or make decisions that are harmful and hurtful to them physically, emotionally nor spiritually. You will "hear" what they are saying and react in a way that's in their best interest without being harmful or hurtful to yourself. Hearing is about what you discern in the message and that message should be lined up with what God is saying to your spirit.

God will always speak of "peace and love."

Are you Hearing Me?

Bobbie Willis

"If you abide in me, and my words abide in you, ask for whatever you wish, and it will be done for you" (John 15:7).

It sounds so simple: "abide in me" Christ already knew that the world would have trials and tribulations. The scripture John 15:7 makes it sound easy to do, but sometimes it is not. It is a decision of the heart. Our hearts should desire an intimate relationship with Christ. In desperation our soul should thirst for Him. Every believer should abide in Christ. To abide in Christ means that we believe and trust Him for everything we desire. When we abide in Him, it allows us to pray with confidence and to witness prayers being answered.

Christians should allow His Words to fill their minds and direct every path that comes up. We must be rooted in Him. Each passing day is an opportunity to lean on Him. When you abide in Him, you will learn how to have joy in sadness. He will be your light when darkness is all around. In poverty, He will be our provider. He is our Comforter. No matter what is going on in your life, Christ will always be with you. To effectively abide in Christ, we must study His words. If we remain in Him, He will remain in us.

It is of utmost spiritual importance that we always maintain a secure attachment to the Lord. "I am the vine; you are the branches."

Dawn Wilson

In life, we often go through trials and tribulations, for which we often look to the world in search of answers. Often, we are given advice about what others might do if they were in that situation. With our ears tuned to the world, we cannot hear the only solution that comes as a whisper from our creator. He patiently waits for us to tune out negativity, and search for His light that will guide us when we are lost, His strength when we are weak, and the power of His love that conquers all evil! Why not turn your problems over to the One that drew the blueprint of your life versus those who cannot resolve their own problems? If not, we will continue a path of hardships. The pain endured will eventually take a toll on our lives. The unresolved problems and hurt cause barriers that isolate us from the ones we love! Throughout my life, I have experienced issues I couldn't fix, pain that was crippling or sorrow that consumed me. It wasn't till I realized what the real issue was. I had lost sight of my Father! In "Matthew 14: 28-30, "Jesus was walking upon the water, and Peter said, Lord, bid me to come unto thee upon the waters." Peter walked boldly toward him; eyes fixed on Jesus. But, when he saw the wind, he was afraid and, beginning to sink, cried out, "Lord, save me!"

Fix your eyes and thoughts on Jesus; keep the faith and focus on our Lord and Savior. Hear His voice in the times of heartache, and pain, and like Peter, with eyes fixed upon the Lord you will prevail! When you can't find the answers you seek, turn your problems over to God. This is where you will find your strength.

James Wilson

The resilient, faith-full man is a man who pulls from a well of his foundation in faith. Whether it be his family, his faith, or the knowledge from the experiences he's gone through, there is something that gives him his deeply rooted fortitude to face the daily challenges of life. The keys I've adopted over the years to maintain a level of resiliency have been, without a doubt, my faith in God. I go to that well repeatedly because I know what the opposite of that has done for me. Absolutely nothing! With the way this world operates, there is a sense of limited time here due to the fact of diseases, gun-violence, horrible healthcare, and many other issues, but these are things that worry people constantly.

My question to you would be, "How do you handle all of that?" Well, were the same question asked of me, my answer would be because I'm assured that, as the scripture says, "He that believeth in Me, though he may die, he shall live. And whoever lives and believes in Me shall never die." (John 11: 25-26) Is it just faith? No. The Bible says, "faith without works is dead," so you must work at it. How? Romans 10:17 says, "faith comes from hearing, and hearing through the word of Christ." Read your bible daily. With technology as it is today, access is at your fingertips. Join a local church to continue to grow and mature in Christ. Share what you know or how it has worked for you. The Great Commission, Matthew 28:16-20, tells us to go forth and make disciples of men and that comes from sharing what faith has done for you. And in this faithful work, the level of resiliency you develop can feel astronomical.

Jae Joi Wingfield

As we grew up, many of us were taught to "find happiness." We spent our childhood and young adult lives pursuing things we thought would make us happy, only to find that happiness was fleeting and often unfulfilling. We were misled and should've been seeking joy instead.

Happiness is that temporary excitement or pleasure we feel when something good happens. Happiness is circumstantial and requires the continuous occurrence of "good" to be sustained. Joy, on the other hand, is an enduring sense of peace that exists regardless of what is happening. When we are joyful, we can find beauty in each day; or at the very least remain hopeful for the future. Joy is not a temporary nor circumstantial emotion; it is a state of being.

To achieve joy, we must take control of our thoughts and emotions. As we navigate life, many things happen that are outside our control, but the one thing that is within our control is our reaction. In fact, science proves that (in most situations) only 10% of our emotional state can be attributed to what happens to us. The other 90% is our biological wiring and how we react.

We must do the work to rewire our brains to see the good in each day, to feel hope for the future, and to appreciate the lesson in each setback.

Without the rain, the rose would not bloom.

Without the wind, birds would be unable to fly to new horizons.

When the leaves fall and the trees appear barren, they are in a state of rest and renewal so that when spring arrives, they may bloom fuller than before.

Remember to smell the roses, marvel at the birds, and bask in the shade of lush trees.

Dr. Tonya T. Wise

"Trust in the Lord with all your heart, and do not lean on your own understanding. In all your ways acknowledge him, and he will make straight your paths." - Proverbs 3:5-6

As business professionals, we often find ourselves juggling numerous responsibilities and passions. We are known for our ability to wear multiple hats, pursuing various endeavors simultaneously. Yet, during this multifaceted life, it is crucial to seek divine guidance, allowing God to illuminate the torch we should carry in the fire. Our heavenly Father knows the depths of our hearts and the unique gifts He has bestowed upon us. He understands our multifaceted nature and for us to channel our energy and talents in ways that align with His purpose. In pursuit of success, we must surrender our desires to control every outcome and trust that God will direct our paths. Through prayer and seeking His wisdom, we can discern which torch to ignite and nurture amidst the flames. God's hand is not limited by the constraints of time or our limited perspectives. He sees the intricate tapestry of our lives and how each thread weaves together to create a beautiful masterpiece. When we acknowledge God in all our ways, we invite Him to guide our decisions, illuminate our paths, and grant us clarity amid the chaos. As we entrust our dreams, aspirations, and endeavors to Him, He will provide discernment and align our passions with His divine plan.

Prayer: *Gracious Father, in the complexity of our lives, we surrender our multifaceted talents and ambitions to You. Grant us the wisdom to discern which torch to ignite, as we acknowledge Your presence and seek Your guidance. Help us to trust in Your perfect timing and plan, knowing that You see the bigger picture. May our pursuits be aligned with Your will, and may our diverse passions bring glory to Jesus. Amen*

Dasia Wood

Our surrounds may shake with chaos or stand still with peace. We endure rain and sun and yet we still grow. We can be our own chaos as well as our own peace. We could be our own rain as well as our own sun. Everything works together for our good. We can chase after joy or embrace the joy that is already within us and let it shine through. We can choose to feel an infinite amount of joy in all areas of our lives as well as a moment of happiness during those special memorable times.

The wonderful thing about joy is that it doesn't have to be temporary. We can carry it with us everywhere if we choose to. Joy is that warm and fuzzy sensation that fills your heart and makes you smile from ear to ear. It's like a burst of happiness that radiates through your entire being. When you experience joy, everything seems brighter and more beautiful. Joy can come from the simplest things, like spending time with loved ones, achieving a goal, or even just enjoying a peaceful place.

It's contagious too! When you're joyful, it spreads to those around you, making everyone's day a little brighter. Joy is a reminder to appreciate the good things in life and to find happiness in even the smallest moments. So, let's embrace joy and let it fill our lives with laughter, love, peace, sunshine, and an endless number of smiles.

Melissa Wood

While we aren't given exemption to trials as Christians, God does give us an instructional manual that tells us everything we need to do to prepare for the trials of our lives. Just as people who live along the coast must prepare for hurricanes before they make landfall, we too must prepare for the trials we are to face in life before they are even on our radar. The first step in preparing for our trial is to know what we believe and why we believe it. Before the storm begins to rage, know what God's word says. Root yourself in the promises God defines in His word. By anchoring yourself in truth now you can stand firm when the storm begins by remembering the truths in which you have grounded your faith. Secondly, know and recognize the truth as the storm hits. Satan is lurking. He is not going to be slow in trying to convince you that all you believe is false. He will bring fear and doubt, but you can resist his attacks by recognizing what he is trying to do. You can counter his lies with the truths of God's word.

Finally, remember the cross. The cross took away any power that fear or doubt can bring in any storm you have to face. It gives you the promise that you are never left to weather your storm alone. It gives you promise that whatever God brings you to He will bring you through. Now, while your storm is brewing, prepare and plan so you are ready when its landfall is looming. Grow the roots of your faith deep in His word and saturate them with the fertileness of His promises every day. Anchor your faith, in the one who loves you most. Remember that the testing of your faith through your trials builds your endurance, your endurance produces your character, and your character produces your hope.

Dr. Rhonda Wood

Life's journey takes us through various seasons, each with its own challenges and blessings. In this ever-changing world, one thing remains true: the promise of joy. As women of faith, we are called to seek and embrace joy in every circumstance.

Psalm 30:5 reminds us that sorrow and weeping might endure for a night, but the dawn brings with it the gift of rejoicing. Just as night transitions to morning, our trials give way to triumphs when we anchor our hearts in the eternal hope of God's unwavering love. Joy is not dependent on external circumstances but is rooted in our relationship with our Heavenly Father. It's a fruit of the Spirit that grows as we cultivate gratitude, resilience, and trust. Even amid trials, we can find joy by focusing on the goodness of our God, who turns our mourning into rejoicing.

As women, we often carry the weight of many roles and responsibilities. In the busyness of life, we might lose sight of the joy God desires to pour into our hearts. Nehemiah 8:10 reminds us that the joy of the Lord is our strength. It's not merely a fleeting emotion but a divine gift that fuels our spirits, enabling us to overcome trials with resilience and grace. When challenges arise, take a moment to reflect on God's faithfulness. Recall the times He has carried you through past trials and trust that He will do so again. Invite His presence into every aspect of your life, and let His joy be your strength.

Remember that joy is a gift waiting to be unwrapped in every season. Embrace it through prayer, worship, and a heart full of gratitude. May your life reflect the joy that comes from a deep and abiding relationship with our Heavenly Father.

Matrice Woodall

.Grief, molested, raped, drugs, cheating partners, sickness, lied on, church hurt etc. All these things have enormous potential to make someone devastated and give up on life. I've been through 8 of the 9 I have named so I've had my share. I have experienced some dark places in my life. Dark places others have gone and died. I have survived trauma after trauma and yet here I am.

Isaiah 12:3 says, with joy shall ye draw water out of the wells of salvation. The only one I know that can give you that kind of joy is Christ.

Your joy can only be restored through Christ. There are many places of joy in salvation and the only way to get to that kind of joy is by receiving Christ into your life and having a true and real relationship with God. There is a place in God you can go and experience Him in such a way . . . that secret place where He talks with you, comforts you and He tells you that you are one of His own . . . that place where He holds you, loves on you and gives you unspeakable joy.

People will fail you and only make you happy but for a moment. All else will fade away, but God will never fade nor fail you. We look for Joy in all the wrong places and we always seem to come up short. Earthly things are temporary, even our lives. We are limited human beings and what makes us expand (go from little to big) is God. God causes us to expand beyond our limits and we are nothing without Him. God remains forever. He is an everlasting God who can give you everlasting joy.

Debra Woodley Thomas

We show our faith in God and confidence in His provision when we stand still and trust Him. We recognize that He is in charge and will care for us. It means saying, "God, I rely on You to look after me. God, I give You everything."

Trusting God and standing still can be challenging. We live in a world that is constantly moving and changing, and it can be tempting to act on our own and try to solve things ourselves. But God has a plan for us, and He knows what is best for us.

It is powerful when we surrender and trust God. We are allowing Him to work in our lives. We are allowing Him to guide us and show us the way. We are allowing Him to be our strength and our hope.

We enable God to do the impossible when we stand still and trust Him. We let Him move in our lives and do things we could never accomplish ourselves. We let Him work in ways that we could never foresee.

We can't always predict what will happen, and it can be hard to let go and wait. But when we stand still and trust God, we are placing our trust in Him, and we are letting Him do amazing things in our lives.

"Trust in the Lord with all your heart and lean not on your understanding; in all your ways submit to him, and he will make your paths straight." (**Proverbs 3:5-6**)

April Woolsey

The most powerful thing you can do right now is to be patient with yourself while things are manifesting for you. One or more bad chapters doesn't mean your story is over; it's just beginning. Sometimes you must go through the worst to get to the best and having a negative mindset won't give you a positive way of life. It doesn't matter what broke you, hurt you, tore you to pieces, shattered your mind, let you down, discouraged you, left you alone, disappointed you and made you question who you are. Your blessings will come in your healing process. You have to be willing to accept what is, allow yourself time to heal and move on! Respect yourself enough to say that you deserve peace at this point in your life. It's ok to outgrow people who aren't growing with you. Stop being afraid to lose people who do nothing for your life but give excuses, cause you pain, make you feel like you're the problem, leave you hanging, and add drama. Standing up for yourself doesn't make you argumentative or mean, and saying no doesn't make you uncaring or selfish. It says you love yourself enough to live a happy and meaningful life! You must make choices to take a chance, or your life will never change. If you haven't felt your best lately, have been going through some tough situations, but still get up every day and refuse to give up, keep pushing, because you got this. When you focus on the good, the good gets better. Never forget that you deserve to be loved and respected. Never dim your light, just to make others more comfortable, and don't allow them to take up space in your head when they don't belong there. So, the only time you should look back is to see how far you've come and where you're going to next!

Iris Wright

"But I will sing of thy power, yea, I will sing aloud of thy mercy in the morning for thou hast been my defense and refuge in the day of my trouble." Psalm 59.16 KJV

As a young girl I grew up in the church believing in God. I believed that God would provide me with protection from harm and my enemies. I believed in His love and grace.

Around Nov of 2001 I was facing over twenty years' incarceration for a crime that I did not commit, and my daughter was taken from me. Eventually I stopped trusting Him.

Sept 6, 2002, I went to court by myself with no Attorney and all my charges, but one was dropped. I was given one-year unsupervised probation and was told what to do to get my daughter back. I was still unhappy because I was innocent and should have been found not guilty.

Later I realized that God was in that courtroom with me; I could have gotten twenty years. During my healing process, God allowed me to see that He was still with me and never left my side. He helped me obtain the strength that was needed to fight for my daughter, to keep my other children and to love and trust again. Most importantly, He helped me evolve into the strong person I am today. I realized that I needed to rebuild my personal relationship with Him and to trust Him again.

I thank God for the knowledge, strength, wisdom, grace and love He has given me. I will forever love and trust Him with all my heart.

Joyce Wright

God is your Father; He is also your Friend. When you are in a physical relationship with someone, you both feel excited, fulfilled, and grateful when you spend time with each other. This is how you would feel, and it is how God feels when you just spend time in His presence. Sometimes, you may just empty your mind of all that concerns and worries you and just breathe. As you breathe, take God's word as His love letter to you. So, hold it to your heart as you talk with God. However, you shouldn't rush off after talking, wait to listen as your Father and Lover talk back to you.

The presence of God is everywhere. Take advantage of this absence of restriction every time you feel overwhelmed. When you're on the road and feeling drained and discouraged, draw your mind inward and acknowledge the presence of God. When you're unable to handle difficult situations, take a pause and speak with your Father. He's ever-present, ready, and willing to listen. Allow your Father and Lover to soothe your racing, fearful and bruised heart.

God speaks to us by His Spirit. This Spiritt is called Comforter (Psalm 94:13). Allow Him to console and ease your heart. Never believe that your busy schedule and activities can stop you from dwelling in His presence. Make deliberate and conscious efforts to take some time away. Begin in bits. Through consistency and joy, you derive from His presence, you'll soon increase your time with Him. The more you dwell, the more you are taught ways to maneuver the stormy paths, the more you are taught the ways of life that inevitably bring joy. Your lost joy will be restored in full.

Shadawn Wright

2 Timothy 1:7 1 John 4:18 Has GOD ever instructed you to complete an assignment, but there was a spirit of FEAR hovering over you? He gave you the instructions and resources, however you felt fearful and anxious at the thought of completing the assignment.

You can admit it. You are not alone! When this happens, it is the enemy trying to keep you from obeying GOD.

2 Timothy 1:7 KJV states, "For GOD hath not given us the spirit of fear, but of power, and of love, and of a sound mind". This scripture reminds us that we can overcome any obstacle the devil tries to put in our way.

The spirit of power gives us strength to push through self-doubt, anxieties, and strongholds that fear uses to attempt to overwhelm us. We have the power to break down barriers and obey GOD's instructions. According to 1 John 4:18 KJV, there is no fear in love, but perfect love draws out fear. When we surround ourselves with love, fear does not have a chance to consume our minds.

Having a sound mind releases all doubt and transforms the way we think. It is trusting GOD knowing that He is in control of everything. What am I saying? We do not need to fear anything in this world. GOD said He will never leave or forsake us. Release that spirit of fear! GOD did not give it to you. He gave you power, love, and a sound mind. Stir up your gifts and complete the assignment GOD has put in your heart to accomplish. He is with you!

Made in the USA
Columbia, SC
25 February 2025

b145960f-7aae-4252-8121-fff60fc50b65R03